ROSE'S WORLD

Rose Bloom

ROSE'S WORLD

Rose Brenda Lavis

iUniverse, Inc.
New York Lincoln Shanghai

ROSE'S WORLD

iUniverse books may be ordered through booksellers or by contacting:

iUniverse
2021 Pine Lake Road, Suite 100
Lincoln, NE 68512
www.iuniverse.com
1-800-Authors (1-800-288-4677)

Because of the dynamic nature of the Internet, any Web addresses or links contained in this book may have changed since publication and may no longer be valid.

The views expressed in this work are solely those of the author and do not necessarily reflect the views of the publisher, and the publisher hereby disclaims any responsibility for them.

ISBN: 978-0-595-47559-9 (pbk)
ISBN: 978-0-595-71195-6 (cloth)
ISBN: 978-0-595-91827-0 (ebk)

Printed in the United States of America

Contents

ACKNOWLEDGMENT

Thank you to Reverend Valerie Reay for your input, inspiration and your insight in helping complete Rose's World.

INTRODUCTION

Rose's world is a series of events, which are true. Rose was a child who has survived a dysfunctional family and an abusive childhood, the daughter of a mentally ill mother and a violent alcoholic father. Rose has survived and blossomed into an Empowered successful adult. The names of the children have been changed, with the exception of Bernice and Rose.

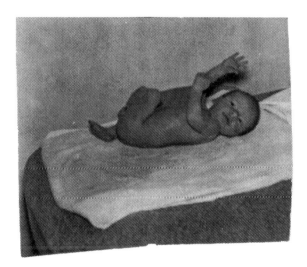

Rose 11 days old

1

ROSE'S WORLD

Most children's stories begin with "Once Upon a Time" and end with "And they lived Happily Ever After." This one is no different. I am here to tell you that living happily every after is very real. There is no circumstance, which cannot be overcome. We all begin our lives "Once Upon a Time." We call this day our birthday and we all can choose to "Live Happily Every After."

Most babies are born into situations were their arrival is a much anticipated joy. Others are born into situations were there may be less excitement but they are loved and accepted. Rose was born into a family were she was considered a burden and not wanted. She was born to a mentally ill mother and a violent alcoholic father.

Rose was the second oldest of five children, one older sister, one younger brother and two younger sisters. The age span between Rose and her older sister Bernice was eighteen months and between Rose and her brother David was eighteen months. The other two sisters were five and nine years younger. Because of family circumstances and the large age gap between the older and younger sisters, they grew up not knowing much about each other.

If it is possible to categorize children, Rose and Bernice were born into the considered a burden and not wanted category. David although born into the same family was in the extreme hated category. The two younger sisters were also considered a burden, because of the huge age difference they were also in the left over, you're in the way, look after yourself or be looked after by your siblings category.

The photo in the introduction is a picture of myself (Rose) as a baby. As you look at this picture, I hope what you see is a beautiful little baby. In sharing this picture, I want you to know it took me more than forty years to be able to look at that picture and see a beautiful little baby. Each one of you was born, "Once Upon a Time" as a beautiful little baby. There is no circumstance so great that can stop you from choosing to live, "Happily Ever After."

It took me more that forty years to see that I was born a beautiful baby. No different than all beautiful babies when they are born. Rose was brought home to an environment where she was not wanted and considered a burden. My siblings and I were considered the cause of every problem our mother had. Before the age of five, the belief that I was ugly, useless and nobody wanted or would every want me was imprinted on my soul. Growing to be invisible became a means to survive.

What I want you to know is I was always the same beautiful little baby. Had I been raised in a different environment I would have had a different view of who I was. The baby never changed. The eyes viewing the baby changed.

The fact that my mother saw me through her eyes and her eyes were attached to her mentally ill brain meant that the problem was her brain. Had she not had a mentally ill brain she would have seen a different picture when she looked at her beautiful baby.

Today as a mother and a grandmother who has raised two children, foster children and taken in street kids, life has shown me that there is nothing a child can do that makes them not valuable or not worthy of being loved. Every human being is born, "Once Upon a Time" as a beautiful baby. It is possible for every life to choose to live, "Happily Every After."

2

IMPORTANT BEGINNINGS

My earliest childhood memory was the first time I met my father. My mother had taken my brother David who was eighteen-months-old with her to meet him at the train. My older sister Bernice and I were very excited to meet our daddy. The reason my mother took David with her was our dad had never seen him. Daddy was coming home from jail. David had been born while he was in jail. I recall my mother telling us that she was taking David with her because daddy had never seen him. This must have meant that our father had seen both Bernice and me although I do not recall every seeing him before this day. If David were eighteen-months-old I would have been three-years-old.

This day defines most of my childhood relationship with my father. He was here for a while and then he was gone for a while. He was always coming home from somewhere. My father was a violent alcoholic who would drink for days or weeks at a time. When he was home, it usually meant he was out of money. There were times when he had a job and would come home with money. Most of the time, my mother relied on welfare. There were many occasions when my father would take the welfare check and be gone or he would sell whatever we had, which wasn't much so he could buy alcohol.

My second early childhood memory was my first day of school. I was six-years-old going into the first grade. At this time, Kindergarten was not a part of the school system. It was only available for children whose parents could afford to pay.

Turning six-years-old a few weeks before school began, still able to feel childish enthusiasm I remember being very excited about going to school. All of the children were sitting on the floor while the teacher was telling us some of what we would learn in first grade. She was telling us that we would learn the alphabet and what sound each letter made. We would learn how to count and how to add numbers etc.

Raising my hand, the teacher acknowledged me. I was excited to tell her that I already knew my alphabet. As she listed different items, we would learn I raised my hand a second time and told her of other things I knew. Raising my hand a third time, at six-years-old and excited to be in school I wanted her to know what I knew. She was frustrated with my interruptions and told me to go and stand in the hallway.

Standing in the hallway feeling rejected and unwanted. Although I was a child, acting like a child, being natural, saying what you thought or how you felt was not accepted at home. Already adept at being invisible, trying to be perfect so no one would notice me or blame me for anything at home. On the first day at school in the first hour of school at six-years-old, the message was clear. I had to be invisible here too. I had to be invisible everywhere. My mother was right. I was no good for nothing, no one wants me and no one would ever want me; in order to be tolerated I had to be invisible. This would be the one and only day for me to speak in class without being asked first. In order to survive I would say only what I believed anyone wanted to hear.

This first grade teacher had no way of knowing that the child she sent into the hallway that day was already spiritually broken. Surely, her intent was not to zap the last scrap of childish enthusiasm from an already abused six-year-old. If we all as human beings treated everyone we met whether it is an annoying child or a grumpy, adult with patients and dignity we may help to empower rather than to crack a fragile soul.

My elementary school experiences consisted of many different schools. Living in a family with no regular source of income meant when we were actually living together we moved constantly due to none payment of rent. Due to my mother's mental health issues, she had several stays in various psychiatric wards.

During the times my mother was not able to care for us we were sometimes left with my father, left with any drunk my father could find to take us in, with various relatives and several times in the Children's Shelter. This was before conventional foster homes were available. Children's Shelters were the equivalent of an orphanage only not all of the children were without parents. On most occasions other than the children's shelters, my sibling and I were not kept together.

The result of these countless moves and changing circumstances my life consisted of always being the new kid in class. There were some schools I attended for as little as two weeks, others a month or two. With each new living arrangement or each trip to the shelter, there would be a new enrolment in whatever school was appropriate at the time. Leaving one school in a classroom where children were printing letters, which I could do, my next enrolment would be a classroom where the children were writing. I had no idea what the words on the blackboard said as they were in hand writing. Having missed the transition from printing, I eventually taught myself how to write. To this day and I am a grandmother my handwriting consists of some written and some printed letters. It is difficult at times for me to read what I have written.

There were several times I did not attend school at all. Left in a skid row hotel room with some drunk or at the home of a hooker my father befriended there would be no one to take me to school. Children have little sense of time. As a child being left anywhere and everywhere, each situation seemed like forever. There was no way for me to determine if what seemed to be forever was days, weeks or months.

3

HOME ALONE

Rose's world was one of constant change. Changing schools, the houses where my family lived constantly changed. On one occasion, we lived in a building, which was condemned. There was a notice taped to the door, which read condemned! There was one occasion when Bernice, David and I were left totally on our own. I am assuming that my mother was in the hospital again. Wherever she was, she was not home with us. Perhaps she thought my father was looking after us there was no way for me to know. We were all old enough to be in school I would have been eight-or-nine-years-old. How long we were alone is uncertain, although the memory of us getting up and going to school on our own for several days is clear. Where our younger sister was during this time is unknown, she would have been too young for school and she was not with us.

It was dark; we were all sleeping when a police officer knocked at the door. A neighbour had called the police to say we were alone. We sat in the back of the police car on our way to the children's shelter. It was dark to me it was the middle of the night.

Arriving at the shelter all of the children were asleep. Carrying a stuffed animal with me a woman at the shelter took the stuffed animal and put it in a bag. She told me it would be returned when I went home, keeping it was not allowed because it might be dirty.

I am sure we all arrived at the shelter looking un-kept and not cared for; that is exactly what we were. Taking a bath in the middle of the night and taking away my stuffed animal made me feel dirty. Knowing I was unwanted at home and barely tolerated everywhere else this was just one more place that took me because they had to and really did not want me.

The next morning I was given a dress to wear. We brought nothing with us from home. Thinking the dress was ugly; putting it on made me feel uglier. Once again I was going to start a new school wearing someone else's clothes feeling like I stood out in this ugly dress, how would it be possible to be invisible? How long we stayed at the shelter on this occasion is unknown. There were a lot of dresses and many school days. It may have been a few weeks or a few months.

One occasion that we were left alone for the day, we had a house fire. This was one of three fires I remember as a child. Two fires in different homes a few years apart, both caused by David playing with a lighter or matches. My drunken father caused the third fire.

On this occasion, it was daytime; I am not sure where my mother was she was out for the day. David who was maybe five-or-six-years-old at the time had used a lighter to light his mattress on fire. He still slept in a crib with one side removed because it was the only bed we had.

David although he was born into the same family was in the extreme hated category. He was abused physically and mentally by my mother as we, all were. David was also absolutely despised a hated by my father. My father would beat him, other times he would completely ignore him, shove him against a wall or punch him in the stomach. He would shout at David, "I hate boys I hate you!" I remember hiding and crying while my brother was the target of both of their rage.

It is not rocket science to figure out why a young child in such an environment might light a mattress on fire. David came running out of his room screaming, "Fire, fire!" Bernice and I called the fire department took David and ran out of the house. Bernice had her picture in the paper with an article about the fire. The article said we had been home alone, yet no one questioned why three young children were alone.

I was nine-years-old when my youngest sister was born and we were again left alone. Today as an adult with two grown children, recalling the time when my own daughter was born and my son was not quite three-years-old. Pregnant for nine months I knew that at some point I would go into labour and would have to go to the hospital. My Husband would be with me for the birth so we arranged for someone to care for our son when the time came.

Scenarios like this are played out thousands of times by families with more than one child. It is impossible to understand why when my mother was pregnant with her fifth child, with four children ranging from ages four to ten at home; did she not arrange for someone to care for us while she was giving birth. This was at a time when a mother stayed in the hospital for up to ten days when she had a baby.

My mother woke me up in the middle of the night. She said she had to go to the hospital. She was going to have the baby. I have no idea how she got to the hospital. She told me to wait until she was gone, phone the police and tell them that we were alone. She said the police would take us to the shelter. Once again in the middle of the night at nine-years-old, I am riding in the back of a police car to the children's shelter.

Looking back today, asking myself, was my mother that alone. My mother had several sisters, my aunts living in the same City at the time. There were times when I had lived with some of them. Bernice and David had also lived with different aunts at times.

I was listening to my mother on the phone as she was talking to relatives or who ever she knew to see if they could take us again. The reason she was sending us away this time was unknown. This conversation had been heard many times before, sitting outside the door of a social worker or a shelter worker's office with my stomach in my throat as they made phone calls trying find some one to take one or more of us.

On this day, my mother was talking to one of her sisters. She hung up the phone and screamed at me, "she has money, she doesn't care, she doesn't want you either." I had been to this aunt's house only once or twice with my mother, she lived in a nice house. My mother always referred to this aunt as having money, being rich and not caring.

The one thing that stood out to me about my aunts' house was that it had carpet on the floor. This was the only house I had ever been in with wall-to-wall carpet. This was the only place where we drank real milk. If we had milk, it was mixed from powder. On one, occasion my aunt asking if I wanted a cookie. I was young maybe five-or-six-years-old. I took two.

I knew by the look on my mother's face that I was in trouble. She didn't say a word in front of my aunt. As soon as we left my aunts' house, she was enraged. She was screaming that she had never been so ashamed of me. What an ungrateful pig I was because I had taken two cookies. She screamed she would never take such an ungrateful brat anywhere with her again.

My aunt does have money; she also had four children of her own and two foster children at the time my mother had phoned her to ask if she would take me. She would have jeopardized being able to keep her foster children had she taken in any more.

My mother's reasoning was so twisted that she found something wrong with everyone in her world. I am sure her sister tried to explain the circumstances as to why she could not take in any more children. My mother interpreted what she heard as, "she's rich, she doesn't care, she doesn't want you, nobody wants you".

Whether I was in the back of a police car on the way to the shelter again because my mother believed her sister was too rich to care we will never know. I do know some of her family took us in at different times. My mother may have given up asking or maybe she did have a plan for someone to care for her children while she had another baby. She may have planned to have me call the police and have them take us to the shelter.

4

COMING HOME

It amazes me now to think back at how many times I lived at the shelter and how many different places had taken me in. Most of all it amazes me that as chaotic, violent and unhappy home was somehow each time it was time to go home I was excited.

Being a child, I wanted to go home. A part of me always thought that this time would be better. A part of me had the expectation that my mother would really care or really want me this time. What I really wanted was to have the mother she could never be. Being so young there was no way for me to comprehend her world or mine. What is unbelievable to me is that not one Social Worker, Psychiatrist, Shelter Worker, Police officer etc. ever stood up and said no more. No one ever said these children are not going back. Each time I returned home in reality it would be as bad or worse than the time before and there would always be a next time to be sent somewhere.

There are no memories of my mother ever working until I was in my early teens. Although my mother did not work, Bernice and I from my earliest memories were expected to cook and clean and take care of the younger kids. My mother did have a sewing machine. She did sew clothes for us. Because my mother was mentally ill, she blamed everything down to the tiniest details in her life on someone, anyone.

She had a pair of scissors she used for sewing. No one ever went near her sewing things. My mother would constantly fly into a rage screaming wanting to know who took her sewing scissors. She would always find them were ever she left them last but this would not stop her from flying into a rage the next time she couldn't find them.

Flying into a rage, she would scream, "Which one of you ungrateful brats took my scissors? I know you did it, where is my belt? You better find those scissors right now." "I hate you all! I'm going to give you all a way!" She would actually pick up the phone and scream "I'm going to call the shelter right now and you can all go back." We would all be crying, shaking, begging her not to send us away. This scene and others like it were played out over and over and over again, sometimes daily. Sometimes she snapped was back in the hospital and we were sent away again.

Another item that was a constant, "who took it?" was the potato peeler. I was the one who did most of the cooking and potato peeling. It was constant screaming, "what did you do with the potato peeler this time? You're so stupid you probably threw it out with the peels last time you used it." There was no way of knowing from one moment to the next what would set her off. Every movement and every word I said had to be calculated. Doing my best to be invisible. It was not always possible. She would accuse us of what ever it was today as a group. If no one did it then she would just hit us all with a belt.

One occasion about age-eight-or-nine, I was playing in my room. There are very few memories of times when I actually just played as a kid. Spending a lot of time in my room, which was usually shared, there were a few stuffed animals and a doll or two to play with. Talking to the stuffed animals believing that they had feelings, always being careful to talk softly so no one would hear or just talk to them inside of my head. Being alone in my room talking to a stuffed animal was a good way to be invisible.

On this occasion choosing to actually play with my dolls, the dolls were sitting on the bed with the stuffed animals. Involved with the dolls and my imagination I must have been talking to them aloud. My mother heard me and came in the room. She snapped at me, "What are you doing?" I said, "playing." She laughed at me and said, "You're playing with dolls." "What are you a baby?" She then proceeded to tell everyone in the house, "Look at Rose she's a baby she's playing with dolls." I was an eight-or-nine-year-old girl. Feeling like some kind of a freak I wanting to crawl in a corner and never be seen again.

Today in my fifties living a wonderful empowered life I have to really work at playing. Consciously telling myself it is okay to do something just because you enjoy it. It is okay to have fun. The one thing that my kids who are now adults say to me is, "come on mom lets just do whatever it may be." "Mom you're no fun."

Hospitalized on more than one occasion with stomach ulcers starting at eight-years-old numerous social workers and other professionals were involved over the years with my family, yet no one, not one person ever stood up and made a decision that would have been in the best interest of the children. As a child, part of me believed I wanted to be home. Looking back, clearly we should have never been given back.

5

GET A JOB

Due to our mother's inabilities to cope, Bernice and I were expected to do most of whatever housework and cooking was required. As you can imagine in this environment the house was usually in the same physical state of chaos as the emotional environment. Bernice and I would do the laundry; wash the dishes and the floors, sweep, and pick up after the younger kids. David was not expected to do anything as he was a boy and was considered totally useless. Our two younger sisters were too young, which left Bernice and me to deal with being the housekeepers.

As our mother relied on welfare to pay the bills with little or no help financially from our father, there was never enough money. As mentioned in early chapters we often moved after being evicted for non-payment of rent.

Bernice was about eight-years-old, which would have made me about seven when our mother told us she had no money and we would have to go out and look for work. She told us to go and knock on doors and ask people if they had any work we could do. This was in the early 1960's when knocking on a neighbour's door or entering a stranger's home was not considered dangerous.

We went door to door knocking and asking if anyone had any work we could do. Most people smiled or said, "Isn't that cute." There was nothing cute about it. We needed to come home with some money! Finally, we knocked at one house. The mother answered, there were children playing who were older than we were. I asked if she had any work we could do. She actually said yes. We could clean her basement.

We cleaned the basement and did some vacuuming. When we were done, she was going to pay us a dollar each. In the early 1960's two dollars was a lot of money. She looked in her wallet and realized she did not have any small bills. She said, "I'm sorry I don't seem to have the right change." "I will have to go to the bank, can you come back Monday and I will pay you?" This was a Saturday and the banks were closed. There were no ATM's at this time so Monday was the only option.

We knew we could not go home without some money. We had to tell the lady the truth. We had to tell her that we needed the money today because we were supposed to buy beans and wieners for dinner before we went home. The lady went to the grocery store and got us the two dollars.

There was only so far two kids could walk in the same neighbourhood so we would often knock on the same doors each week. One older couple thought we were cute the lady would say to her husband, "Look it's the little girls again aren't they sweet?" She never had any work for us but she seemed to enjoy us knocking on her door.

One weekend we knocked on her door, she said her housekeeper had quit, we could dust and vacuum if we liked. We did, we now had a steady job. We went back every Saturday and cleaned their house. Even after we moved out of the neighbourhood, we would take a bus on Saturday to clean their house and make a few dollars.

At seven-and eight-years-old, this was the beginning of a never-ending demand that we should have a job. I was eleven-years-old when we moved from Alberta to BC. My father had moved to BC and for some unknown reason although they were apart more than they were together my mother felt the need to follow him. We worked every weekend for this older couple until we moved to BC.

I was in grade six when we moved. We no longer had this couple to clean for and were not bringing home any money my mother constantly demanded that we find a job. At eleven-years-old, she would tell me, "You don't need to go to school. If you can find a job you can work you don't need school."

As the only job available to an eleven-year-old was babysitting, I became the neighbourhood babysitter. It paid 50cents an hour. Knowing by age seven that working and bringing home money made me at least acceptable. My mother never went into a rage over me going to work. The message that was ingrained in me was that my worth was directly tied to how well or how much I could work and if money could be made. If there was no work for me I was useless, to work and bring home money made me at least tolerable.

This self-image was carried with me into the adult world. My self worth was directly tied to how much I worked. If I was not working, I had no worth. Not just if I was or was not employed. Arriving home after working a full day there would be cooking and cleaning, being sure to find something to do until bed-time. My mother was not there in the room to push me as an adult. Psychologically pushing myself based on the pictures playing in my head, telling myself the more I did the more acceptable I would be to the world and to myself, was a permanent drive for most of my adult life.

My early adult life was a reproduction of my childhood without the physical abuse. My mother was not there to fly into a rage and be mentally abusive, yet somehow I had taken her place. Never showing emotion or anger, I had learned well to keep myself invisible.

Without realizing it, my mother's voice had been traded for my own. It was my voice telling me how stupid or inadequate I was. It was my voice screaming, I could have done better I should be doing more.

Telling myself everyday that I would never be like my mother; would never treat anyone the way she had treated me. She blamed the world and everyone in it for every problem in her life. I made a conscious decision to never blame others. Going from one extreme to the next in my determination not to be like her no matter what the circumstance.

Promising never to treat anyone the way she had treated me. I forgot to include myself in that promise. Internalizing everything that may not be going right at work or at home, telling myself I should have or shouldn't have done something different, believing only what was required was to work the hardest, do the most, not complain and never say how I felt, by eighteen I was once again hospitalized with ulcers.

6

THE DRAMA QUEEN

Looking back on my childhood, I understand that my mother's actions were caused by her mental illness. My siblings and I although we were available targets, were not the cause of her problems. There was nothing we could have done or not done to help her see us or see anything differently. My mother looked at the world through eyes that were attached to a distorted mentally ill brain. The circumstances in her life, in her childhood that may or may not have been the cause of how she viewed the world I may never know.

One thing I did come to realize was my mother on some level seemed to require the drama she created. As Dr. Phil would say, "what is the pay off?" What was she getting from creating chaos? I believe a part of her needed the attention. There was a part of my mother that was a drama queen.

There were several occasions where my mother created such drama out of her own mind, for reasons that were likely not known to her. One such occasion was Christmas Eve. I was maybe seven-years-old and still believed in Santa Claus.

In chapter 4, I described the feelings of excitement whenever it was time to return home from where ever I may have been, even though it always ended in chaos. At seven-years-old, there was the same excited feeling of anticipation knowing my daddy was coming home. It always ended up the same way, yet as a child I wanted daddy to come home.

This Christmas Eve we knew that daddy was coming home. I had no idea where he was or where he had been, only that he was coming home for Christmas. My mother told us he was driving home through the mountains. A seven-year-old could only guess where the mountains were.

She started telling us that the mountains were dangerous. She started talking about accidents. She gave me a phone number and told me to call and ask what the weather was like in the mountains. Why she did not call herself is a mystery.

This was the number to call for highway conditions. I was a kid and had no understanding of mountain routes. Asking the lady on the phone what the weather was like on the roads in the mountains; of course she asked, "which roads, and which mountains." I told my mother that she wanted to know which roads and which mountains. She answered, "the mountains going to Calgary." Relaying this information to the lady on the telephone, she could not provide me with the correct information.

My mother is almost eighty-years-old today and she has never learned how to drive. She had no idea what road or which mountain she was asking about. When I hung up the phone, she was angry.

My mother spent the rest of the afternoon into the evening talking about bad roads and accidents. She built up her anxiety and ours to the point where she was telling us, "Daddy is probably drunk; he should have been home by now. He has probably had an accident." "The roads in the mountains are full of snow, they are dangerous. Your dad is probably drunk and he is going to drive off a cliff. He is going to kill himself." These were not just words she was saying; she was near hysterics, pacing with worry.

The more worried and frantic she became the louder she spoke. I went to bed on Christmas Eve crying to myself telling myself, "I don't want my daddy to die!" "Please don't let my daddy die!"

I realize today that this incident was caused by my mother's paranoia. Why she had the need to share her paranoia and fear with her children to the point that we were as frantic and scared as she was I do not know. There was a part of my mother that fed on the chaos and the drama she created. There are two other incidents were I recall being part of the paranoid dramas my mother had created.

At eleven-or-twelve-years-old, we were living in BC and were already on the second or third place we had lived since leaving Alberta. We lived with my father for a while. The pattern of daddy being home for a while and gone most of the time was repeating itself.

I had seen him a few times since we moved into our latest house. My father would often turn up with some drunken friend at his side. Sometimes his friends would be men other times they would be women. It wasn't until my teen years that I realized the women my father brought home were hookers. Not your high priced call girls. These were literally skid row hookers, the type of woman that would trade herself for a drink out of your brown paper bag. Sometimes he brought them home as friends when my mother was home. I recall many times when my mother was in the hospital my father drinking and partying with a variety of skid row hookers.

He had invited one woman over a few times since we moved into our current house. My mother was there. My dad wasn't living with us at that time but he did come over. I have no idea what happened prior to this particular night. Was there something that I had missed that day that had started my mother's paranoia?

The house we lived in was on a very short block. There were maybe five houses on our side of the block and the same across the street. This was a dead end street with the house we were living in being the second house from the dead end. The front of the house came almost to the sidewalk. There were no driveways or garages, only street parking. The house we lived in was three stories. It had a basement a middle floor and bedrooms upstairs. One upstairs bedroom window faced the front looking out onto the sidewalk.

It was dark and I had been sleeping. I woke up as my mother was talking. For some reason she was up stairs. Her room was on the middle floor. She had the upstairs bedroom window, which faced the street open. She was yelling to someone outside. I could hear what sounded like a car door shut.

She woke me up and told me that dad's girlfriend the one he had brought to the house was outside. She told me she was trying to break in and wanted to kill her. At one point in the hysterics, my mother was saying that someone was in the basement. She was sure someone was in the basement!

Whether or not we had a telephone at this time is unknown. I remember being terrified. She told me to go to the front bedroom window and scream for help. Scream for someone to call the police. She must have woken up the other kids; as there was more than one of us screaming out he window "help! Police! help!" in the dark.

Our screams must have been heard as the police arrived. We were all crying; trembling, scared to death someone was outside or in the basement, someone who wanted to kill us. Listening to the police tell my mother to calm down. Telling my mother that they had checked. There was no one in the basement. There was no sign that anyone had tried to break in. One officer was assuring her that no one was out side. I remember his words to my mother. "Calm down, you have these children scared to death."

The third incident although it involved no hysteria and no screaming was emotionally traumatic for me at eleven-years-old. I have no recollection of where my sisters were at the time. My mother called me; we were living in the same house as the screaming incident. She was actually talking, not mad, not screaming. She told me she felt like she was going to kill herself. She said she needed me to take David, go to the police station and tell them if they do not do something, she was going to kill herself.

It is assumed that many of the times my mother was in the hospital she may have been suicidal. Always knowing my mother had problems at eleven-years-old this was the first time I had ever heard her say she wanted to kill herself. Never questioning why she wanted us to walk to the police station. Why did she not make a phone call? If we did not have a phone, why not send us to the neighbours to make a call? I now believe my mother had a real need for attention. On some level she fed on the drama, she was creating.

David and I walked to the police station, which was about fifteen blocks from where we lived. We were ten-and-eleven-years-old. We told the man at the desk that our mother had sent us to tell them she was going to kill herself. The man at the desk asked why we had come the police station. Why didn't we call an ambulance? I answered, "I don't know, my mother told us to come here." The police did call an ambulance and my mother was taken to the hospital again. David and I walked the fifteen blocks back home.

There are two other situations, which stood out as examples of my mother's irrational and unpredictable behaviour. The type of incidents that I am describing happened as a daily occurrence throughout my childhood. These were shorter and less dramatic than the stories above, however the mental and emotional toll on me as a child was no less devastating.

I was thirteen-or-fourteen-years-old at this point in my life my mother was working. She had a factory job and worked full time. To her credit, I know she worked hard for her money. With all of the other issues in her life, she managed to eventually put a down payment on a house. It was in a run down neighbourhood but I give her credit for accomplishing something in her life, which to many others in her situation would have seemed impossible.

It was still my job to do the cooking. My mother expected dinner on the table when she walked through the door at 4:30 p.m. There was never a pre-planned menu or any instructions of suggestions as to what was to be cooked. I was expected to see what was in the house and make dinner.

The events that took place for her that day are unknown. She walked into the kitchen and flew into a rage. Dinner was ready as always. I had cooked rice rather than potatoes. This was not the first time I had ever made rice. She bought the rice; it was in the house to be cooked. She started in on me, "what the hell did you cook rice for?" "You're too damn lazy to peel potatoes!" "I work all day and have to come home and eat rice!" "I don't know why I ever come home. I hate you!" she was still yelling about me cooking rice for dinner well into the evening.

It must have been November or December as this next incident involves Christmas. I do not recall how this incident began. Perhaps she overheard me say something about needing a pair of gloves. It was wintertime. I made my own money babysitting and would have never asked my mother for anything. It had been engrained as a toddler not to ask for anything. I may have been talking to one my sisters and my mother overheard that I needed or wanted gloves.

She told me that if I needed gloves that the Army & Navy Store had a big box of different coloured gloves on sale. I had seen these gloves in the store. They were thin cotton, almost like a gardener's glove in florescent pink, orange and a bright yellow with the stitching showing on the outside. I made the mistake of saying that I had seen the box of gloves on sale and that I didn't like them.

My mother flew into a rage and walked away. She returned a few minutes later and threw a pair of orange gloves at me. She screamed, "here's your Christmas present you ungrateful brat, and don't think your getting anything else."

There was no way for me to know that she had bought me gloves for Christmas. Christmas was far enough away to expect that she had shopped at all. Had I opened those gloves on Christmas morning I would have been eternally grateful and told her I loved them and would have worn them, because I knew the consequences of anything else.

7

DADDY'S HOME

As mentioned in chapter 2 my relationship with my father was off and on. He was gone more than he was ever home. I honestly cannot remember a time that my mother actually said something, anything good about my father. There was many times as a child that I believed my mother was right. Believing that all of our problems everything that we needed and did not have including a father that lived with us, everything wrong with my world and hers was my father's fault.

My father was absent for long periods of time. After we moved to BC, he was more absent than present. He lived with us when we first arrived and then again for a period of time when I was about twelve-years-old. Most of the time in BC, we lived with our mother.

As I write *Rose's World* as a fully functioning adult, it is blatantly clear that my mother was an abusive, disturbed woman. Her ability to cope and rationalize was deeply impaired. It was not possible to reason with her as her picture of the world was so distorted. I do not believe that any sane, rational thinking person could possibly see what my mother sees as she looks at her world.

My father was no angel. He had his own set of dysfunctional issues. He was an alcoholic who drank constantly. There were times when he tried AA or a detox centre. When every my father announced that he had quit drinking and he made this announcement many times. He would follow his announcement with, "I only drink beer now."

I do not know the circumstances that brought my mother and my father together. There must have been a time in these two lives when they had dreams. What every brought them together, whatever the cause of my mothers disturbed mind, what every the cause of my father's alcohol dependant life, I do not believe that either one was the cause of the others circumstance. There was a point in each of their lives when they lacked the tools required to create a life of abundance and love.

A genuinely empowered person has a life of abundance and love and requires no one to blame for his or her failures. It is when we allow our failures to define who we are that we begin to see ourselves as flawed or failed. It is not possible to be human and not to have failed at something. In one lifetime, each one of us will have failed many times. It is what we learn from our failures an how we define our successes that empowers us.

The following are incidents, which occurred during the times my father was home. Some are taken from times he lived with my mother, others are times he was caring for us when my mother was in the hospital.

The chaos, paranoia and drama that were a part of my daily life did not end when my father was home. My father's anticipated arrival to me was always exciting. As I described in chapter 4 home was always the same or worse every time I went back. With my father's coming and going it was no different. There were times when his being home was horrifying. It always ended with his leaving again. Yet as a child, some how there was still excitement when daddy was coming home.

On some level, my mother must have wanted my father to come home. No matter what the circumstances of his leaving each time she welcomed him back. I do not recall ever hearing my mother say anything good about or to my father. Looking back at their relationship as an adult, reflecting on the parts of their relationship witnessed as a child.

There had to be more to this relationship than I was able to understand. What I recall is my mother treating my father the same or worse than she treated her kids. She called him useless, lazy, good for nothing, she would scream, "your not a man!" she would snap at him and question everything he did or didn't do. When my father would yell, "I'm leaving!" my mother would scream, "fine put your tail between you legs and run! Your good for nothing anyway!" It did not matter what the argument was about. I am not sure they always knew what they were fighting about; these words were repeated thousand of times.

My father was an extreme alcoholic. As I have already said, he drank constantly. There were times when he was employed although I do not recall any of his jobs lasting very long. Several times with various jobs he was supposed to have, my mother would call him or have me call him where he was supposed to be working. The calls always ended with, "he doesn't work here any more." My mother would be furious. I know she was counting on him bringing home a pay cheque.

There were times when my father would return home after being absent when he would have money. I recall him giving me a dollar. The first time he gave me a dollar I went to the store and spent it on candy. Later that evening when I was sleeping and he was drunk. He woke me up and asked for his dollar back. He said he needed it to buy more booze. He said he needed to borrow his dollar back and he promised he would pay me back as soon as he could. I told him I spent the dollar on candy. He was angry and stomped out of my room.

On every occasion after this when he returned home and gave me money I knew he would ask for it back. He always did. I honestly believe that on some level my father cared for his kids. In his mind when he gave me a dollar, he wanted me to have it. When he was drunk and needed more booze, as he would ask for his money back; saying that it was a loan, I believe he was sincere. My father was so spiritually broken he did not have the ability to follow through with his intensions.

When my father drank, he could become violent. He would become physically violent with my mother and my brother. He was never physically violent with me and I do not remember ever seeing him physically violent with my sisters. The only time my father ever said he loved us was after he beat up our mother. She would be in the hospital and he would tell us he was sorry. He always said, "your mother made me so mad, she made me hit her." He would say, "I love your mother and I love you kids."

He would beat my mother with his fist. She was hospitalized several times for bruised or broken bones. David never ended up in the hospital but my father was both physically and mentally abusive to him. I do not recall ever hearing my father say he was sorry he hit David. He never said he loved David. He said many times about him and to him, "I hate boys I hate you."

Although I do not know a lot about my fathers life when he was away from home I know he had times when he was violent that did not involve my mother or my brother. He arrived home one time with a broken foot due to being in a fight. On one other occasion, he knocked on the door and woke us up in the middle of the night. He was drunk. His face was covered with blood. He had been in a fight and had come home in a mess. My mother was yelling at him for being stupid she was yelling, coming home looking like this was going to scare the kids. I am not sure I recall any other time she was concerned about scaring her kids.

I believe on some level my father cared for his kids and my mother. There were several times when my mother was in the hospital and he was supposed to be taking care of us. It wasn't until I was in my early teens that I realized my father spent most of his time away from home living on skid row. In BC, he lived on the now infamous lower east side, Hastings & Main Street area.

My father would entertain various drinking friends when my mother was away. The one thing that I can honestly say my father did well was picking a guitar. He played old time country and he was really good at it. I used to love to hear him pick Orange Blossom Special. He would have a drinking party and would play and drink with his skid row friends and hookers all night.

Waking up in the morning after one of dads drinking parties, wherever we lived at this time, the bedrooms were up stairs. I looked out of the upstairs window in the morning to see our furniture a couch and recliner on the front lawn. I asked my dad why the furniture was out side and he answered because we had a fire.

My father or one of his partygoers had fallen asleep with a lit cigarette. He said someone driving by saw the smoke and banged on the door to wake them up. The couch and chair were on fire. They took them outside and put them out with a garden hose. I obviously slept through the excitement. Some one was looking out for us that night.

My father would leave me many times with various friends or people he knew. Where he left the other kids, I do not know. I do remember him taking me to his hotel. I know now that these were skid row rooming houses or hotels. He would introduce me to his friends and ask them if I could stay with them for a while. I do not recall anyone every saying no. How many different times and different places I was left is unknown. There were too many to count. Being young, anywhere from six-to-ten-years-old at different times I do not remember how long I stayed at each place. It always seemed like forever.

My dad would not leave me completely alone with his friends. He would show up every once and a while and then go out again. It amazes me now that I do not recall any one of these people being anything but kind. I recall sharing hamburgers from the hotel restaurant at times. Not one person who cared for me in a skid row hotel room ever abused me in any way. They took care of me as my dad had asked until he came to get me.

I cannot say the same for some of the friends that my father brought home with him. On more than one occasion, he brought friends home to stay. Sometimes when my mother was home, these friends would sexually abuse Bernice and me on a regular basis. I do not know if my younger sisters were abused in this way.

The house we lived in, in BC where the screaming out the window incident took place was next door to an older couple. The old man was nice he liked kids. His was the only house on the block that had a colour TV set. This old man molested me on many occasions. Being a child who had no normal adult attention, I was an easy target for an experienced pedophile.

I was twelve-years-old when my mother sent me to my grandmother's house for the summer. This was her mother and her mother's husband or her stepfather. We lived in BC at the time. My grandmother, who I did not know, lived in Saskatoon Saskatchewan. My mother was sending David to stay with someone in Calgary at the same time. She put us on a grey hound bus together. David got off in Calgary I went on to Saskatoon alone. I did not know either my grandmother or the man who was supposed to be my grandfather. I was to stay with them for the summer. A few days after my arrival, the man I called grandpa started to molest me. I can still remember his tongue in my mouth and the smell of the chewing tobacco he used.

My mother left home in her early teens after her mother was married to this man. I often wonder if this was not the reason she left. I asked myself, would she have sent her twelve-year-old daughter to stay with a man who had molested her. Unfortunately given her state of mind and her need to find someone to take her kids yet again I believe she would.

As I have mentioned before my father would do what ever he could to feed his drinking problem. There were many times when he would be home long enough to take the welfare cheque and be gone again. This would leave my mother with five kids, no way to pay the rent, no money for food and evicted again. It is not hard to visualize my mother or any mother in this circumstance feeling alone, stressed and suicidal.

Although I do not know for sure it was likely a situation such as this that lead us to live in a condemned building for a time. I have very few recollections of my mother actually cooking but there is one occasion that stands out. This was a time were we literally had no food. I do not recall my younger sisters being there. It is possible they were not born yet. My mother had a bag of flour. She mixed the flour with water and a little oil to make dough. She rolled the dough out very thin, as there wasn't very much. She cut the dough into long strips and made noodles. This was all she had so she made noodles.

Whether my father had taken the welfare cheque or whatever the cause, it is amazing to me that this woman had the ability to make something from nothing to feed her children when she had to. My mother had the ability to survive. She had the ability to care on some level. What she lacked was the ability to care for and love herself so that she could in turn love her children.

There was one occasion when my mother was in the hospital I do not recall were I was staying at this time or how long any of us were away. I do recall coming home. While we were away, my father had sold everything in the house. Literally everything, I am assuming he had the equivalent of a moving sale only no one was moving. When my mother returned home, the house was empty. He sold the furniture, he sold the TV and he even sold the beds.

What ever the reason and I am assuming it was money for alcohol, everything was gone. How my mother every coped or recouped her belongings one can only imagine. I do know that every fight from that day on, as they were screaming; my mother would always add, "your no man! What kind of a man would sell your own kids beds?"

One of the worst beatings my mother ever survived was after we had moved to BC. I was twelve-years-old. My older sister and I had returned home late in the evening around 10 o'clock. My father was in the house. He was in one of his speak softly I am sorry kind of moods. He told us that our mother wasn't home. She was in the hospital. He had beaten her up. Of course, he said he was sorry and that he loved her, that he loved us, and that it was her fault, she made him hit her.

He had beaten her so badly this time that she was in the hospital for some time. How long I do not recall. I remember taking a bus to see her, her face was swollen, purple and her chest was black. Her eyes were puffy. She had a broken jaw and several broken ribs. It is difficult to understand why my mother who had spent as much or more time on her own as she had spent with my father endured such treatment. Their relationship for as long as I could remember was physically and mentally abusive and draining for them both.

Arriving home shortly after the incident my mother was sitting at her sewing machine. She very quietly said to me, "Your father and I are getting a divorce. I will keep the little ones but you and Bernice are on your own." I was twelve-years-old Bernice was thirteen. It was around this same time that Bernice had met a friend who belonged to the Navy League Wrennets. This was the equivalent of Sea Cadets for boys only this group was for girls. Bernice joined and talked me into following her.

After being in so many different schools, there was no attachment to school for me. I had learned from a very early age that I was never around long enough to make real friends. In the older grades, changing schools became more difficult. Older children were not as accepting of the new kid in class. Consequently, this newfound group would become my circle of friends.

The last incident with my father before my leaving home at age fifteen was an incident when I was about thirteen-or-fourteen-years old. He was not living with us at the time but he was coming over every once in a while. My father had called on the telephone a few times this day; he was clearly having an argument with my mother.

She hung up after one of the phone calls and said, "dad was on his way over; and that he was going to kill her." In her panicked and hysterical state, again she told us he was coming home to get his gun and he was going to kill us all.

My father did have a rifle behind the door in the bedroom and he did have bullets. I do not recall who called the police this time it may have been Bernice. I know my mother wanted someone to call the police and tell them that dad had a gun and was going to kill us.

The police came and confiscated the gun and the bullets. Looking back at this now, it is not logical that my father intended to come home to kill my mother and his children, yet he would call first to let her know where the gun was. Either this was another of my mother's paranoia incidents or my father was just as illogical and irrational as she was.

8

ALTERED PERCEPTIONS

The years following the gun incident, I do not recall my father being home at all. Tagging along with Bernice I had attached myself to this new group of Navy League friends. As the saying goes, "**birds of a feather flock together**." The flock we became part of included one or two kids who had what I considered to be a normal life. The majority of the kids that we hung around with on a regular basis were from dysfunctional homes. Some had no fathers others had off and on again parents etc.

At twelve-years-old, my perception of the world consisted of my experiences. I saw the world through the eyes of a twelve-year-old girl who's only references to family, parents, school, jobs etc. was what I had experienced. There was no way for me to know how distorted and dysfunctional my world had always been.

The first time Bernice and I were invited to one of our new found friends home, this was a girl and her brother both in the Navy League. These were the kids I referred to as having a normal life. They lived in what I now know was a middle class home in an older Vancouver neighbourhood. This was literally the first time I ever knew a kid that had two parents that lived together all the time. Their father not only lived with them but he had a job. He drove an ambulance. The first time I walked into their house I told my self-wow they are rich, coming to this conclusion because their house had wall-to-wall carpet. The only other house I had ever been in that had wall-to-wall carpet belonged to my Aunt and my mother always said she was rich.

It was a more natural attraction for me to spend most of my time with the kids in the group who came from dysfunctional families. At twelve-years-old I thought nothing of coming home at 2 a.m. or not coming home at all for two or three days at a time. No one ever asked where I was. Usually turning up late Sunday night or early Monday morning to go to school and be gone again Friday after school.

We would routinely get together at which, ever house had no parents at home. As the kids I chose to be with had families with parents who drank or did drugs it was not difficult to find a house with no one home. From twelve-years-old to fifteen I was drunk every weekend all weekend long. We would drink rot gut wine, lemon gin and navy rum mostly because they were cheap. I was shy and preferred to be invisible even with this group. Most of my time was spent sitting in a corner by myself; drinking until I puked and passed out. We all did the same thing. I may have been drunk but I was accepted. There were a few times that I skipped school to get drunk. Always-smart enough not to skip too many classes and affect my grades.

My drinking days came to an end at fifteen-years-old. Working as a waitress at a fast food restaurant, still in school, working Friday nights and weekends. It was at this restaurant that I met the man I married. I was fifteen-and-a-half and he was seventeen when we met. He was in grade twelve and had a job flipping hamburgers on the weekends.

I had everything in common with this tall good looking seventeen-year-old. His parents had divorced when he was seven-years-old. He lived with his mother while his two older sisters lived with their father and his new wife. His mother had since remarried and had two children with her new husband. Both his mother and his stepfather were alcoholics. His stepfather was an on again off again parent. At the time we met, Jason was living at home with his mother, younger brother and sister, working and trying to finish high school. His stepfather was not living with them at the time. We shared stories of our dysfunctional families and childhood horrors. Jason had a stepfather who hated him. His stepfather had two children that were his and one that was not and he let everyone know which one was not his.

We spent every day together. I was now going to Jason's house on Friday night and coming home late Sunday night. His mother was an alcoholic but she was a happy drunk. She was a real comedian who had no boundaries for herself or her children. She would sell beer by the bottle to any kid who knocked on her door in the welfare project where they lived. She would actually make Jason's brother sleep on the couch so we could sleep together in the room they shared when I would stay for the weekend.

Jason graduated high school a year before I did. After he graduated, he got a full time job and moved out of home. Jason shared an apartment with a roommate to cover expenses. I began staying at the apartment with him and wanted to quit school and get a full time job so we could live together. If I paid half the rent, he would not require a roommate. I am forever grateful that Jason talked me into finishing school.

We did move in together. I changed schools to one that had what they called a semester system. This allowed me to take classes in the mornings and work in the afternoon. Making it possible for me to live with Jason while completing grade twelve. I was the only one of my mother's five children to ever graduate high school.

Choosing not to attend my graduation ceremony, I knew my mother was not likely to come. The school policy was that I had to attend with someone who went to the school, which meant leaving Jason at home. The last day of my grade twelve year was a Wednesday. Three days later on Saturday June 23, 1973 at seventeen-and-nineteen-years old Jason and I were married.

Looking back today, it is so clear how distorted my view of the world had been. At the time that I met Jason at fifteen-years-old, I actually believed that he had everything. My world had been so small and everyone in it was broken in some way, not only did I believe that this seventeen-year-old had a normal life; I believed he had it all. This may sounds ridiculous to anyone who has never shared my reality.

Jason at seventeen-years-old had graduated high school. This was the first person in my world that had ever achieved anything. He had an alcoholic, violent stepfather who was sometimes home and sometimes not. My attitude at this time was big deal. I believed everyone had a father or someone that fit this picture in his or her life.

I expected that his past life should have no long-term emotion affect on him, as I believed I went through as bad or worse and it did not affect me. We often talked about situations from our past. It was just that; it was the past. I think we were both naive enough to believe that we had come through our lousy childhoods unaffected.

I loved this new person in my life. For the first time since my birth, I felt wanted. The reason that I believed this boy from a dysfunctional home had it all was, Jason may have had an abusive stepfather but he also had a mother who was always there. I did not see an alcoholic with no boundaries who sold alcohol to eight-year-olds out of a welfare project. I saw a happy mother who was always home. I heard the stories of his mother protecting him from his abusive stepfather. I saw what I believed to be at the time a perfect mother who loved her kids. My world was so deprived of anything that I would now describe as normal. I lived in a world where welfare was the norm. To actually be living in a welfare project was something my mother had aspired to. Our family never made it off the waiting list. The reality in my world was if you were fortunate enough to be living in the projects as we called them. This meant you always had a home. Without a welfare project home, the welfare cheque did not always cover the rent. This meant constant evictions. When we could pay the rent there was no money left for food. My mother had often told me if you lived in the projects, you had it made. Your cheque actually covered your rent and paid for food and you never got evicted.

At the time, that we met Jason had been living in the same apartment in this project with his family for more than two years. To me that was a stable home forever. Jason was going to graduate high school and he had a minimum wage job. What more could a person ask for? He had it all!

It is so clear as I look back now through wiser, older eyes, how distorted my view of the world had been. To me at the time at seventeen-years-old I was sure I had the world figured out. There was no way for me to know that my world, which was based on my experiences, was so small. I had no way of knowing that my experiences were the exception and not the norm.

My mother is now eighty-years-old. Somehow, she has lived eighty years in her own small world. Living from her distorted perceptions. She has always been apart of a completely wonderful world she has been unable to see. She believes the entire world and everyone in it is sharing her experiences. She believes she is the norm.

Wherever you are in your life, dare to open your eyes. Dare to see the whole world. Dare to see your world from as many perspectives as you can find. Question it all, choose to learn, choose to look at everything from all sides.

The only way any of us can possibly look at our worlds is through our own eyes. We view everything in our lives through the filters of our experiences. Dare to admit that your experiences may have been distorted at some point in your life.

It is through sharing experiences, good or bad, accurate or distorted that we are able to truly see each other and ourselves. The only tool required for a full-empowered life is an opened mind and the willingness to see. Dare to soar through life with the strong steady wings of an eagle. Dare to soar with both eyes open.

Have you ever seen an eagle madly flapping in the breeze? An eagle does not flap or flounder and eagle soars. An eagle soars on strong steady confident wings making slight adjustments for the wind. An eagle eagerly searches always with both eyes wide. An eagle searches for what he knows is already there. The eagle has no doubt that the ingredients to sustain and strengthen his life are within his reach he has only to soar long enough and wide enough to find them. We all have the ability to soar. Choose to soar through life with the determination of an eagle. Choose to soar with both eyes open.

9

EXPECTATIONS

I had not seen by father since the gun incident, he was not staying with my mother and I was no longer home on a regular basis. I was married three days after finishing high school. Jason and I had been living together and had always talked about getting married. We both were marrying for love although the reason for the timing was we needed money to buy a motorcycle.

About six months before my graduation, we had a car accident. We were on our way home from a weekend with friends at a lake. Jason was driving, he went around a curve too fast and we rolled the car. Jason was not hurt I had three-damaged disks, two in my neck one between my shoulder blades and a dislocated shoulder. I used a neck brace for more than a year. Because of the accident, we no longer had a car. I did not have a driver's license at the time. Jason needed a vehicle to get to work as he worked too far away for public transit.

Jason's father who we had visited together a few times said if we were to ever get married, he would give us $300.00 for a wedding present. This was 1973, $300.00 was a lot of money. A brand new Toyota off the lot with all the extras was about $3,000.00.

After the accident, Jason was having a hard time finding a way to get to work. We decided that we would get married and use the $300.00 to buy a used motorcycle. It was summer and a motorcycle would get him to work. That is exactly what we did.

Jason had just celebrated his nineteenth birthday and I was seventeen when we married. In BC, you are legally an adult at nineteen. He did not require permission for a marriage license I did. My mother provided her signature however the law requires both parents to sign. The signature had to be witnessed by a Notary, a police officer or Reverend etc. I had a friend who went to church she arranged for the Reverend from her church to witness my fathers signature.

My mother gave me a phone number to contact my father. He was drunk when I called to explain that we were getting married and required his signature for the marriage license. My father agreed to meet me and sign the consent. He had someone with him at the time that I phoned. He wanted to me to say hello to his girlfriend. I was polite said hello. She was obviously intoxicated.

Providing my father with instructions to the church where we were to meet and explaining that his signature had to be witnessed by the Reverend. I asked him very nicely if he could not be drinking when he showed up and if he would come alone without his girlfriend. He was drunk at the time so he agreed.

My father did actually show up at the right place at the right time and he did sign the consent form. He was drunk and he brought his drunken girl friend with him. My father still chose his girl friend from skid row. She was dressed in a hot pink very mini, mini skirt with a dirty white blouse, complete with bleached blond un-kept hair and was wearing black nylon stockings with several large runs and holes. There were bruises on her legs and tattoos on her arms. The two of them together as they walked into the church looked like a couple of wino's that needed to sleep it off. This is exactly what they were.

This was the first time I had met this Reverend. He looked at me; he looked at the two of them and he said, "I guess the mother signs here." I could not believe the words came out of my mouth but I actually said, "That's not my mother!" The tone in my voice was one of disgust. My father signed the form and the two of them left the church. Either he was so drunk he hadn't heard what I said or for some reason he chose not to notice.

As disgusted and embarrassed as I was it felt good to actually say what I had been thinking. For one brief moment, I felt like it was okay to stand up for myself and say what I was feeling.

There were only two other occasions that I recall seeing my father after being married. The first one was a phone call at work three or four years later. I had not seen or heard from him since the summer of 1973.

I was working as a secretary in the offices for a major department store in down town Vancouver BC. The one thing I had accomplished during high school was becoming a competent typist and completing office and clerical courses. My father called me at work one day. My mother told him where I worked and had given him the phone number; she always seemed to know where he was no matter how much time had gone by.

He sounded reasonably sober. He wasn't calling to see how I was or what was new in my life he was calling me to borrow money. He used the same words that he used when I was a kid and he wanted his dollar back. He said it was a loan until payday and he promised that he would pay me back. He never did say where he was working or when payday was.

Feeling obligated to say yes, just as I had felt obligated to keep his dollar and return it every time he asked when I was a child, I agreed to lend him some money until payday. Expecting that he would come to the office and pick it up. He asked if I could meet him on the corner on my lunch break. He said he was not allowed in the department store because he had been charged with shoplifting in this store.

His life had not changed since the first time I remember seeing him when he was coming home from jail and I was three-years-old. He had been in jail for stealing. There I was standing on a street corner in downtown Vancouver waiting for my skid row father to meet me so I could give him money to buy booze.

No longer a child, yet somehow feeling the same excitement that I felt as a child when daddy was coming home, I was meeting my father after not seeing him for three or four years. A part of me expected and even wanted him to be happy to see me. There were expectations that he would ask about my job or my husband or some part of my life. As with every time daddy came home the result would be a disappointment.

The first thing my father said to me after, "did you bring me some money?" was to tell me how disappointed he was that I had cut my hair. He proceeded to tell me how homely I looked now that I wore glasses. There was no thank you for your help, I missed you or how have you been. Walking back to the office feeling used, ugly and stupid for not saying no when he asked for a loan that I knew he would never pay back and would never appreciate.

The next and last time to see my father was in 1980. No longer working in Vancouver, I lived in a small town in the Fraser Valley and had not seen or heard from him since the day we met on that street corner. Picking up the phone one morning it was my father.

Every instinct in my body was telling me to hang up or say, "What the hell do you want?" I found myself doing what I had always done, being polite asking him how he was and why he was calling. He started by telling me that he had quit drinking again. I had heard this story a million times. He was telling me he was staying at a detox centre a few miles away from the town where I was living.

That little voice inside of me was now saying maybe he has changed, give him another chance. He told me that the place he was staying had a shuttle bus, which takes the clients into town for the day. He was in the town where I was living. He wanted to know if I would meet him for coffee. Somehow the old pattern of being excited and having some kind of good expectations when daddy came home seemed to override the fact that I knew he used me the last time, and that he would disappoint me again, I still agreed to meet him.

We agreed to meet for coffee. I told him I was bringing my son his grandson. Daniel was two-years-old at the time. This was the one and only time my father every saw his grandson he never met his granddaughter.

We met at a local coffee shop. The instinct that I had ignored, the instinct that told me he did not want to see me he wanted something from me, was once again correct. He told me that he had missed his shuttle bus and asked if I would drive him back to the detox centre.

He said he wanted me to meet his workers and he wanted to show his grandson to his friends. Once again, I said yes. It was about a twenty-minute drive down a narrow country road. We were on the road almost on the grounds of the Centre. He asked me to stop the car for a minute. I pulled over and stopped the car. He got out of the car, walked into the trees, took a brown paper bag out of his coat and hid the bag in the trees.

My father did not miss his bus. He had no desire to introduce anyone to his grandson. What he needed was a ride back to the Centre because he would not have been able to take his booze on the bus. He stopped to hide his bottle so he could later walk down the hill and get drunk.

He did quit drinking. This time instead of, "I only drink beer now," it must have been I only drink rye now. He did tell the truth about one thing he was staying at a detox centre.

That was the last time I saw my father. In the almost twenty years which passed from this day until he died I never saw him again. He died the way he lived, in a skid row Vancouver East Side hotel room, passed out drunk choking on his own vomit.

My mother attended his funeral with my youngest sister and David. David attended his father's funeral with an escort as he was in jail at the time. Bernice, 1 younger sister and I chose not to attend. They held his funeral in the bar at the skid row hotel where he had lived and died. The Royal Canadian Legion paid to bury him, as he had been a Veteran of World War II.

I do not mourn my father's death. I mourn his life! I do not know my fathers history, his childhood story. I do know that by the time I was born for whatever reason my father was a man whose spirit had been broken. He may have had childhood experiences that contributed to his sense of self worth. Whatever the reasons, my father lived his entire adult life in a constant state of struggle and uncertainty. I cannot speak to what he actually felt. I believe he felt lonely, unwanted and unworthy. He spent his lifetime attempting to drown his sorrows in alcohol.

I mourn my father life. I mourn the moment in time in his life when he chose to see the world with his eyes closed. The moment in time; when he chose to feel only the pain in his life. My father spent a lifetime, his lifetime, medicating his world to mask whatever pain he believed he was feeling. He was unable to see that he was living in a world full of beauty. He was a part of a world that is full of love. He lived an entire lifetime in a world full of caring, loving, laughing, productive, energetic, enthusiastic people of which he saw none.

I mourn the life my father could have known had he dared to open his eyes, had he dared to experience and be part of the whole world to which he had been born. My Father shut his eyes and closed his mind at a time in his life when he had experience only a fraction of what the world had to offer. He concluded to himself that the entire world was exactly as he was viewing it through his experiences. I mourn the life he could have had, had he only known that his experiences at that point in time were distorted and only temporary. The cause of the distortion does not matter.

. We all live in a world full of love and wonder. We all live in a world full of pain, hurt and anger. We all live in this world side by side sharing the same time, sharing the same space. Yet, we experience such different outcomes. We all see the world through the only eyes we have. We all see the world filtered through our own experiences. There are many people who have been hurt by people or circumstances, which legitimately were out of their control. Many people legitimately have someone to blame for unfavourable circumstance in their lives.

We all must choose which part of this whole world to live in. I choose to see the whole picture. The world I live in is a world of love. I live in a world of sharing and caring. This does not mean that I do not also live in a world with disappointments, pain, hurt and sometimes anger. These are all a part of life.

I choose to see that all of life's circumstances are temporary. Life itself is temporary. I will soar through the disappointments and the pain, as an eagle with both eyes open knowing there is love and wonder already there for me to find if I will only soar long enough.

To choose to go through life focusing on the pain, focusing on the medication or focusing on who to blame is to be an eagle able to fly yet unwilling to open his eyes. Everything required to sustain his life and flourish is there, yet an eagle unwilling to open his eyes is not able to see and will surely experience a life of lack, a life of hardship and will surely perish.

Only one thing is required to change in order to live a full, empowered, happy life. You have only to change your mind. There is a completely wonderful world waiting for you if you are willing to soar with both eyes open.

10

ROSES MAP FOR THE FUTURE

Married to a man I loved; my childhood was gone but not forgotten. I was the only one who could see the pictures playing in my head. My life and our future were mapped out in my mind.

What I did not know was I was the one drawing the map using seventeen years of distorted accumulated knowledge. Certain I knew which road to take and which roads to avoid; I was determined to complete the chosen route mapped out in my mind. I was careful not to include any roads on my map that had been previously traveled by my parents or myself.

As it is only ever possible to see through your own eyes and through your own experiences that is exactly what I was doing. Viewing my current life through eyes attached to my brain that was full of distorted perceptions of the world.

Dr Phil says, "We teach the world how to treat us." This reference is for adults, as adults through the choices, we make and through our actions or reactions, we set the tone for our relationships.

Although no longer living with my mother I had taken her place, telling myself how stupid I was or how inadequate, how I could have done better, how I should be doing more. The only picture in my head of being worthy was a picture of me doing it all.

Determined to be the perfect wife, having no idea what it meant to be a wife let alone a perfect one. The definition in my head of what it meant to be a wife was I was responsible for making him happy. Whatever Jason's needs may be it was my job to fill them.

If I loved Jason and I did, it was my job to meet his every need. My definition of a successful marriage was it was up to me to do what ever it took to make him happy so he would not leave me. I started this relationship, our relationship as a couple with pictures playing in my head, which did not include or acknowledge

37

me. I now know that the life I had mapped out in my mind was not the route to a perfect marriage. Striving for the perfect relationship, doing what I had always done, giving more, doing more, working harder, requiring nothing for myself; yet unable to see that I was working on the wrong project.

I had not mapped out a route to a perfect relationship as a couple. I had mapped out and had been working on a relationship between a man and his maid. My physical self was included in the picture while leaving out my wants, my desires and my needs.

I was still the little girl who had learned to be invisible; the little girl who knew that to ask for something, anything, was to be ungrateful and greedy; still the broken little girl who believed that I was worth less (worthless). To ask to let my husband think that I may require something, anything from him would make me a burden. A part of me did not want him to give me away as I had been given away so many times as a child. I had to be perfect if I wanted Jason to stay.

Jason had no way of seeing the life I had mapped out for us in my mind. My taking on the roll of doing it all meant he did not have to! I had no needs no request no expectations. What ever he did or did not do was acceptable to me. As I had no expectations, he had nothing to aspire to in our relationship.

My father was an alcoholic his mother and stepfather were both alcoholics. Completing my lifetime of drinking between the ages of twelve and fifteen, meeting Jason gave me a reason to not spend my weekend's drunk. There were several years in our marriage were we both had a dislike for alcohol.

My teen years was a time when experimenting with marijuana was just beginning. I had tried it and only wanted to go to sleep. Jason tried marijuana for the first time when he was eighteen before we were married.

Jason smoked marijuana on a regular basis. We both had a strong dislike for alcohol because when a person drinks it changes their personality, when Jason smoked marijuana he was so quiet and mild it was like taking a tranquilizer. We did not see this as a negative change or as a problem.

What I did not know was at eighteen-years-old before we were married Jason had already experienced that moment in time in his life where he had closed his eyes to the world. Jason had already concluded to himself that the entire world was exactly as he was viewing it through his own experiences. He was already living a life of pain and medication.

I was not able to see how broken my world was. Believing my childhood was over and that I now viewed the world without the affects of my past. I was wrong. My perception of myself was subconsciously distorted and my perception of Jason's life was equally distorted. Other than conversations we had about our past

I had concluded that none of it mattered. While I believed that Jason's past was equally over and had no effect on him, unable to see that Jason's image of himself was as distorted as mine. Thinking Jason had it all together, Jason saw himself as being less than.

What Jason was feeling inside I do not know. The pain and rejection from his own childhood was distorting his view of the world as was mine. At eighteen-years-old when he discovered marijuana, he also found his way to medicate his pain.

Jason's eyes remained closed as my father's eyes remained closed, with his need for medication increasing.

Jason is now in his fifties and has yet to open his eyes. The map of my future, our future was engrained in my mind. The picture of our future was complete down the smallest detail. This was not a dream, a wish or a desire. This was a blue print. My life was like a mission that I could not fail. Using the only tools, I had; I would do what ever it took, for as long as it took, to make it all happen. I was still that little girl walking down that sidewalk knocking on doors determined to come home with some money or I could not come home at all.

It was not my mother insisting that I keep going until I had what she needed. This was not my husband insisting that I create a world for us all on my own. I shared my pictures with Jason yet chose to make myself solely responsible for every detail. I told myself what our lives required and insisted on taking responsibility for doing what it took to make it happen. Anything less would mean I was once again a failure.

Without knowing it, I chose to live beside my husband rather than with him, never allowing Jason completely into my world. Absolutely believing that to ask for help was a sign of weakness, I was completely determined not to be a burden. I was determined to create our perfect world; so, he would keep me.

It never entered my mind that to Jason, coming from a childhood with some of the same unwanted issues that he may be interpreting my actions, as a sign that I did not need him. Was it possible that unknowingly in my doing it all; Jason was left feeling as though he was less than. Could Jason have interpreted my actions as I chose to do it all because I believed he was not capable?

I loved Jason and told him I loved him everyday. Jason's life consisted of going to work every day and coming home to medicate himself with marijuana and television. Jason made the choice to medicate his pain before we were married. I know that I am not responsible for his choices or the outcome of his life.

I was living everyday in my life, yet I was not completely present, physically I was there; part of me was present on some emotional level. I was always able to walk through the daily details.

Rose was not present. I did not exist even to myself; so adept at becoming invisible I was emotionally detached even from myself. My blueprint the blueprint in which I had painstakingly drawn every detail was just that. It was full of details. It was full of exacts. If I do this, the result will be that. The feelings that I thought were mine were just as controlled and calculated as rest of my life.

I was living my life in fear. This was not an external threat. This was internal. The fear that had taught me to be invisible when I was a toddler; was deeply implanted in my soul. Learning to be invisible, to show no emotion, to analyse every word before speaking; was a survival tool. It was a tool that I had used so often it no longer had to consciously be turned on, this tool was used so often that I no longer ever turned it off.

While mapping out my foreseeable future and creating an exact blue print of my life requirements. I was not building a future I was building a fortress with a moat; believing that by working harder, doing more, doing it all, I could build a future for us. This life long project I was fully responsible for, was to protect me, if I were perfect if everything was perfect Jason would stay, he would never leave.

The need for this project was only in my distorted mind. Still hearing the voices saying no one wants you! No one will ever want you! Believing my worth; was determined by what I was able to produce, being so intent on hanging on to Jason, yet somehow never taking the time to really know him, never taking the time to know myself. Living my life on the surface, present only in the details of each day. I was barely, present in the emotional part of my own life.

I loved my husband. I know now that the emotions I shared with him were as guarded as the rest of my life, incapable of showing my true feeling, ideas, thoughts and emotions even to me. The love I was able to give was as complete as was possible for me at the time.

Living every part of my life with my invisible tool turned on full; I had given up being fully a part of the present. In my quest to secure my future from an imagined possible threat I was not able to see that as I was struggling to keep my husband happy, as I was struggling to create the perfect world for both of us, I had locked myself out of my own life and his.

Jason had already closed his eyes and was living in his own world. He was concentrating on medicating whatever pain he believed he was feeling. I was busy building a fortress to keep him in, when his spirit had already left. So determined that it was my job to make Jason happy, I was so busy doing my job that I did not see that this man was anything but happy. He was living the daily details of his life as I was. Jason was not present in his life or mine. He was content due to medication. Although we did not know it, we were two broken people trying to put each other's pieces together. We were both working on puzzles of each other without knowing how the complete picture was to look.

There is nothing or no one so broken they cannot be healed; it is only possible to fix or heal whatever the project may be with the correct tools. We were both working with broken parts and broken tools. This does not make the result impossible; it does make it more difficult and in some cases a life long project.

11

UNCLAIMED ACCOMPLISHMENTS

One of the plans for our future that we shared and spoke of even before we were married was having children. We both wanted a family. I saw myself with four children, three boys and a girl. Jason's picture of a family included two children. We both shared a dream of the families we never had. We talked about how our children would never experience being unwanted. We would insure that our children would grow up feeling loved, wanted, happy and secure. Our children would never experience the worlds we had both left behind.

I cannot speak as to Jason's feelings or motives for wanting to be a father. I had some subconscious drive to not only be a perfect mother but to somehow make-up to the world for the life my little brother endured as a child. There was a deep need at the time to prove to myself, but mostly to my mother, that it was possible to raise a boy. I made it my mission to prove a boy can be raised to be a loving, caring and successful man.

Jason had often spoken of his father leaving when he was seven-years-old. He was the youngest of three children and lived with his mother. His two older sisters lived with their father and his new wife. Thus, he had very little contact with his father growing up. As an adult, he did see him on occasion. I do not know his fathers history. All I know of his father and his new wife was that they were both alcoholics when I met them.

Being a child Jason's understanding of his father leaving when he was seven-years-old was the same understanding of most young children. He believed somehow that it was his fault. As an adult, he still believed he somehow was the cause. He often would say that he only wanted two children because the third was always a problem. Jason was the third child. Somehow, he felt his being born was the cause of his parent's divorce and his father leaving.

Jason told me the story several times of his father having an affair with the woman he later married. He remembered hiding under the basement stairs as a child watching his father and the woman who became his father's new wife kissing etc. As an adult, he understood that his father had divorced his mother and remarried because of this affair. Emotionally he still believed he was some how responsible. Jason never lost the belief that a third child caused all future problems.

As I had carefully mapped out every part of our relationship, every part of our married life the blue print in my head included children. We were both working at full time jobs. Jason had started a four-year apprenticeship program, which would result in a trade ticket and a good wage; I was employed as a secretary for the same department store.

This was the early 1970's; a time when women were opting for careers and daycare centres. We were both determined that I would stay home, because neither one of us wanted some daycare centre to raise our kids. As with all other aspects of our relationship I was determined that this too was a project I must complete for us, and so it was up to me to create the perfect environment if we were to have children.

We had purchased a car and Jason traded in his $300.00 wedding motorcycle for a brand new Honda 500. We had jobs we had transportation; he would soon be qualified to earn a wage that would allow me to stay home. There were only two other items in my blueprint required for us to start a family.

The most important item in my plan was a house. I was determined to own a house, while Jason felt this was out of our reach. Owning a house would be nice, but it was not a requirement for starting a family.

For me this was not just a desire to own a house. I had given up having any wants and desires as a child. To me to own a house was an absolute necessity. It was as necessary to own a home before having children, as it is necessary to have air to breathe. For me to bring a child into this world without owning a home meant a life of constant moving. I saw my children having to change schools, their lives being in the hands of landlords, many, many, landlords.

We had no savings, no down payment. We certainly were not going to be one of those couples whose family would help with the financing. I could not imagine a life without children and could not, would not, return to a life of constant moving and constant change! I would not do this to my children! This was not a choice! I was absolutely passionate about having children and completely driven to find us a home.

The home I was looking for was some small shack in a run down neighbourhood. It would not be fancy but it would be ours. I envisioned us fixing it up and one day being able to sell it for something better. I was looking for something anything that we could call our own and that we could afford. I did tell myself that ideally it would have three bedrooms and would preferably be a house without a basement. I had memories of old houses with scary cellars or underground basements.

The only reference in my mind to houses, were those in the neighbourhoods that I had lived in as a child. Other than my aunts' house and the one friend with wall-to-wall carpet, I did not have much occasion to be in someone else's neighbourhood. We had lived in two different apartments one before and one after we were married, and were currently living in a basement suite in a reasonable neighbourhood. This neighbourhood was not fancy but it was well out of our financial reach to purchase a home.

Although I had the map for my life my blueprint in my head, there was no realistic plan for how we would be able to buy a house. Reading every newspaper ad and every real estate ad, I could find. I read, "for sale by owner," "build a log house" or "buy a mobile home." If it had real estate in it, I read it. I read every description of "Mortgage Company" ads, "money to loan ads," "rent to own, lease to own." There were ads detailing how much money down how much money a month. It all seemed way out of our financial league.

The more I read that was out of our reach the more determined I became. To most people including Jason the logical thing to do was to give up and wait for our financial situation to improve. There was a voice inside of me that kept saying you will find the one, there has to be one that is just a little more run down or the one seller with a different circumstance.

To give up to me would mean to give up having children! That was never an option. Doing what I had always done. I tried harder and looked further I looked and looked and looked.

I had been looking for close to two years with the same results. Then one day I found a "for sale by builder" ad that caught my eye. It read $500.00 down assumable mortgage no qualifying. This was for houses being built in a small town two hours away from Vancouver, for this reason I discounted the ad and kept reading.

A week or so later the same ad appeared again. It wasn't until coming across the ad for a third time I called the number. Talking to the builder on the phone, he was selling brand new three bedroom no basement homes for $43,000.00. The builder had taken out mortgages on the homes, which were assumable with no qualifying. All that was required was $500.00 down. I finally did it. I found us a home. It wasn't a run down shack in an old neighbourhood it was brand new, three bedrooms and no basement. It was perfect and it came with wall-to-wall carpet!

The last item required on my list was a dishwasher. Why this item was on my list, I am not sure. There may have been a part of me that actually added a want to my blue print. Whatever the reason we purchased a dishwasher from the department store where I worked before we moved into our new home.

We made the decision to move to this small town. It was the perfect place to raise children. We bought the last house on a dead end road. The road ended where a farm field began. We had chickens and a rooster next door. We moved in the spring, had our third anniversary in June and I turned twenty-one in August. I had been married three years, bought my first house and had not yet turned twenty-one-years old.

I was still working in downtown Vancouver and Jason was working in New Westminster. We would ride together to where he worked, which was about an hour and a half away from home, and I would continue on by bus to Vancouver. Later I discovered that it was possible to take a Grey Hound bus each morning to Vancouver. It was a two-hour trip one way, leaving home at 6a.m. and returning home at 7p.m. every day. This continued for the next two years.

This little town thirty-years later is a City and now many people commute to Vancouver on a daily basis for work. At the time, that we moved into our first home everyone thought we were crazy. My boss could not believe that anyone would come so far every day for work.

To look back now I am able to see that coming through the childhood I had survived, graduating from high school, working as a secretary, being married and purchasing my first home all before turning twenty-one were each amazing accomplishments.

The first time we invited Jason's mother out to see our new home. This was a woman who since her divorce when Jason was seven-years-old had lived on welfare. She remained on welfare until well into her eighties when she moved into a nursing home.

His mother complained about how small it was. It was only 1100 square feet, it was so far away and it doesn't even have a basement. She commented on how hard it was on Jason to have to drive so far to work every day. This type of reaction I would have expected from my mother. I had always thought of Jason's mother as being wonderful.

I was never able to see any part of my life, as being successful, never seeing any part of what I did as an accomplishment and this was no different. I had found us a house. A new house yet somehow, it was and I was still less than (not good enough). I did not celebrate my accomplishments, telling myself somehow I could have, should have done better.

As I mentioned earlier Jason did not believe owning our own home was a necessary prerequisite to starting a family. We had not used birth control for the two-year period that I was searching for a house. I was not what you would consider a sickly person but I was also not the picture of health. Being thin as a child amongst the long list of negative descriptions and names, my mother called me was skinny.

As a child and well into my adult years feeling stressed would make it impossible for me to eat, my childhood was full of with daily worry, anxiety and fear. You have heard people refer to having a pit in their stomach. When I was upset which was most of the time my stomach would tighten like a rock.

As an adult I continued to tell myself that every time something wasn't going right at work or at home it was because I should have, or shouldn't have, done something different. So sure I had to work the hardest, do the most, not complain and never say how I felt. Keeping everything inside by eighteen I was again hospitalized with ulcers.

At five feet, five inches tall and weighing at my heaviest 107 pounds. Two years of desperate house searching had put yet another stress on my already fragile mind and body. At sixteen, before we were married I had my first surgery for ovarian cyst. Like everything else in my life, I went through the details without attaching any importance or emotion to the situation; this surgery only affected me and I was of no importance to anyone.

During my two-year house-hunting project, surgery was again required on my ovaries. I again went through the surgery like it was no big deal and it did not matter. I had completed the necessities on my list of must haves before we had a family; all that was left, was to actual get pregnant. As my time was not required to look at real estate listings, we were actually acknowledging that two years had gone by and we were not pregnant.

I made an appointment with a specialist to be sure that everything was all right. Over the next two years, surgery was required seven times on my tubes and ovaries. One surgery included removing one ovary and my appendix. After losing my left ovary, I had concluded that I would never become pregnant. Unable to conceive with two ovaries how would it be possible to conceive with one? In addition, the remaining ovary had scar tissue from surgery. The specialists said he was not sure that it was functioning.

We began talking about adoption and the possibility that we may never have our own children. It took four years of trying and nine surgeries before finally becoming pregnant. I continued to travel the busses and work in Vancouver until two weeks before my due date to deliver our first child. Nineteen hours of labour and we were blessed with a beautiful baby boy. My need to prove to the world that it was possible to raise a boy with love and acceptance had begun.

My mother arrived a week or so after Daniel was born to see the new baby. She handed me a book on horoscopes and said, "This is so you can look up what to look out for, so you can know what kind of problem he will be and how to handle him." She followed it with, "thank god he is not a Scorpio." Scorpio was David and one of my younger sisters horoscope signs. At this time in her life, my mother believed if you were born a Scorpio or a Pisces, which was my fathers sign, there was just nothing anyone could do for you. You and your life were hopeless. Perhaps it helped her deal with the guilt she felt for how she had mis-treated David. Telling herself and everyone else that it was no ones fault he was just born that way.

My mother no longer had kids at home and was at a time in her life where she read the *National Enquirer* for her news, checked the horoscopes to see what was wrong with every sign except hers of course and cut medical articles out of the *Enquirer* to take to her doctor. She said that doctors are just too busy to keep up with all the new cures and that her doctor was always so grateful when she brought him an envelope full of articles to read.

It just so happened that Jason and my mother shared the same horoscope sign. She made sure that we knew that there were two types of Taurus's there were her type and his. It amazes me how the universe works. I had a psychological need to prove to the world, my mother and myself that it was possible to raise a wonder-ful successful boy. I was blessed with a son and I am today blessed with not one but two beautiful grandsons. One is a Pisces and both are beautiful, loving, car-ing, happy children.

Although we had a successful pregnancy, the Specialist told us that it might not be possible to have more children. He explained that the best time to con-ceive a child is sometimes right after giving birth. He advised that if we wanted more children we might want to start trying right away. Six weeks after Daniel was born, we started trying to have another child. Another part of my life's blue print was complete. I was now the stay at home mom in my blue print and was planning for child number two.

12

PARTIAL AWAKENING

The emotions, buried deep inside were all pouring out as I held my first child. I was bursting with love, caring, wants, desires, expectations and needs. I was able to show and express all of these things as they pertained to my child. Sitting in my rocking chair with my newborn son sleeping on my chest looking at his angelic face the bond and the love that I felt for this little person was incredible. For the first time in my life, I felt no need to hide the feelings spilling out of me.

Not only had my need to prove to the world that it was possible to raise a happy boy begun. I had unknowingly started a new chapter in my life. My need to be invisible had shifted. Still unable or unwilling to have or show any needs, wants or desires for myself. I was now able to express the needs, wants or desires of my child for my child. There was a part of me that had become empowered. It would take another twenty years before I would include myself in this empowered picture.

Looking back today, I know that my bond with my newborn son was an extreme. As with all other things in my life I was still viewing him and our future through the distorted pictures in my mind. This was the first time in my life that I had someone with whom I could be completely unguarded. Absolutely loving my husband, the love I was able to show him was always guarded. There was the need to protect myself from the perceived threat in my head that if I were not perfect he would leave me.

With Daniel, as with all children there was no threat. It was not possible for my son to determine whether I was perfect. It was not possible for him to choose to leave me. The bond and the love that I felt for him was not threatened by real or imagined circumstances. I was experiencing unconditional love for the first time. My new life and my love for children, all children, were just beginning.

The feelings of intense love and the bond between us were unstoppable. It was not possible to imagine a time or a circumstance that would change or lessen the feelings I had for my child. I wondered if there was ever a time with any of her children that my mother felt this same bond or any bond. It was not possible to imagine a circumstance bad enough that I would look at Daniel and see a burden, or see his face and think ugly or that I would every trade my feelings of incredible love for feeling of hate or disgust for my own child.

Was my mothers mind and spirit so broken before she had her first child that she was already looking at her world and everything in it through a mentally ill mind? Again acknowledging to myself how distorted my mothers thinking had always been. It would take another twenty years, until I was in my forties before I was able to actually believe that my mother, from before I was born had been and still is mentally ill.

With these newfound incredible feelings of love for my newborn son, there was a newfound purpose for my life. Jason loved his son and was a caring loving father. My relationship with Jason was built on the love I was able to show, still keeping any real emotions hidden. Jason's relationship with me was built on the love that he was able to show still feeling somehow that he was inadequate. My husband was still working and coming home to medicated himself with marijuana and television. We both shared the love we had for Daniel and were both anticipating having a second child.

I know that the extreme attachment I had for my newborn son and my total attention and devotion to his every need was on some level understood by Jason. I also know that Jason was feeling even more left out and unnecessary, once again choosing to do everything for both Jason and Daniel. I was going 100 miles an hour responsible for even the tiniest detail. All out, of my choosing to believe in my distorted mind that I was responsible for creating the perfect life now for all three of us.

While I was going 100 miles an hour Jason was on the sidelines. He was a necessary and appreciated part of the pit crew yet he felt left out of the race. He did what was expected of him, which was to go to work and come home to the family we had created. In my need to create the perfect world, all on my own Jason felt left out.

Somehow, I had left out of his life and mine the part that I needed him. I had left out the part in my life and his that I needed anything, still protecting myself from becoming a burden to him so he would not leave. I was so busy protecting myself from an imagined threat with no realization that I was creating exactly what I had feared the most. Busy creating an environment where Jason had all his physical needs met yet I had no idea that emotionally he may have had a need to be needed. Jason may have wanted to feel like he also was capable of and needed to take care of our son and me.

It had been ingrained in my thinking that for me to need anything made me undesirable, greedy and a burden. There was nothing in my mind that told me my husband may have a need, may have actually wanted to care for the needs of his wife and his child. Living in the world I had created, busy looking after Jason our home and our child. Jason went to work came home and medicated himself into a permanent state of tranquility.

I cannot speak to what Jason was thinking or why he made the decision in his life to medicate himself rather than be a live part of whatever life brings. The moment in time when Jason chose to keep a part of himself hidden from the world and medicated. The moment in time when he chose to live his life with his eyes closed to a possibly different future that we could make come true, had happened when he was eighteen-years-old before we were married. We were both living in worlds we had created for ourselves, based on the choices we made. We were both using distorted thinking from our dysfunctional past to tell ourselves that we knew what we were doing and we knew where we were going in our lives.

We each had our own map; we each had our own blueprint. We had no idea that we were beginning what we thought was the same trip from different starting points. We thought we were on the same road. The trip was over before either one of us figured out that; we had created our maps without having the necessary directions.

Although we had planned for me to be a stay at home mom the financial reality of living on one wage was very different from the original plan. At the time, that Daniel was born maternity leave was available for only three months. I was not planning to return to work and was not eligible for unemployment benefits although I had worked for the same company for the past five years.

We were both determined that I would stay home. Jason took a second job. For the next year, he would finish working at 4:30 p.m. and have to be at his second job for 6 o'clock. He would arrive home after midnight and have to leave home by 6:30 a.m.

Daniel was about seven months old when I opened an in home daycare. The town where we lived had a program, which would approve homes to care for children. This allowed Jason to leave his second job. My in home daycare would operate for the next five years.

There would be up to six children in my care including Daniel. I loved kids. As our house was full of children on a daily basis, ours was the house in the neighbourhood where all the kids played.

We were still determined to have a second child. Returning to the specialist to see if there was anything, more we could do. I took fertility pills for three months and was not pregnant. The doctor doubled the dose for the next three months. I was not pregnant. The specialist explained that it was not safe to take fertility pills for a longer period and said that the one ovary I had left had scar tissue from previous surgeries and he believed that it no longer functioned.

Once again, we were discussing adoption. The Specialist signed the required papers stating that I was no longer able to have children. We applied to adopt a second child. As we already had one child, we were not eligible to adopt a baby. The social worker quoted abortion versus live birth statistics and explained that there were so few infants available for adoption that only couples with no children were eligible to adopt a baby.

We were eligible to adopt a special needs child. Our best option for adoption would be over seas adoption; this option would cost several thousand dollars we did not have.

We agreed to adopt a special needs child. Daniel was just under two at the time. Adoption regulations state that an adopted child would have to be the youngest child in the home. This meant that we would have to wait for a special needs child under two to become available. As there was a shortage of infants available for adoption, special needs children under two-years were also given to childless couples first. Approved and placed on the waiting list for a special needs child we had been on the list for about ten months when I became pregnant. We were ecstatic! We were going to have a second child.

Although I had trouble conceiving, my first pregnancy was healthy. I loved being pregnant. I was healthy, continued working and had gained forty pounds carrying Daniel. I had expected that my second pregnancy would be the same.

With my second pregnancy, I had morning sickness. There was morning sickness in the morning, morning sickness in the afternoon and in the evening. I was sick all the time for the full nine months. Regular visits to the doctor once a month would mean me stepping on the scale to see how much weight I had gained. As my pregnancy progressed there was very little weight gain. Being sick or nauseated continually was affecting my ability to eat. I was also still caring for up to six children each day. There were several months were I had actually lost weight. Although I was sick and concerned during my second pregnancy, I was thrilled to be carrying my second child. A child we thought was not possible.

More than two weeks over due, the doctor was considering inducing labour. Finally, I delivered the most beautiful baby girl in the world. She was barely six pounds but she was healthy and she was ours.

As we left the hospital to take this little miracle home, one of the nurses commented. "You have a millionaires family a boy and a girl" she was so right. We both felt like millionaires. We had won the lottery of life. It had been three years since Daniel had been born and we had been trying to conceive since he was six weeks old. We now had the perfect family. Jason's picture of his family was complete.

The picture in my mind of my perfect family included four children. We had been blessed with two beautiful children, which I adored, It had been so difficult to conceive that neither one of us considered that we would ever have another child. I continued to raise our two children and run my daycare and Jason continued with his job. The picture we had talked of creating was now complete.

13

UNCALCULATED CIRCUMSTANCE

Our daughter Laura was just over a year old when I became pregnant for the third time. So excited I told myself that the doctors were wrong. They said I was not able to have any more children. We had the signed papers from the specialists stating that I was no longer able to conceive; and here I was. Not only had we had a second baby but I was about to have my third. I was both surprised and thrilled to be carrying my third child.

In my third month, unlike my second pregnancy I had not experienced any morning sickness and was expecting to be healthy, with a repeat of my first pregnancy. The doctor was not even able to explain why I miscarried. There may have been something wrong with the baby was the only explanation available.

We had two beautiful children that I had struggled to conceive. We believed we would not have any more children. In my third month of pregnancy, not yet able to feel the baby kick, yet loosing this baby was devastating. My life had been filled with stressful, difficult times as a child and as an adult. I had struggled, endured and survived situations without attaching any real emotion to any of it.

The feelings and emotions that I had allowed myself to have after giving birth to my children were now on the surface. No longer buried deep inside; I grieved for this unknown baby as if it were a child I had known and lost. I fell into a deep depression.

During my early teen years, I had entertained thoughts of suicide. As I am still here, it is obvious that I did not act on these thoughts. Although there was so much to live for I had a millionaire's family, I was again feeling suicidal.

Unable to deal with the emotions that I now allowed myself to have, there were such strong, caring, loving, emotions when it came to my children this was not a situation I could deal with by stuffing my feelings deep down or becoming invisible again. I had no coping mechanism for dealing with emotional pain, as until now I had not allowed myself to have any real emotions.

Jason was not able to understand my emotional distress, as I had never shown him until now that I had an emotional need for anything. He left me alone to grieve and cope as I had always done everything on my own. How or when this depression ended and I was able to cope with life again I do not recall.

Although this was not a pregnancy, we had planned or expected. I now had a longing to be pregnant again. After Laura's birth we were so grateful for the family we had and were told may never be, I had come to terms with never having another child. There was now an unexplained need to make up for the child I had lost.

It was during the time of my depression that the economy took a nosedive. It was 1982; interest rates were climbing. This was the year we were due to re-mortgage our home. The interest rate at the time of the renewal was 18%, which meant a substantial increase in payments. Had our renewal date been two weeks later it would have been 22%.

The unemployment rate was rising with company layoffs in the news every night. Several families were loosing their homes. Finally, Jason's Company was laying off, most of the companies that did the same work as Jason had lain off workers already. Job opportunities were slim. My daycare depended on working parents and I had already lost some children, as their parents had been laid-off.

Living on unemployment was pretty tight. I had asked this first and only time for help from the Christmas Bureau for gifts and a turkey for my children. I will never forget the feeling and the pit in my stomach as I stood in that line. It brought back so many painful memories from my childhood; I was again feeling less than, again feeling worthless and not good enough. I would have never done it for myself. I was there for my children.

Jason had been laid-off for a few months when he received a phone call from the Company where he worked. They did not have enough work to take him back but they had received a call from a Company in Bella Bella BC looking for a good man. The Company recommended Jason and were calling to pass on the information.

Jason called the number in Bella Bella and took the job. He had never heard of Bella Bella and neither had I? It was on a small island about 300 miles north of the tip of Vancouver Island. The only way in was by plane or boat. He flew to Bella Bella and began work. Jason had been working away for a few months when he called to say the job could be permanent and asked if I wanted to move to Bella Bella.

The local job prospects had not improved so I said yes. We rented out our house for a little less than our mortgage payments. With the current economy, it was the best we could do. I packed up the kids and we took a ferry trip to Bella Bella BC.

Bella Bella was actually a very remote Indian Reserve. The Island that we were moving to was Denny Island, which was about a 20-minute boat ride from Bella Bella.

Denny island had a year round population of forty people. It was a privately owned Island, which housed a fishing resort. Jason had the job of diesel mechanic to maintain the engines on the fishing boats. This island was absolutely beautiful. The company owned a few run downs mobile homes which housed the workers.

In the summer months, the resort operated a small hotel and restaurant mostly for American tourist who wanted to fish for salmon or watch the whales. The summer population was a bit higher as the hotel staff would stay on the island.

We lived in a company mobile home, which was on the edge of the school-yard. Denny Island had a one-room school. Grades kindergarten through grade seven depending on the age of the children at the time. School population at the time we were there was about seven children.

This was a new experience for all of us but it was a wonderful one. The Reserve at Bella Bella had a hospital and a general store. The store had limited groceries and received supplies once every two weeks when the freight boat arrived. All supplies required had to be delivered by freight boat or by plane. To order a hundred dollars worth of groceries by plane would cost you more than hundred dollars for the freight charges.

We ordered large quantities of canned goods and dry goods by boat, stock piling for a couple of months in advance. Any clothing or household items that were required were ordered through the Sears catalogue and were a long time coming. You just ordered everything in large as it would take too long to return or reorder anything.

The trip to Bella Bella to buy groceries was by the Denny Island Sea Bus. This was a boat provided by the hotel and shipyard for transportation. Technically, there was a Sea Bus schedule. In reality the Sea Bus went when it went and it came back when it came back. The standard saying to all new comers was everything here runs on Bella Bella time. If I wanted to travel to Bella Bella on the day the freight boat arrived, I would walk down the hill to the hotel with the kids at 6 a.m. and wait for the boat to leave. It may leave at six, it may leave at seven it may leave at nine the return trip would be the same. You walked your groceries from the store to the boat dock and waited for the remainder of the day for the Boat to arrive for the return trip. Daniel and Laura would play on the dock or we would watch killer whales from the shore.

After the boat docked on the return trip, I would carry Laura on my back and groceries in both hands up what we called the goat trail, which was a shortcut up the hill to our home. The first Christmas after moving to Denny Island my children received a wagon, which made future trips up the hill much easier.

The Band store in Bella Bella was supplied with what ever arrived on the boat. Fresh produce and milk were available only for the day the boat arrived. Anything required that the store did not carry, you did without or you made. I made our bread. If you wanted a hot dog or hamburger bun, you made it or you did not have it. You very seldom every saw an egg. I learned several ways of substituting eggs and other items in baking and cooking.

Arriving with my children in Bella Bella in the spring of 1983, we celebrated our tenth wedding anniversary and Laura's second birthday in June.

The time that Jason had spent unemployed and away working on his own had been an emotional strain on him. He had medicated his problems with marijuana for years. The few months that he spent on his own in Bella Bella before we arrived, he had spent working and drinking.

By the time I had arrived with the children, he had developed a pattern of working and drinking until he passed out, eventually finding a marijuana connection even in a remote place like Denny Island and Bella Bella. Jason had now spent months medicating himself daily with alcohol in place of the marijuana and would continue his alcohol and marijuana use for the remainder of our relationship.

September of this same year, Daniel would start kindergarten in the Denny Island one-room school. As you can imagine finding teachers for a remote one-room, school was a challenge. It was equally challenging to find teachers for the schools on the Bella Bella Reserve. In the just under two years that we lived on Denny Island, I had one of the most incredible learning experiences of my life.

The teacher for Daniel on Denny Island was a first year teacher. He had taken the job as a learning experience for himself, his wife and young daughter. He was a nice guy who was young and inexperienced. His teaching skills involved handing out a worksheet, then going across the road to the trailer where he lived, and keeping his wife company.

There were days he did not show up at school all day. He would send his wife who was not a teacher, nor employed by the school district, to watch the kids. Needless to say, there was not much teaching going on.

Since Daniel's birth, I had a new found ability to speak up and say what I was thinking or feeling as it pertained to his needs. I was still not able to speak up or acknowledge thoughts or feeling pertaining to myself. Although I did not approve of or agree with this teachers teaching ability I was able to tell him how I felt and why and still maintain a working relationship, which included my caring for his daughter on occasions.

My time spent on Denny Island and in Bella Bella opened my eyes to some of the daily realities of life for the residents of this remote Reserve. I met some wonderful people and made friends I will never forget.

The driver of the Sea Bus and his wife became good friends. They were a young couple with a baby. They were permanent residences of Denny Island. Her parents were also permanent residents. Her parents had adopted two special needs brothers. This young couple were foster parents although when we first met they did not have foster children staying with them.

Through this couple and on my many trips to Bell Bella I met new people and began to learn about the culture. It broke my heart returning on the Sea Bus one day. Two teachers from the Bella Bella Band School were travelling to Denny Island. This boat holds maybe a dozen passengers. It is not a large boat and it is difficult if not impossible not to be apart of any conversations taking place.

These two teachers were young and they were white. Most teachers and doctors working on the Reserve were white and had taken the job either as first year first time employees or for the experience. I listened to these two men discussing their day and their students. The comment was about completing another day, "keeping the animals corralled." One of them actually said, "They don't really expect me to teach them anything do they?"

I would later learn than although the Reserve had an elementary and a high school the high school was not an accredited school. This meant that if you graduated your marks and achievements would not be recognized by accredited post-secondary institutes.

There were two families living on Denny Island who were already making plans to leave as their children were in grades five and six in the Denny Island school and they knew that staying would mean sending their children by Sea Bus to the unaccredited Band high school, teaching them at home by correspondence, or moving.

I never forgot the comments made by these two teachers. I may not have been native but I knew how it felt to be a child that someone thinks of as less than. I could not understand how two grown men, supposedly educated adults, could look at a group of children and not see how beautiful they all are. Why would anyone choose to teach as a profession when he has no respect and no real feelings for the children they were to teach?

Angry at these ignorant men, I could feel the hurt that each of those children must have felt, being in a daily environment with a person they look up to for caring and guidance; It broke my heart visualizing these little children being looked down upon as animals who require being subdued and corralled.

Sadly I would learn that this attitude although not shared by all Bella Bella teachers was shared by far too many who had ventured to this remote community for what they called a new experience. How is it possible to experience or learn from any culture or any person that you have already determined to be unworthy? The men who were called teachers; not only did a great disservice to their students, they also robbed themselves of the opportunity to share in what truly is a magnificent community full of wonderful people.

The Bella Bella Reserve had the only store and a small hospital. The hospital was where you would go even for a regular doctors appointment. My first visit for a doctor's appointment I was provided with the usual forms to fill out and return to the receptionist. Returning the forms, watching as they were placed in a manila folder, the woman behind the counter then wrote the word "white" in large letters across the front of the folder. She must have noticed the surprised look on my face as she explained that "white" meant that I was not status native and therefore was required to show medical coverage.

There was a similar experience when I inquired about vitamins for my daughter who was two-years-old. The response was, "we cannot sell you vitamins as they are only for our children." I would later learn that the vitamins at the clinic were not for sale; the government paid for and provided them to the native children at no costs. As a non-native, I would have to find another way to purchase vitamins for my daughter.

Without the explanations it is easy to see how printing "white" across my folder in bold or stating that vitamins were for native children only; could have been interpreted as racists. After all, I was the minority white person visiting their Reserve. Reflecting on this experience, telling myself if everyone had an experience of being on the side of the counter where you feel like the minority, if everyone had the experience of feeling worth less it might open our eyes and our hearts to a new understanding and a new way of looking at all people we meet whatever the circumstance. There is no one who would choose to feel that they are worth less, each one of us deserves, is worthy of being treated with dignity and respect.

A few months after our arrival in Bell Bella, the couple that were foster parents received a call, asking if they would take in two young girls who were sisters. The oldest one was two and the youngest was sixteen-months. As this couple had a baby at home who was nine-or-ten-months-old at the time, she felt it might be too difficult for her to care for all three little ones.

We had become friends and I had looked after her baby and other children on the island on occasions. She knew I loved children and had previously run a day care. Explaining the situation, she asked if we would consider becoming foster parents to the two-year-old. This little girl was the same age as Laura. If each family were able to take one sister, they would be close enough to see each other on a regular basis. After discussing it with Jason and completing the necessary contacts and approvals from Social Services, we now had our first foster child.

It is impossible to forget the lump in my throat and the pain in my stomach as a child each time I waited and listened to phone calls asking someone to take me. Knowing how scared and lonely it felt to spend day after day in a children's shelter wanting to go home. Remembering how it felt to want someone anyone to want me.

The request for me to take in a foster child brought all of my childhood emotions to the surface. I could not imagine saying no to a child who needed a place to go. Telling myself, I would never be the voice on the phone detailing the reasons it was not practical for me to take in a child. From this day, forward I never turned away a child who needed a place to stay.

Jason although he had medicated himself with marijuana for years and was now adding alcohol to his medications was always a gentle loving man. He had just begun to drink alcohol on a regular basis. We had been married ten years and he had always been a good father he had always enjoyed the houseful of children. Jason's alcohol use at this point did not result in the chaos and violence that was my father's life. When Jason drank, he would sit quietly and fall asleep.

The two little girls who were now in our friends and our care were native children whose mother and grandmother live in Bella Bella. The Band had a system of placing children in foster homes on the Reserve whenever possible. The circumstances with these two children did not make placement on the Reserve possible at this time. If the girls could be placed in foster homes on Denny Island, they would still have reasonable contact with their mother. The only other option would have been a foster home on Vancouver Island, which was 300 miles away.

As removing the children from the Reserve was not the preferred method of care the Band Counsel had to approve the placement. Bella Bella is a small and very close knit community everyone on the Reserve was aware of the decision to place two of their children with white families on Denny Island.

I loved children and felt very competent in my new roll as a foster mother. Looking back on this experience today, I had a lot to learn. The two girls in our shared care spent as much time as possible together. Both children were fetal alcohol syndrome children and both were very developmentally delayed with health issues. This was my first experience with children who were alcohol or drug affected. All of the future children I would care for would be in one or both of these categories.

As the only medical facility and store was on the Reserve, I would now attend doctor appointments with three children in tow, as would be expected; the community had mixed reactions to their children being sent away for care. Most of the people understood the circumstances and were grateful that the girls were cared for. It was not possible to walk down the street to the hospital or shop in the Band store without everyone stopping to say hello to me and to little Jeanie.

On one occasion an elderly women approached me in the store. I do not know her relationship to this little girl. She was very agitated and upset. She walked up to me called me an eff'n Honkey and said I had no business looking after their kids. I later learned that Honkey was a term the natives used for white men which is equivalent to calling someone a nigger.

Perhaps it was because my own mother had called me worse for years. I simply said, "I am sorry that you feel that way" and walked away, there was no upset or anger, talking to myself, stating she is entitled to the way that she feels.

They say hindsight is 20-20, had I had the knowledge at the time that I have today I would have dealt with this foster care situation differently. Years of experience have now taught me that not only were these two children severe fetal alcohol syndrome children but their mother who was only seventeen-years-old at the time was also a fetal alcohol syndrome child.

The first time I met the mother of these two little girls she was shy, soft spoken and obviously very uncomfortable having to visit her daughter in my home. Still seeing the world through the only eyes I have. My eyes were still filtering everything that I saw through my distorted brain. Although some of my ideas and thinking from my childhood had shifted, my picture of the world at this time was based on my experiences. A part of me believed that my experiences were no different that anyone else's experiences.

Although I would have never said it or showed it to this mother I knew the background of these two little girls and was fully aware of their medical histories, the neglect and abuse they had endured and they were both still babies. The picture in my mind, blamed their mother for their circumstances. I knew their mother was seventeen-years-old before we met.

My expectations of what it meant to be seventeen-years-old and a mother of two were again based on my distorted history; I had not lived at home for two years and was married at seventeen-years-old. Telling myself that if I had had children at seventeen there was no way I would have been this irresponsible and neglectful. There was no reference in my mind as to what it meant to be a seventeen-year-old. To me being seventeen meant being a responsible adult. My children were still young I had no contact with teenagers other than when I was one. Telling myself if I could do it with no parental help then there was no earthly reason why this seventeen-year-old mother could not do it if she cared.

What I saw at the time, as a mother who did not care, was in fact, a mother who was a child herself. This mother did not neglect or abuse her babies because she did not care. She had no idea how to care for them. Although I knew her background, this was my first experience with fetal alcohol syndrome.

I know today that this seventeen-year-old child who had two children of her own to care for was just as neglected and abused as her babies were. Depending on the severity of her own fetal alcohol syndrome, she may have never been capable of caring for her children without guidance and assistance from someone who cared enough to teach her to first care and love herself so she could in turn care and love her children. If it were possible to go back, a do it over today, I would have offered to take in the mother and the children.

I would like to share one more heartbreaking situation with this little girl. Jeanie required medical care, which was not available in Bella Bella. She required medical tests, which would require a trip to children's hospital in Vancouver. The appointment was booked and we made the ferry trip to Vancouver. Although Jeanie and Laura were both the same age, they were developmentally miles apart. Depending on the severity of fetal alcohol syndrome, it can cause several mental and physical developmental delays. Jeanie had both. Her ability to walk and speak were both impaired. The medical test we were here for did not include either her walking or her speech.

When the tests were over, I was consulting with the paediatrician and was asking about Jeanie's developmental issues. My concern was that if she did not receive help with her speech she might not have been ready for kindergarten when she was five.

I never forgot the words this doctor, who is a children's specialists said to me. He actually said, **"Well if this was your daughter we would be worried because she may not be ready for school and may need speech therapy. But all this girl will ever be is an Indian on a Reserve so it doesn't matter."**

These shocking words, which I never forgot, broke my heart. If he spoke those words to me today I would have stood up and not only told him what I thought. I would have reported him to everyone and anyone who would listen to me. At the time feeling shocked, hurt, sad, disappointed and disgusted I left his office and returned to Bella Bella without saying a word.

Holding this precious beautiful little girl sleeping in my arms on the long ferry ride home, childhood memories were churning in my mind. Feeling that little Jeanie not only had a mother who did not care but she was living in a world where her teachers and even her doctors did not care. I was asking myself how is it possible for me look at Jeanie, and see such beauty, and feel such intense feelings of love and caring and someone else sees only a "useless Indian". As I rocked little Jeanie in my arms envisioning my mother holding myself little Rose, seeing only a burden, only a worthless lump.

Having already made an unconscious commitment to somehow make up to the world for David's experiences, I now had a burning heartache, a burning passion to care for them all. I wanted every child everywhere to know that somebody cared. I cared.

The short time that I had the privilege of caring for little Jeanie opened the door for me to care for several alcohol and drug affected children many of whom where native. I can honestly say I loved each and every one.

14

UNEXPLAINED HEARTBREAK

A lot had happened in my life in a short period. I had suffered a miscarriage, my husband had been unemployed, we had moved to a small Island that we did not know even existed and we were now foster parents. The thoughts I had about having another child were not completely gone, but they were no longer weighing heavy on my mind. The possibility of my becoming pregnant was always there but we both believed it was highly unlikely.

During our time living on Denny Island, I became pregnant for the fourth time. Explaining to the doctor about my history and my recent miscarriage, the doctor repeated the same dialogue spoken at the time of my miscarriage. He said that normally when you miscarry in the first three months it indicates that there was something wrong with the baby. I had had two successful pregnancies and there was no reason to believe that this one would be different.

We were careful not to tell our children or anyone that we were expecting another baby until I had passed the three-month point. Feeling wonderful and big as a house just as I had been with my first pregnancy, the schoolteacher's wife and a friend from Bella Bella were both pregnant at the same time. There was no explanation for the events that followed.

In my seventh month of the pregnancy, feeling great, I woke up one morning and had started bleeding. We immediately went to the hospital in Bella Bella, remaining in hospital for a couple of days before I flew to Vancouver. The Bella Bella hospital did not have an ultra sound machine at the time. The doctors were not able to tell me much about what the problem was or how the baby was.

The two days spent in the Bella Bella hospital it just so happened that my roommate was my friend who was also pregnant. She was also having complications. She was the granddaughter of the head of the Band Council and had taught me a lot about native life and customs. Her grandmother had been the

63

one who had signed the permission for us to care for little Jeanie. We had some wonderful conversations as she visited her granddaughter in the hospital.

Taking my first ever airplane ride from Bella Bella to Vancouver, I had contacted my regular doctor in the Fraser Valley and arranged to be admitted to the hospital in Abbotsford. As with everything else in my life, I did this alone. They did an ultra sound and told me that there was no heartbeat. My baby was dead.

I was absolutely devastated; there was no explanation or reason why. The doctors determined the safest thing to do would be to induce labour. Not only did I know my baby was dead I now had to deliver him. I delivered a tiny baby boy. He looked just like Daniel. He had all his fingers and all his toes he just wasn't breathing his tiny body was purple. We had already chosen his name it was Adam Michael. After the delivery, I required surgery. I asked the doctor to tie my tubes at the same time. Knowing I could not ever go through this again. The test they did on Adam showed no conclusive cause of death. No one could tell me why I had now lost two babies.

Had Adam lived he would have been in his twenties today. The tears would not stop as I was writing this paragraph.

Leaving the hospital and returning to Bella Bella in a state of deep depression, I did not want to see anyone I did not want to talk to anyone. Had I not had two beautiful children to raise I would have ended my life. Both the teacher's wife and my Bella Bella friend had healthy baby boys.

Continuing to go through the details of each day caring for my children, I was in such deep mourning for not one, but two children, that I felt I was not really alive.

Once again, I chose to make this a problem for myself alone. This was something that I had to get through by myself. The voice in my head was telling me to be strong for my children. I could not let my children see that I was sad I could not let my children see me cry. Not wanting them to be sad I did not want my pain to become theirs.

As Denny Island and Bella Bella were so small, both communities had heard about our loss, trying desperately to keep my grief to myself, to become invisible again, wanting both my physical and emotional self not to be seen.

Some time had passed I was waiting by the dock in Bella Bella for the Sea Bus to return me to Denny Island. She did not tell me her name, but a wonderful native woman came up to me and said that she was sorry for our loss. I had not wanted to talk about it, which meant that people who knew me did not know what to say. No one including myself said anything it was almost as if nothing had happened. This wonderful woman put her arms around me and said, "I am so sorry, I feel so sorry for you." Although believing I wanted to be alone what I really needed was for someone to say exactly what she said, I needed someone to hug me and say they cared.

As I had returned to Bella Bella in a state of severe, depression Jason was not able to understand or help me through my grief. I would not let him in. Deeply depressed and unable to see, that he too had suffered a loss. We did what we had always done. I dealt with my problems alone and Jason increased his medications.

I do not recall how the conversation began; I do know this was another item Jason added to his personal list of failures, which he felt required numbing with alcohol or marijuana.

Being so involved in my own pain, I was not aware that Jason blamed himself for Adam dying. Whether he was over come by grief or alcohol or a combination of both he was in tears as he told me, it was his fault that our son had died. He said that he really did not want a third child. He still believed that a third child would be the cause of all future problems and that deep down inside he had not wanted this baby.

Jason never forgave himself for not wanting his own child. I know that it was not Jason's thinking or anyone else's fault that Adam died. Heaven must have needed one more tiny angel.

When our first grandson was born and Laura was considering names. Jason suggested that she name him Adam. Laura was so young at the time she had no idea the meaning that name had to her father or me until I told her the story. She did not name our grandson Adam but I know Jason still grieves as I do and it had been more than twenty years.

Unknowingly Jason had at eighteen-years-old closed his eyes to the world in front of him and concentrated on grieving, remembering and living with his mind in his past. He had medicated his life to a state of existing in the present and remembering the pain of the past. Jason had long ago lost his enthusiasm for today and tomorrow.

Jason's perception that the third child was the cause of all future problems, his perception that he was the cause of his fathers leaving was based on the fear and emotions of a child. As an adult Jason knew that logically he was not the cause of his father's affair and that, no child, whatever the order of their birth, could possibly be responsible for the decisions of their parents.

Jason was seeing the world through the distortion of his past experiences. He believed that what he saw and experienced in his past was destined to be his future. Jason chose to medicate his problems. It is not possible to numb your mind and open it to clear logical thinking at the same time.

My husband was not able to open his eyes and his mind to see the world through new experiences and new ways of thinking. Jason believed that the third child would be and was the cause of all future problems. His belief was so strong that he created exactly what he believed.

Adam was our third child although he did not live. In Jason's mind, this third child had created the worry and anxiety that he felt when he thought he did not want him. In Jason's, mind our third child also created twenty years of future grief for the son that he lost and obviously loved.

In reality, our third child was not the cause of Jason's irrational fears for the future. Adam was a beautiful baby who lived inside of me for seven short months. He was a precious gift if only for a short time. He was not the cause of Jason's problems or mine in life or death.

Adams short life and death were only a problem in Jason's mind because he chose to see a third child as a problem. Jason commented years after we were divorced that things between us were never the same after we lost the last baby. He believed that our losing the third child was the cause of our divorce.

We all create the world that we live in through our individual choices. We are not always able to recognize why we make choices. We are not always able to see that at times we also choose our pain.

Choose to live your life in the present. Acknowledge your past, learn from your past and refuse to live in your past. Live each day with your eyes wide open, challenge yourself to think with an opened mind. Allow yourself to entertain new ideas.

Look at your life and everything in it as a gift. If you see a gift, it will become a gift. Life is what you say it is and what you make it. What ever your circumstances, you are living the life you have created. It is not possible to be anything else. Whether you are able to see the choices you have made or you are living today from unconscious choices made in your past. You and only you have the ability to choose. Choose to change your mind.

Life is what you think it is. Life is what you choose to make it. Choose to make yours magnificent.

15

IT IS ALL IN HOW YOU LOOK AT IT

We lived on Denny Island for just under two years. It was fall when we returned to the home we owned in the Fraser Valley. The economic situation was not great but it had improved. Jason was now employed. Still living in what I call a zombie state; although not severely depressed I was just numb. Going through the motions of the required every day circumstances, I was not really there. Physically alive, physically present yet I was emotionally dead.

I loved my children and my husband. I was unable to feel a thing; it was like living life in a permanent mental fog. I was able to make dinner, read my kids a story and hold a conversation all while being emotionally absent. Since childhood, I had been an expert at doing what was required while emotionally detached from everything in the room.

I would notice every pregnant woman in town. There were times when it seemed like everyone was pregnant except me. Seeing a mom to be or a mom with a new baby in the grocery store, there was a part of me that wanted to and needed to burst into tears. I would go through the details of putting items in my cart with the words, "don't do this, don't get upset, don't let the kids she you sad, don't let the kids see you cry" repeating in my head.

It took more than twelve years for me to be able to tell anyone, it took more than twelve years before I could say aloud that I had lost my baby. I do not recall the conversation or even to whom I was speaking. However the subject came up; I do remember telling whoever it was that I had lost not one but two babies. Playing the same don't get upset, don't cry message in my head at the time, I vividly remember driving home from where ever this was with tears streaming down my face telling myself that it has been twelve years there is no reason for you to cry.

Living on Denny Island had been an amazing experience that had changed a part of who I was. There would have been the same devastating feeling of loss no matter where we lived when I lost Adam. It was truly a gift having the opportunity to live in such a remote peaceful place, having the opportunity to embrace a slower softer life style, meeting so many gentle easygoing loving people. Coming from a world of chaos and worry, coming from a world where everything and everybody was either coming or going, where everyone was required to be doing something.

To compare these two worlds it is like one world is full of stress, spinning at a hundred miles and hour with everything regulated by the clock or some schedule of some kind and the other world is standing still looking at the ocean and watching the whales. If there are no whales, you just watch the waves it makes no difference. Both are equally tranquil and beautiful.

The people I met in Bella Bella had as many or more problems as you or I have. They have daily details to maintain in their lives as we all do. The difference I admired was in the way they saw their world. The world I saw and interpreted was a world that flows; the world that runs on Bella Bella time.

This was a world where the boat goes when it goes and it comes back when it comes back. If you require something, you find a place to order it. It arrives when it arrives. There is no schedule; there is no expectation of arrival or departure times. It just doesn't matter. If you order something that is supposed to take three weeks to arrive and three weeks go by, you don't make angry phone calls or threaten to cancel your order. You just wait. You just know that you ordered it and it will be here, the when makes no difference.

If you go to the store, you buy what they have. If they do not have what you are looking for you just don't buy it. Life really can be just that simple. Life is all in the definition. You only have something to worry about if you choose to worry.

If I were able to maintain even a fraction of the patience, caring, wisdom and the tranquil spirit that I had observed I would truly be blessed.

My Bella Bella, experience had permanently changed some of my previous behaviours. You would think that after living in a place for almost two years with only one small grocery store, no clothing stores, no department stores, not even a drug store that a person would have a desire to shop. I cannot explain it, but after living in Bella Bella for some reason, I had absolutely no desire to shop. Returning to the Fraser Valley not only was there no desire to shop I disliked shopping.

Shopping only for groceries or if absolutely necessary for the kids, otherwise avoiding shopping. The more time that went by, the older I got the more I avoided going to the store. I discovered there is a part of me that would make a good hermit.

Life slowly returned to what it had been before we moved to Bella Bella. I was caring for our children and Jason was back working. Our house was once again the house where all the children played. The neighbour behind us, our back yards joined, had two children and boy and a girl. The girl was close to Laura's' age the boy was, three years older than Daniel, our children became good friends and spent equal time playing between the two homes.

Daniel was a child who preferred playing with older children. He loved playing with this boy. I always taught my children no matter how young they were that they were responsible for what they did. They were capable of making decisions and they were responsible for the decisions they made.

Daniel was taught that if he chose to play with a boy who was three years older than he was then he had to be able to determine if what they were doing or playing was right or wrong. I taught him that if the older boy or the older boys friends were doing things that he knew were wrong he was to come home.

Daniel understood that it would never be acceptable to do something and then say he did it because the older boys told him to. I explained that he was able to determine for himself whether something was wrong and even though older children told him to do it, he was capable of saying no and capable of coming home. Daniel understood that if he was not capable of choosing appropriately for himself that would mean that he was too young to play with older children and it would no longer be permitted.

There were many occasions with the children in my daycare and in the community where parents were too eager to make excuses for their children's behaviour. It would be the parent not the child saying, "I know he only did it because the older kids told him too." Unknowingly this teaches children that it is acceptable to find excuses for their behaviour rather than teaching them that they are capable of making the right choices and are responsible for the choices they make.

We had a new family move in across the street from us. They had two boys the younger boy was the same age as Daniel the older boy was three years older. This family had problems. The parents would often have screaming arguments on the front lawn with some very disturbing things said to each other. Both parents had issues they were dealing with. The mother although she had problems was a nice person. This was a small friendly community. She was a stay at home mom her children played at my house as did most of the neighbourhood children.

It is not possible for children to live in a home with parents who deal with their problems in front of them not to be affected by their environment. This was a very loving mother and father. The issues they had were between the parents. The mother was very protective of her boys and either did not have the skills to control their behaviour or perhaps she was over compensating for other issues. These boys could play and have fun with other children they also at times displayed some very disturbing behaviours.

The younger boy who was in first grade drove their car into their garage. The mother was upset one day and told me that she caught her son slicing up the couch with a knife. When she asked him why he was doing it, he said he lost his car and was looking for it.

Daniel and Laura were enrolled in several activities in the community. I was one of the moms who were eager to volunteer for the soccer team or swim club whatever the activity. While sitting at the swimming pool watching my children at swim club practice, a mom with a son about the same age as Daniel sat down and asked me a question.

The boys who had moved in across the street from me were also in swim club. This mom had observed Daniel and the younger boy playing. It was no secret that these two boys had some behavioural problems.

She asked, "Aren't you worried about your son playing with that boy?" I answered, "They play together all the time. They live across the street from each other." This mother explained that her son was a follower. Her son was so influenced by other children and was having such difficulty staying out of trouble that she had taken him out of school and was now home schooling him. She said, "I would never let my son play with a boy like that."

I explained to this mother that Daniel knew that he was permitted to play with this boy when the boy was playing nice. If the boy was doing things that were, wrong or being mean etc. my son was to come home and not play with him at that time. Daniel was capable of determining what was appropriate and what was wrong. Even the youngest children have a sense of right and wrong.

As the boys lived across the street from each other, the alternative was to decide for my son that he was to never play with this boy. This would not teach Daniel how to choose what is and what is not right for himself. This would also lead to these two boys possibly being rivals. I did not want to create a situation were I was teaching these children to dislike one another.

These boys were in the first grade. Whatever the boys issues may be he is still a child. If Daniel plays with him when he is behaving appropriately and tells him that he will not play with him when he is doing things that are wrong this may help to teach this young boy what appropriate behaviours are. I was not willing to be a part of isolating and rejected a young child for any reason.

We continued our conversation. I explained that I wanted Daniel to be capable and confident. I wanted my son to be able to make appropriate decisions for himself no matter what the situation. As it is not possible for me to be with Daniel all the time, it is not possible for me to follow him to school and make his decisions for him and that it was essential that he learn to think for himself.

As much as I hate to admit it I knew there would be a day even in elementary school when Daniel will be asked to try to smoke a joint or a cigarette or take a pill or steal something. Whatever future situation he may encounter I want my son to be capable of choosing what is right for him. It is essential that Daniel be able to say no with confidence. This mom said that she wanted the same for her son.

I asked her, "How is your son going to be capable of making his own decisions when he is ten or twelve, or as a teen if he has never had to make one?" "If you choose his friends, remove him from school to protect him from choosing the wrong friends and the wrong behaviours how will your son learn to choose for himself?"

Our children deserve to be taught how to think and care for themselves. That is our only job as a parent. As much as we love and cherish our children, they are not ours to keep. Our children must be given the tools to think, choose and be responsible for their behaviours and their lives.

An empowered adult is a person who is capable of making decisions while weighing outside influences and making appropriate choices for themselves. It is not possible to blindly follow others or to blame others for your circumstances and consider yourself a responsible adult at the same time. Responsible empowered adults are the result of raising responsible empowered children.

Both of my children were being raised in a home where they had other children around them on a regular basis. Both of my children where in swim club and were enrolled in various age appropriate activities. Daniel was a very outgoing and energetic child. Laura who was not yet old enough for kindergarten had a quieter more subdued nature.

Since our return from Bella Bella, I had noticed Laura becoming increasingly shy. She was comfortable at home and playing with the children she knew, she was beginning to not want to include herself in other activities.

We would enter a room full of children playing at a parent and tot group and she would stand on the side lines or be stuck to me. I was concerned that if Laura was this shy and uncomfortable she may have difficulty starting kindergarten without me.

I accompanied Laura to each playgroup and encouraged her to join in and play, there were some days she refused to participate at all. It was on one of these days that the instructor came over to me and said that I should not be too concerned if she did not want to join in. She suggested that if she was not ready perhaps I should let her go home and join the group again when she was a little older.

I explained to the instructor that this is precisely why Laura has to be here. I said that my daughter could choose whether or not she wants to quit this group on the day that she is able to run into the room and go down the slide with a smile on her face without feeling shy or stressed. Until that day, she has to continue to attend. I know when that day comes she will choose to stay. The Instructor looked at me as if I were from Mars. She obviously disagreed with my way of dealing with the situation.

I knew that whatever Laura's fears or concerns were they were imagined; there was no real threat to her in the room. I knew she was capable of interacting and playing with children as this was something she did on a daily bases. She was apprehensive about a new place and children, which were not familiar. It would be much easier for her to adjust to this new phase in her life with me at her side over the next few months than it would if I left her at the kindergarten door with tears in her eyes to fend for herself.

Laura had no way of determining whether the way that she felt was real or imagined. She needed to experience for herself that she could join in, play, and have fun like the other children. She could choose to believe what she feared or she could choose to experience and see for herself that her fear was not based on reality.

Laura was too young to psychoanalyze any part of her life. By allowing her to give into her fears, her fears may indeed become her reality. We continued to attend moms and tots together. Laura not only was able to run into the room and go down the slide. She was on the trampoline she was singing songs. By the time the class ended, she could not wait to sign up for the next one.

I know that the instructor meant well when she suggested that I not force my daughter to do something she was not comfortable doing. It is my job as a parent to do what ever it takes to prepare my children to survive in this world without me. To allow Laura who was too young to discern what is a real or imagined fear to choose to give into her fear would be to rob her of her full potential.

To allow her to remain shy and fearful of new situations would be to allow her to believe that she was somehow not capable. To expect her to deal with this on her own at the kindergarten door could possible make what could be a wonderful independent experience an emotion struggle that she may not know she has the ability to win.

I wanted both of my children to know how amazingly capable they are. Children will rise to expectations. Had I allowed Laura to remain shy and not capable that is exactly what she would have believed she was.

16

OFFERING A HAND UP

It was spring and a realtor knock on our door. He was looking for new listings. He explained that because we were paying such a high interest rate that it was possible for us to sell our home, buy a larger home and have the same payments or possibly lower payment as the interest rates had dropped significantly.

We had never considered selling our home; we decided to take this realtor up on his offer. If he could find us a larger home with the same or lower payments, we would be willing to sell.

He did find us a larger home in the same town. It had three bedrooms and two bathrooms with a full above ground basement and a garage. It was not new but it was only a few years old. The payments were less than we had been paying. We sold our home and moved across town.

Settling into our new home, we were again considering being foster parents. I enrolled and completed the foster parent course at Fraser Valley College, which was one of the requirements. Daniel was in school; Laura was not yet old enough for kindergarten.

The first child we took in was a five-year-old-boy. This child was with us on a special program. This young boy was a fetal alcohol syndrome child. Alex was born with his brain affected by his mothers alcohol use while she was pregnant. He had a mother who loved him but due to her own issues at the time was not able to care for him. He had been living with an aunt who was loving and very capable, however she had severe health issues at this time and already had two children of her own including a son who had special needs. We agreed to take him until his aunt was well enough for him to return.

Alex did not have the physical features of some severe fetal alcohol syndrome children. His emotional needs and behaviours were considered extreme.

Shortly after Laura started kindergarten, a long time friend bought and was operating a local restaurant. She asked me if I would be interested in working for her. She offered me school hours so I was able to be home with my children before and after school. An extra income was welcome so I took the job.

I worked in my friend's restaurant for the next five years. After about two years, I became her manager. One of my duties as manger was to hire the staff. Due to my background of struggle, I had a soft spot for anyone who was struggling and often hired people that I now know may have been turned away elsewhere.

I loved the look on someone's face when he or she heard they got the job. This was at a time when jobs were not plentiful, as most restaurant jobs do this paid only minimum wage.

There were not a lot of local jobs even for minimum wage in this town. Many of the people I hired were native Indians. Most were young shy, soft spoken and very eager to learn. Two of these young women stood out to me. The first was seventeen-years-old. She had some experience was an excellent waitress and was exceptionally quiet and shy. This young woman came from a background I could understand. She lived at home with her mother and her siblings. Her mother was an alcoholic. This young girl worked full time and cared for her mother and her younger siblings who were still in elementary school. There were occasions when this employee would come in late or miss a shift without calling.

Sitting down with her to discuss the effect that her actions were having on her job and on my ability to run a restaurant when my staff does not show up. She explained that on the occasions when she was late, it was due to her mother being passed out drunk and no one was there to feed her younger siblings and get them off to school. She stayed with the children and came into work after they were fed and safely off to school.

She needed this job as the money she earned paid for food for her family. The occasion when she did not show up at all was on a Saturday, she did not know where her mother was and refused to leave the children home alone. Telling her that I was proud of her for taking on such a huge responsibility, we arranged for her to work only on the weekdays and to start after 9 a.m. This allowed her to help the children get off to school if required. She would not have to miss work if no one was home on a weekend. She was able to keep her job and her income while continuing to care for her family. She continued to be one of my best employees.

The second woman was in her early twenties. She was working mostly at the counter as a cashier. She too was a quiet very polite young woman. Standing in the area just behind the till, I overheard a loud obviously unhappy customer speaking to my employee. This man was loud and obnoxious. He was not happy with having an Indian serve him. He made a rude comment about her being slow, followed by calling her a fat squaw.

As I listened, my employee was polite and very professional; she did not show any anger. She handed the man his change and said have a nice day. We had a chance to speak once the man left. I asked her why she did not say anything to this man. She answered, "I didn't want to get fired."

Telling her that no one had the right to talk to her the way he did. Calling her a squaw showed how ignorant this man really was. I wanted her to know that she had the right and the ability to stand up for herself no matter where she was and that I would never fire her for standing up for what was right. She never showed the hurt she must have felt. Sharing her pain I may have never been called a squaw, but I did know how being called any derogatory name made you feel worth less.

There was another special employee I would like to share with you. This was a woman in her late fifties. In this job market finding work for anyone in there fifties was not an easy task. I hired this lady on the spot after our first interview. She was full of enthusiasm. She was full of spirit and was an experienced worker.

She was so grateful for the job. Hiring her because I liked her, I had no idea that she was someone who was not wanted in the work force because of her age. This job came with little or no real management training. Without receiving any proper criteria for hiring workers, I looked at a resume for previous work experience, how long a person had kept a job and for current references. For those who were young and inexperienced the criteria were personality and character. I hired most people on a combination of their work history and my instincts.

This woman fit both. She had a great work history and she was all personality. I loved her. She worked for me right up to the time I left this job. On my last day she said to me, "I will never forget you. You gave me this job when no one else would give me a chance and I thank you." Until this day, there was no way for me to know that the decision I made to hire her would have an impact on her life. I was glad that my hiring criteria were based on my personal instincts rather than some proper learned protocol.

This employee said that I had changed her life. One young employee would change my life forever; I hired an eighteen-year-old native young man. He had no experience but it was summer and we were hiring students for jobs, which required little training. He seemed eager to learn and was grinning from ear to ear when I told him that he got the job.

This was a small town and I was fairly well known between my job, my kids school and activities and foster care. I knew several teacher, councillors and social workers. One of the school councillors who worked with native students helped me to know the difficulties of the seventeen-year-old woman I told you about. This same councillor spoke to me after seeing this young man working for me.

This young man had mild fetal alcohol syndrome. She had worked with him and his family while he was in school. Richard had not seen his mother since he was a very young child. Richard and his younger brother were being raised by a violent alcoholic father and their aunt, their father's sister. This councillor had known the family situation for years.

She said the boys even in elementary school were alone; they were often living on the streets, and locked out of the house for weeks at a time. They were growing up struggling on their own. She was happy to see that he had a job and was hoping that this would be an opportunity for him to permanently be on his own. She felt it was not safe for either boy to be at home.

This councillor had no idea of my background, she knew me as a mother and a foster mother to a fetal alcohol syndrome child. She was a regular customer at the restaurant so she also saw me as a manager. When she told me Richards story it broke my heart. Some of what he was still living I had already survived.

Richard had no way of knowing that I was aware of his circumstances and his background. I would make a point of having as many conversations with him as possible. It did not matter what we were talking about I just wanted to get to know him and make sure that he was all right. The more time we spent together and the more conversations we had, I was beginning to realise how young this young man really was.

I still had the picture in my mind of seventeen-years-old as being a mature responsible adult. This young man was older than seventeen I had expectations in my mind that he would be able to think and reason as an adult. I knew that he was considered mild fetal alcohol syndrome; I still had the expectations of holding conversations with a young adult.

Richard had not worked for me for very long when he started showing up for work late, looking like an unmade bed. After the second or third time he turned up late, I spoke to him. He had been late as he was sleeping on the street or sometimes at a friends place. He had no alarm clock and came to work as soon as he woke up. He had no way of knowing that my heart was breaking as he told me his story.

As we became comfortable talking to each other he told me that he had not seen his mother since he was about five-years-old. He did not have much of a memory of her. Richard's mother lived on a Reserve in the North West Territories. His father was white. His father had taught his son from the time he was five-years-old that his mother was nothing but a useless drunken Indian and a slut. This young man was actually taught to think of and call his own mother a slut. He would often make derogatory remarks about native people.

It was after one of his negative native remarks that I asked him, "How can you say that when you are an Indian?" He stood up straight and in a very determined tone stated, "I was raised to be white," to which I replied, "you are half white, you are still half Indian, you look like an Indian you should be proud of who you are!"

The more I got to know Richard the more I liked him. The more time and conversations that we shared it was becoming clear that although this young man had the body of an eighteen-year-old man, he still had the mind and the emotions of a very young child. Richard was very much a sad, lonely, hurt little boy doing his best to survive.

Spending time with Richard was showing me that the world he was living in, the world that he understood in his mind was just as distorted and illogical as the world that I had lived in as a child and young adult. I knew from the conversations we shared that he believed his experiences and his world was the same world that everyone else lived in.

We were developing a close friendship; I knew that Richard had already survived several years of abusive and difficult living conditions. It was possible that he would be just fine fending for himself from this point forward. Somehow being aware of his circumstances there was something telling me I had to do what ever I could to help him.

As the summer progressed, I became more worried about Richard living on the streets or between whatever friend was available at the time. The money that he made would not be enough to pay full rent a damage deposit, hydro, groceries etc. We discussed whether he was looking for a permanent place to live. He was trying to find a place he could afford so he would no longer have to live between the streets and his return trips to his father's home if he could time his stay between his fathers drinking and his violent outburst.

Discussing my concern regarding Richard with Jason, we contemplated adding a bedroom to the basement and offering him the room for a nominal rent, he could easily afford on his salary. This would give Richard a place to stay and if he was paying rent he would feel independent, he would fell as if he was living on his own. This would also allow him some time to perhaps save for a damage deposit etc. so he could live on his own.

Explaining to Richard that I knew of a place that he could afford to rent and explaining that it was not an entire apartment or a house it was only a room in a house. He would have to share the kitchen and the bathroom with the family that lived there. I wanted to be sure that he was ready for a place to be on his own. Knowing that if I told him it was my place, he would say yes, as we had developed a relationship and he was emotionally needy.

Richard needed to choose for himself without emotional attachments involved. I told him to think about it and let me know if he was interested. He wanted to know about the family that lived there. All I told him was that I knew them and that they were nice people. He said he wanted to meet them and wanted to rent this room.

It did not take long after he moved in to realise that Richard functioned on a mental and emotional level of the average twelve-year-old. He really was just a scared little boy in side.

17

BROTHERLY LOVE

Richard changed the way that I looked at my world. Until now, I had no idea that it was possible to be seventeen-years-old or older and still be a child. I began to really look at the other teens in my employ. My children were still young this was the only place for me to have contact with teens. Until now, I had considered them all to be adults, considering the kids that I hired for summer work some as young as fifteen-years-old to be adults. The only thing I had to compare my definition of what it meant to be a teen was my own experience. Up to this point in my life believing my childhood ended somewhere around the age of twelve. A part of me told myself that I was never really a child.

Beginning to acknowledge to myself that it was possible that although I believed I was a fully capable adult when I left home at fifteen that perhaps what others saw was I was still a child. Questioning myself as to how normal it was to leave home at fifteen and be married by seventeen, Until meeting this young man, I had somehow remembered my teen years as me having it all together.

Knowing Richard's history and seeing how his childhood experiences were affecting his ability to think and function as an adult made me reflect not only on my own abilities but also on David. There was no doubt that David had endured a childhood from hell, I was there. The parts of his life that I witnessed were full of physical and emotional abuse constantly aimed at this little boy. There is no way of knowing what he endured for the many times as a child we were apart. I have minimal knowledge of David's life as a teen or an adult.

I have a few pictures of David when he was a child. Looking at them today and looking at the pictures of my own son. I see David was a tiny, thin, beautiful blond haired little boy who was always so sad. I knew my mother looked at me with eyes that saw a burden, ugly, useless, worthless. As disgusted as it makes me feel now that I am a mother, at the time as a child I somehow understood it or at least accepted it as normal.

Even as a child I knew the way David was treated with, such hatred was very wrong. I was only eighteen-months older than my brother but I always knew what they did to him was wrong. Feeling sorry for David and wanting to help him, there was nothing I was able to do.

After leaving home and considered myself a responsible, adult I had often thought of David. I knew that David had began sniffing glue when he was nine-or-ten years old and that he had been in juvenile detention off an on for various break and entering type crimes. I also knew that by age twelve David had graduated to heroin.

I always wondered how it was possible that the schools, the courts, the police, the social workers all knew the circumstances for this young boy, yet no one ever said he was going to stay in foster care.

Why had no one ever stood up and said you cannot send this child back? After leaving home, the only parts of David's life I was aware of seemed to be when he was arrested again for something. My brothers drug habit escalated, as did his crimes. I am only aware of some of his teen and adult difficulties. He did hold up three gas stations in one night with a sawed off shotgun. Apparently, he was so high he had no idea what he was doing. David was arrested just sitting on the street with the gun and the money.

Although I knew the childhood David endured, a part of me actually believed that childhood ended at about twelve-years-old. Believing I was a responsible adult at fifteen-years-old when I left home, and actually believing that although I had not endured the hatred that David endured that I had gone through a less intense but similar childhood. Telling myself that if I could survive without breaking into homes and sniffing glue then there was no reason why David who was basically on the streets since age twelve could not have decided to do the same thing.

Believing that no child is responsible for what happens to him or her. I also believed that once you left home, even if you were only twelve-years-old from that day on you are responsible for yourself. You are responsible for the choices you make. I grieve for David's childhood and wanted to protect all children from abuse. Part of me also blamed David for the choices he made for himself after he left home when I considered him an adult.

It took a lot of years and a lot of learning before realizing that David had medicated his physical and emotional pain with whatever he could find from the time he was a young child. His mind and his spirit were both broken. He was a child, with the understanding and the coping mechanisms of a child; he was left alone to cope with situations no child should have to endure.

David's ability to think, his ability to learn, his ability to reason were all disabled by both internal medications he chose to keep himself stoned; and by the part of his mind that allowed him to be psychologically invisible. There is a part in all of our minds that if required could be turned on to allow us to be mentally detached from our physical circumstances.

It may have been possible for David to make different choices for himself after he left home. Clear choices are only possible with a clear mind. A brain that has been medicated since early childhood is not likely to have the necessary tools the necessary ability to accurately process new information and new ideas.

Most of all, David would have had to have a reason a desire at twelve-years-old to leave his medication behind and feel the real pain. I had the expectation that somehow this should be possible for a twelve-year-old boy to accomplish all on his own.

Until I had my own children, until experiencing through my children what it really meant to be a child. I had no idea that a realistic expectation for a twelve-year-old boy was to play on a soccer team. I now had a completely new way to look at David's world. It is not possible for him or anyone to make adult choices when you have no reference as to what real or adult is.

Richard had no idea that he had taught me to again adjust the way that I had been seeing my world. He taught me to consider that what I believed to be an accurate picture of who I was and who I expected others to be was still my world being filtered through the distorted images of my past.

Now asking myself if it was possible that David was also living his life in an adult body with the world looking at him with the expectations that he function both physically and emotionally as an adult. I was now able to see my brother no matter what his age as being the same scared, sad little boy.

The longer that Richard lived with us the closer we became. The more I saw through his actions and his understanding how much of a child he really was. There were times that Jason and I had discussed how in some cases Daniel had a more logical means of reasoning and he was still in elementary school. It did not take long before Richard was calling me mom. Richard is in his thirties today he still calls me mom and has been my son since he moved in with us that summer.

I knew Richard had a younger brother and had seen his brother a few times come into the restaurant. He was a year younger although he looked and acted much older. There was nothing to indicate that his brother had been a fetal alcohol-affected child. I had mentioned before that Richard although his father was white looked native. His younger brother James looked even more native. When you saw them, together Richard now looked like a half-breed.

James was living the same lifestyle. He had the look of a tough street kid. He had the look that said leave me alone. He also had the look I had seen in David's eyes. He had the look of perpetual sadness. Although I did not know him, I had not even been introduced to him I felt myself feeling his isolation and loneliness. I felt myself viewing James as still being a child, wondering what I could do to help him. There was nothing in me saying that he was old enough to be an adult and should just get his act together. I now had a new way of interpreting what I was seeing while looking at this young man.

There were not a lot of job opportunities in this town, especially for someone who looked like a tough native street kid. Looking back, this restaurant was the only business in town at that time that had any native employees. I really had no idea that hiring native people was any different than hiring anyone else. Even when the customer called my employee a squaw, I thought it was just one ignorant man. Realizing now, I was the ignorant one, completely ignorant of the prejudices in the world around me. I had no negative reference in my world to native people.

I had lived in Bella Bella and loved it. My mother's world was full of prejudices for people who were stupid, worthless, useless, lazy, ugly or rich. I refused to be apart of seeing these things in the people I met. Once again, glad that I was ignorant on this subject and made my decisions based on my instincts and based on individual people not on a particular racial dynamic.

As the year progressed, I had an opportunity to meet Richard's brother. He had stopped at the house a few times to meet Richard and they would go out together. As James was not employed, he was still living on the street or on a friends couch for the night. Richard had been living with us for a few months it was winter. He came to us and asked if James could stay with him for a couple of weeks.

We knew he had nowhere to go and it was cold out side. We agreed that James could stay for two weeks. Although we had met, we were strangers. I had said hi a few times as James waited at the door for his brother. This was not a talkative person. This young man was quiet spoken with a tough demeanour. He was a native teen living on his own on the streets he had to appear tough to survive.

The first night that James stayed with us he was down stairs in his brother's room and in the rec. room where we had a pool table. It was late we had already been in bed sleeping. I woke up to the sound of the pool balls hitting. I had heard this sound many times before this was different. The way the balls cracked who ever was playing pool was taking their frustrations out on the pool balls. I assumed it was our new houseguest and thought this might be a good opportunity to talk to him.

Entering the rec. room, my assumption was correct, our new guest was playing pool alone. He saw me walk in and asked if he was too loud and said, he was sorry if he woke me up. I told him it wasn't a problem and said that I thought by the way that he was hitting those pool balls that perhaps he was upset about something.

James was silent for a moment and then he spoke to me. He said, "I'm not my brother," to which I replied," I didn't think you were your brother." He repeated, "I'm not my brother," he then explained. He said, "I'm not like my brother I don't need you. I don't need anybody I can take care of myself." I was thinking to myself how much this kid was like me. I must have said those words a million times to myself. I don't need anybody I can take care of myself!

Hearing his words, telling myself, I know you can take care of yourself. I also know that you are in my basement, which tells me that you need to be tough and take care of yourself on the outside. You can't show anyone, you cannot show the world that you need anything. Yet if you are in my basement telling me you don't need me I know you at least need my basement. Telling James I understood. I told him if he could look after himself I would leave him alone and that he was welcome to stay. If he ever changed his mind and wanted someone to talk to, I was a pretty good listener.

James who was staying for two weeks stayed for more than two years. He was not like Richard and did not appear to be an alcohol affected kid. He was the younger brother yet he was much more mature and had a normal ability to reason. I had nothing to compare normal teenage abilities. I thought James functioned normally for his age.

Both these brothers had dysfunctional childhoods; both had very different abilities and very different needs. Richard was very much a child; he very much wanted and needed a mother. James was independent, determined, tough and was going to go through life doing it all on his own without asking anyone for anything. Somehow, I understood what each was going through. I could see David's needs in Richard and I could see myself in James.

James although he was not an alcohol syndrome child at the time he moved in with us did have an alcohol problem. He was not employed, although he did work hard at finding a job. Jobs were not easy to find and were even less available to a native kid with no experience that looked street tough. Although James would never drink at our home, he did drink. James would drink to the point where he would pass out. He often blacked out and had no memory of where he had been or what he had done.

In the first two months or more that our new guest lived with us, he kept to himself. The first night in the basement was the longest conversation we had. If you tried to start a conversation or ask a question James would usually respond with a one word answer and body language that said leave me alone. There were several occasions in this time period that James arrived at our door so drunk he had difficulty finding his way downstairs to pass out.

The doorbell rang at 2a.m. one night. Answering the door, two young men were holding James up; he obviously had too much to drink and was passed out. I opened the door and they laid him on the carpeted stairs in the entranceway, which lead up to the kitchen. They said they were just driving him home and left. He was passed out lying on the stairway.

Sitting beside James looking at him and saying to myself, "don't you know how beautiful you really are?" I knew he was drinking to mask feelings he could not let anyone see. I had done the same thing. I completed my drinking between the ages of eleven and fifteen, meeting Jason was my reason to quit.

Watching James as he was passed out on the stairs, feeling his sorrow. I knew he felt totally alone, useless and he wanted to show the world how capable he was yet he couldn't even find a job. Telling myself what I imagined was going through his mind every day. Telling myself that what this kid needs is a reason to live. Wanting to help him find what I had found, a reason to quit drinking. I wanted James to loose the sadness that he carried on his face every day.

James had lived with us for two months or more, keeping to himself not saying much of anything to anybody. I do not remember what the incident was; something happened that could not be ignored. What ever it was I decided that I had to talk to him. He was sitting in a living room chair as I was talking to him with no response. Sitting, listening without saying a word I asked what he was thinking. James did not answer. I continued to say that he had been living here for two months and I did not even know him; and asked him to tell me what he was thinking.

James said he couldn't say what he was thinking, I asked him why? He said, "Because if he said what he was thinking I would kick him out." I told him that would not happen and that he was free to talk to me and tell me anything he was thinking. He sat silent for a while and softly said, "I can't tell you what I am thinking because if I told you what I was thinking I would tell you to (f word) off." My reply was, "James if you really feel like telling me to (f) off, go ahead and say it." "I will not kick you out. If that is the way, you feel you can tell me to (f) off. But then you have to tell me why."

I do not remember what the incident was that started this conversation. I do remember thinking to myself as James said that he felt like telling me to (f) off, wow! Finally! We are communicating! This was a major break through for both of us. I knew he was beginning to feel that he could trust me.

There were at least two occasions that I knew of that James had been arrested and ended up in the drunk-tank over night. One occasion I was told about, one occasion, I received a phone call at 3 a.m. from the RCMP. They asked for me by my first name and James's last name. They said that they were calling to inform me that my son was picked up for being drunk and violent in public. They were calling to let me know where he was and that he would be released in the morning when he was sober. It was 3 a.m. I did not go into the details of our relationship on the phone. I simply let the officer think he was talking to this kids mother.

There was no mention of the phone call when James arrived home later that morning. He was sitting quietly on the sofa when the phone rang. It was a call for James. I could tell by the conversation I was over hearing that he was talking about a job. He hung up the phone and told me that he had applied at a local gas station for a job and they wanted to know when he could start.

Having been previously ignorant about the prejudices towards hiring native people in this town, I was aware of the prejudices towards East Indian people. The gas station that hired James was the first gas station in this town to be owned and operated by an East Indian family. It was the talk of the town when it sold. The talk in the restaurant was about how it would never last. No one would go there and no one would work for them.

James did work for them and they had a great business. They had the best service in town. The owner and his wife would greet each customer and talk to them. The owner's wife would always tell me how beautiful Laura was. She had a daughter about the same age.

The day of this phone call telling James that he got the job was the same day he had just spent the night in the drunk-tank. He hung up the phone and told me that he got the job. James then said softly to me, "this was the day that I was going to kill myself." I put my arms around him and hugged him. He said, "I hate hugs" to which I replied, "I know, but you need one right now."

James now had a job, he was still a person who kept to himself we were beginning to communicate. He still had a drinking problem and was not able to limit how much he drank. When he drank, he drank until he passed out.

James came upstairs one morning after being out drinking the night before. His face looked like a purple balloon. He had obviously been in a fight his left eye was swollen shut his lip was cut, by the way, he was walking his ribs were as bruised as his face. I asked him what had happened. He did not want to talk to me.

Later that afternoon as he lay on the sofa he said he could not remember what happened. He had been drinking and had blacked out and did not remember being in a fight. I sat in a chair next to him and told him how scared that made me feel. He had no idea what I meant. I explained to him that it frightened me to think that he drank so much that he had no memory of what he did or where he had been.

"Look at the condition you are in. You obviously were in a fight with some-one." He agreed with me that that part was obvious. I asked him if he was in this kind of shape what kind of shape did he think the person he was in a fight with was in. He assumed the other guy was as bad or worse than he was.

Asking him if he realized that the RCMP could knock on this door and tell him that he just assaulted or worse killed some one and that he wouldn't even know if they were right or wrong. Explaining that I knew that a person who drinks to the point of passing out and having memory loss has a serious drinking problem and that I was concerned about him.

James was trying to tell me that he did drink but he did not have that big of a problem. I informed him that I knew that at least on two occasions he drank enough to end up arrested and spending the night in the drunk-tank. I asked him if he knew what kind of people end up in a drunk-tank?

I knew from Richard that James had the same negative image of what it meant to be native in his head. James had an even stronger dislike for anything native, although he absolutely looked native. Both brothers would make the statement that they were raised to be white. Richard although he would make such state-ments was willing to admit being native if it meant he shared the benefits of hav-ing a Status Card. Richard had a Status Card, which allowed him to have medical coverage. James had such a dislike for anything native that he refused to apply for a Status Card and did without medical coverage.

I took advantage of James's distaste for being native to help him see what he was doing to himself. Answering my own question telling him that the kind of people who end up in a drunk-tank were drunks. Skid row types like my own father, continuing with I knew that both Richard and him were raised to be white and that he did not want to be seen as an Indian.

Asking James about the night that he was in the drunk-tank and the RCMP called me, what he thought the RCMP officer saw as he was picking him up and driving him to jail. He answered he didn't know. I told him what the officer saw was another drunk Indian. He saw what you said you hate and would never become.

I then asked James why is it when you see a drunk Indian on the sidewalk the comment is always just another drunk Indian. When you see a drunken white man, no one ever says just another drunk white man, explaining that my father was literally a skid row drunk. He was white with red hair but he was still just another drunk. I then asked James why it was; he was ashamed of his mother who he believed was a drunken Indian, yet, he was so proud to say that his father was white. In reality, his father was not only a drunk, but also a violent drunk and a lousy parent.

Asking James if he had ever looked in mirror, He answered, "yes". I asked him, "What did he see?" He did not have an answer. I commented that what he saw when he looked in a mirror was an Indian and that although he may have a white father he looked all-Indian. I explained to him that what the world sees when they look at him is an Indian and said, "You cannot go through life hating half of what you are." "You are an Indian you need to be proud of what and who you are."

Explaining to James that he was what he chose to be. He did not have to be what his parents were or are. I wanted him to see that his life, his future was up to him. I wanted him to see that if he kept drinking he would be a drunk. No, matter how he tried to justify it in his mind.

The world would see what James desperately did not want to be. The world would see him as a drunken Indian. I wanted him to know that he could choose to be anything. First, he had to like himself and he would have to be proud to be who he really was. I hope that the day would come when he could look into the mirror and love the Indian that he saw smiling back at him.

It would be years later when Bernice met our father's stepfather. The man she met would have been our grandfather. He told Bernice that he had raised our father. I do not know whom our fathers biological father was. He said he was married to our fathers biological mother our grandmother. Our grandfather told Bernice that our father's mother our grandmother was a full blood Micmac Indian. Our father was a half-breed. My example of a drunken white man turned out to be a drunken half-breed.

How is it that none of his children knew who their father was? Was my father so ashamed of his own mother? Was he so ashamed that he was half native? Did my father spend an entire lifetime telling himself and the world around him that he was raised to be white? The man who said he was married to our grandmother did not give my sister any reason to believe that our grandmother was someone to be ashamed of.

Was one of the reasons my father hid from himself, hid from life using alcohol as a painkiller because he was ashamed of whom he really was?

How sad it is that entire lives are lived and lost inside of individual minds. How sad it is; that young children are taught to see who they are through the eyes and the teachings of those whose views are distorted.

What a waste that entire lives are lived in such pain when they have always had the ability to look into a mirror and choose to like or even love what they see. Yet, so many of us choose to live with what others see in our mirror. We all have the ability to choose to see who is really looking back at us. We all have the ability to choose not to accept what others think they see as they are looking through their distorted eyes attached to distorted minds.

I may be the product of a mentally ill mother and a violent drunk half-breed father.

I am not my parent's!

I have learned a lot from both of their circumstances.

I am what I choose to be!

I am who I choose to be!

I am proud of who I am and I am grateful for all of the experiences and the people who have brought me to this point in my life.

Life for all of us is what we choose to make it!

Life for all of us is what we say it is!

My life is simply magnificent!

WHAT MATTERS MOST IS HOW YOU SEE YOURSELF!!

18

GROWING PAINS

Our family had undergone several changes in the year or two since we moved into our larger home. We still had Alex living with us. We also had Richard and James living in our home, With Daniel and Laura that was five children living with us.

Jason was employed; our relationship was what it had been for the past fifteen years. He went to work and came home to the television. Since our return from Bella Bella, he would often come home from work and have a beer or two with his marijuana. Jason was still the same loving father and husband that he had always been. He was still quietly living the life that I had set up for both of us since our relationship began.

Working and still dealing with all the daily details of our lives, which now included five children, somehow I still had the mind set that it was all my responsibility. Still after fifteen years believing that, a perfect wife did it all. Still believing if I was the perfect wife, he must have been happy and would always stay.

Jason's life as with all of ours was slowly changing. I had grown emotionally in fifteen years and was seeing my world with very different eyes than when our relationship began at fifteen-years-old. My intense compassion for children had also grown. The more children in my life and the more I felt I was helping in some small way the more I loved it.

What I did not realize or maybe I did not want to acknowledge was we were all growing. Our children were getting older as were we. I was growing emotionally and Jason was growing his dependency on alcohol and marijuana. As our family was growing so to was his family. Jason's mother was now living in an adult welfare apartment. His younger brother and sister were grown and on their own.

Jason's brother was now a young adult and was quite the hustler. He did what ever he could to make a buck. His younger sister who was now in her twenties had moved out of home and was dating a drug dealer.

When I first met Jason's mother she was selling alcohol to children from her apartment in the welfare project. She was always a very outgoing happy, jolly woman. She loved and doted on her grand kids, our kids. I thought she was a wonderful mother. Coming from the example I had as a mother, I thought she was great.

As our children grew and my thinking grew, I began to see her differently. Jason had always accepted her the way she was. She was his mother and he loved her. He never said anything negative about his mother.

There was one occasion when we had been visiting his mother. Daniel was two-years-old; Laura had not yet been born. Jason's younger brother and sister lived at home at this time. His sister would have been about fifteen-or-sixteen-years-old and was showing us her new jeans. She was telling us how she had stolen the jeans. His mother jumped into the conversation and said, "She came home and showed me the jeans she stole and I gave her shit. I told her she should have stolen a pair for her brother too."

Looking back it is obvious that these children were not living in a healthy environment. On the drive home, Jason was saying how disgusted he was with his mother, not because she had encouraged his sister to steal but because she was telling us about it in front of Daniel. He was only two but Jason didn't want him to think that stealing was something to be proud of.

We were both wise enough to want to protect Daniel from this environment, some how we were both accepting that if our son had not been present this situation would have been acceptable.

Growing up in this welfare project, hustle or steal what you can environment Jason's younger brother had learned how to buy and sell almost anything. He was now an adult and his mother was living in an adult apartment on her own. Jason now had a new marijuana connection. He would simply call his mother, ask her to buy what he wanted from his brother, and keep it for him until he was in town to pick it up.

His mother lived in Burnaby, which was two hours away from where we lived. They had a regular arrangement that seemed to work for all three of them. Jason's sister who was also living on her own was now dating a cocaine dealer. Jason's mother was fully aware that her daughters boyfriend was a dealer and that her daughter was not only dealing but using cocaine. This mother and grandmother not only bought and kept my husbands marijuana on a regular basis she was also keeping her daughters cocaine in coffee tins in her freezer.

Daniel was ten-years-old and Laura was seven; we had been married fifteen years when Jason graduated from marijuana and alcohol to cocaine. It would take six months before I would leave. I left him in the fall shortly after Daniel turned eleven and we had our sixteenth wedding anniversary. I spent sixteen years with a picture in my head that I had to do it all to make him happy so he would not leave me. Jason was not happy when we met. If he had been truly happy, he would not have needed to medicate himself into a tranquil state of being for the past eighteen years. I was so afraid of him leaving me that I never really let him into my life. I never really let him see who I was. Jason never did leave me. As with all things in my life and in our relationship I made the decision for both of us. I left him.

Jason told me that his sister talked him into trying cocaine. He went from trying it to being a regular customer making regular trips to his mother's freezer. When Jason smoked marijuana, he was a very peaceful tranquil man. When he drank alcohol, it changed his personality in a way that I did not care for but it was tolerable. He was still a passive quiet man.

He had never shown any signs of being aggressive or violent. My husband was a completely different person when he used cocaine. Over the six months that I stayed, after he began using cocaine he became two very different men. When he was high, he was outgoing, happy and even hyper. When he was coming down, he was loud, moody and irrational. It took a couple of months before I realized he was using cocaine. Confronting him one day, he admitted to trying it with his sister. There was a voice in my head telling me that I had to leave. There was also a voice telling me that I had five kids in the house and could not afford to leave on my salary.

During this time knowing eventually, I would have to leave. I tried to save money and make plans for where we would go. As difficult as it was I called Alex's aunt and explained to her that this was not an environment I wanted him to be in. She said she was now able to take him back. We arranged for him to return to her home.

Richard and James knew something was not right between us. I did not tell them that I knew Jason was using cocaine, telling them that if things did not improve between us that I was planning to leave. More than two years had passed since James had moved in. Both brothers were looking for a place for themselves.

Jason's cocaine use and his irrational behaviours were both increasing. I was back to living with a permanent pit in my stomach being so stressed I was not able to eat. Feeling as I had so many years ago, living with my mother being so careful not to say the wrong thing. Knowing that it was impossible not to say the wrong thing when no one knew what the right thing was, again finding myself second-guessing every thing, I did. I would ask myself if this or that was going to set him off and make him angry.

Jason came home from work on a Friday; it was payday. He walked into the house and literally threw some money at me. He said, "here this is all you get the rest is mine." I picked up the money and told him that this was not even enough to pay the mortgage. He gave me enough to make the mortgage payment. Taking the kids with me, we went to the bank. The money had to be deposited before the Bank closed or the mortgage payment would bounce.

As things had been escalating for the last few months I had been keeping track of the money Jason had spent on cocaine. In the last month before I left, he spent $600.00 that I was aware of on his new habit. Six hundred dollars in one month was a lot of money at that time; money we could not afford to spend and still pay all the bills.

I returned home from the bank to find Jason moving furniture. I asked him what he was doing. He was moving living room furniture into Laura's room. He said he was going to live in there from now on. I told him that he was being ridiculous. He took both hands a pushed me against the hallway wall and slammed the bedroom door shut.

This was the first time in the eighteen years that we had been together that Jason had been physically violent. He was in a very angry, irrational mood. Making the decision at that moment that it was time to leave. I told Daniel and Laura to get into the car. Collecting my purse and the car keys we left. I had no Idea where I was going. Jason heard the car start and ran out of the house. We had two cars at that time. I took the car that was registered in my name. It was the smaller car that he normally drove to work; he jumped in the other car and was chasing us down the road.

This was a small town with not a lot of traffic, driving down one of the main streets with Jason following behind. This was a two-lane road with one lane going in each direction. As he was following me down the road, an RCMP car was coming toward me in the other lane. I pulled into his lane and stopped in front of the RCMP car. Jason stopped his car beside mine. I explained to the officer that I was taking my kids and the car and was leaving. I asked him to keep Jason there long enough so he could not follow me and told the officer that Jason was using drugs and that was why I was leaving.

Jason told the officer that he just wanted to talk to me. We were in the middle of the street and would soon be blocking traffic and this officer was not particularly interested in our problems. I agreed to drive to the local RCMP parking lot and talk to Jason. We both drove into the parking lot. The officer did not follow us.

I expected Jason to ask if I was leaving him, or even say something about me taking the kids. He didn't say a word. He opened the driver side door of the car that I was driving and took two handfuls of tinfoil balls out of the pouch in the driver side door. He then got into his car and drove away.

Jason was not following me because he was concerned about me leaving him. He was not concerned about his children. He was following me because I had taken the car that he had just driven home. It was payday. He had just picked up his cocaine supply and I was about to drive off with it.

Not knowing were I was going, positive that I could never go back. If anyone had said to me six months earlier that I would leave my husband or that one-day we would be divorced. I would have told them they were crazy. I had been married sixteen years. We had been together eighteen years. At this point in my life, this equalled more than half of my lifetime. This day was to be both the end and a new beginning.

I called a friend and explained what had happened and that I had left. This friend was aware of the situation and knew that Jason was using cocaine, expecting her to say come over and bring the kids.

I was in my car with no place to go. My friend told me that she did not want to be involved in my problems and that she had her own children to worry about. She did not want Jason at her door looking for me. She suggested that I call a transition house if I needed a place to stay. I had not even considered a transition house and was hardly a battered woman, I did have two children that needed a place to stay, very little money and no savings account and could not go to a motel.

I could have called other friends. There were friends who asked me after the event why I did not call as they had plenty of room and we could have stayed with them. After calling the first person I thought of and expecting that, she would help only to be told that she did not want to be a part of my problems. I was back to feeling like the child that nobody wanted, telling myself how stupid I was to ask for help from anyone. This was my problem these were my children I should be able to take care of them and myself.

Calling the number for a transition house the local house was full. What a sad statement of our world that even in a small town there is a need for a transition house. An even sadder statement that the house was full of battered women and children. The local transition house arranged for me to stay at a transition house in the next town.

Driving my children to a transition house where we lived for one month; which is the amount of time that a family was permitted to stay. I was grateful that such a place existed.

I was not a battered woman but I had witnessed my mother being battered for years. Listening for years to the endless excuses, my father offered for why he was forced to break my mothers ribs or break her jaw. Hearing the words, I'm sorry, I will never do it again, I will quit drinking; I will go to AA, I will go to counselling. The booze made me do it. There was always an excuse of some kind.

There was always, "I'm sorry" there was even the occasional, "I love you" after another trip to the emergency room. These were words heard so often they had no meaning. My father may have thought he meant them at the time he was saying them. His actions never changed.

There were several women with their children who had come and gone during the month we lived in this transition house. Many of them were from other towns or the City staying in this house, as their local shelters were full. There was one mother I would like to tell you about. This was a woman in her early thirties. She arrived in the evening with four young children. The oldest was maybe seven. She was very quiet and kept to herself. Several of the women wanted to talk about their situations. This woman wanted to be alone.

It was obvious by the bruises on her face that she had been beaten. I do not recall how our conversation began but I was drawn to this woman. We were sitting in the living room together the children were all asleep. There was just the two of us in the room. My exact words I do not recall. I do remember that at some point in our conversation she showed me her bruises. This woman was not just bruised; her entire torso back and front was various shades of black and deep purple. I had seen my mother with the same colour bruises but never to this extent. This woman literally had no flesh colour left.

The first thing that went through my mind when I saw her body was she was lucky she wasn't dead and if she goes back she soon could be. My experience with violent environments taught me that the violence increases. It does not just magically go away. My concern was also for her four young children.

I was not there; I did not live with this woman to witness her experiences. I had spent years as a child hiding and crying while my father beat my mother or my brother and knew this woman was not in this condition without it affecting her children. Also knowing that her husband who did this to her was capable of doing the same thing to her children. It may not have happened yet but it was very likely in their future.

As we talked, she would tell me that this was not the first time she had left her husband and stayed in a transition house. She had made this trip four or five times before. It was not rocket science to figure out the situation was only getting worse and would likely never be any better. I had to talk to this woman my concern was for her safety and the safety of her children.

She was an adult, she was free to choose to stay away or return. Her children had no choice. Her children were forced to live with her choices. I know she felt that she had to return, although she was afraid for her safety. She was more afraid of caring for her children on her own. She was not employed, if she had the skills to find a job that would support her and four children, she did not share this with me. I am sure this woman was far more capable then she felt. She loved her children and believed she was making the best choices possible for them when she left her husband and when she returned.

I explained to her that the situation was not likely to improve. Explaining that what her husband had done to her was assault. I told her that no one deserves to be treated this way. I asked her if she was every concerned about him hitting her children. She said she was concerned. She also said he was really a nice guy and that he loved her. He only beat her when he was drinking.

Trying to explain to her, trying to make her understand that drinking was never an excuse to physically assault someone. I tried to make her understand that her husband was not the only violent drunk who was good at crying, saying he was sorry, saying that he loved her.

He was probably a wonderful man after he beat her. He wanted her to forgive him and not go to the police. She was willing to listen and seemed at this point like she was willing to talk about her situation. I commented that if I were in her situation I would have gone to the police and had him charged with assault. The time to go to the police was right now while she was still covered with the evidence of what he had done to her. I explained that she should have someone take photographs of her bruises. I tried to convince this mother to charge her husband with assault and to make sure she kept the evidence as it can sometimes take months to go through the system and she would likely be healed before her case went to court.

Attempting to make her see that it was possible that if she charged her husband that he would know that there were consequences for his actions. He would know that he was no longer permitted to use her as a punching bag. She did not want to make him mad. I tried to make her understand that if she did nothing the situation would only escalate.

It may escalate if she does something as well. There were no guarantees. Attempting to help her see that she had nothing to loose by standing up for herself, briefly letting this woman know although I was not in the same situation as she was that I had seen violence as a child. I told her that after watching my father beat my mother as her husband beat her that if a man even thought about hitting me I was going to the police.

She had left and returned four or five times. How many times will it take before she was too injured or dead and was no longer able to leave? If she stood up and said no more, it would not be easy, it may not stop. If he was going to kill her anyway what did she have to loose. She would at least be attempting to change her circumstances and most of all she would be making the police and the courts aware of her situation and her children's situation. If he beat her after he was charged, they would know exactly what happened.

I may not have known her husband, as we had never even met. Knowing her circumstances and knowing she wanted to believe that he really loved her. She wanted to believe that he just had a bad day. Perhaps she believed she did something to set him off. A part of her was considering that somehow things would be different next time.

This was no different that being a child living in a children's shelter longing to go home. The part of you that wants to be home somehow is able to override the facts in your memory. You logically know that home will be the same or worse than it was last time. Yet, you are able to tell yourself and able to convince yourself maybe this time will be different. This woman took her children and returned to her husband after only two days.

Because of the violence witnessed as a child there was apart of me that was always tuned in when this subject arose. I would be drawn to television news stories or newspaper articles that involved family violence.

Listening with both interest and disgust for the subject, my interest would peek after an incident hit the news and the parade of experts would be invited to offer up words of wisdom and possible solutions to prevent future such incidents.

One sentence that seemed to be repeated by each expert would infuriate me. Listening to the usual dialogue about how difficult it is to leave such a situation and the reasons why many women feel they have no choice but to stay. Although I did not agree with anyone choosing to stay, I could understand the circumstances and the reasoning behind a woman being unable to leave.

The dialogue would inevitably turn to why do men beat their wives. No matter whom the expert or what there background the same statement was repeated.

Men need to learn how to control their anger. This sentence was usually followed by discussions about counselling and anger management classes.

Hearing this sentence, which is still being used by experts on the subject today I would ask myself, if men need to learn how to control their anger this would mean that the expert is saying that men or the particular man being referred to has anger that is out of control. I ask myself what do these experts consider the definition of out of control.

My definition of a man out of control is a man having no ability to manage, manipulate, reason or think. Any human being who is out of control would mean that they are so angry they literally do not know what they are doing, where they are and they have no ability in that moment to think or choose.

With the exception of human beings who are severely mentally ill, I do not believe there are many adults who literally are not able to control what they do.

Men who beat their wives or their children are in total control! They not only know what they are doing they are choosing when and where they are going to do it.

They are choosing to take their anger out on their wives and their children because home is the one place where they are most likely to get away with it. There is no one else who they could physically beat without ending up in jail.

The world accepts excuses for behaviours that are inexcusable. There is the, he had a bad day at work excuse. He is under so much stress. The kids made him angry. His wife did this or she did not do that, and the ever popular he cannot control himself when he drinks.

Why is it that I have never heard an expert question how it is that a man can work all day, go out to the bar for a few drinks, manage to drive home and it is only after he closes the door that he becomes out of control?

If a man was so angry and so out of control, why do men not punch their co-workers, or their boss? Many men have bosses who cause stress yet there does not seem to be a rash of uncontrolled men beating their bosses. Many men have bosses that are women. I have yet to see the evening news report on men who are so angry and out of control that they regularly beat their boss. How is it that a man is not so angry and out of control, that he does not punch his neighbour on his way into the house?

Men who beat their wives are in total control. They manage to control their anger, their emotions and their temper all day in every other environment except with their wives or their children. They beat their wives and abuse their children because they can! Home is the one place that they can choose to be abusive and get away with it.

There are consequences for hitting a boss, punching a co-worker or a neighbour. There are consequences for being verbally abusive in the work place or in public; it is not tolerated. Unfortunately, home is the one place where the people being abused have emotional ties to the abuser. People are abused and tolerating abuse all in the name of what they believe is love.

The alcohol or drug excuse is no different. In today's society even our court system accepts the, "I was too drunk or stoned to know what I was doing defence." If a human being is not capable of controlling his behaviour to the point of physically assaulting someone when they drink, society should not only expect but also demand that they control what they can. They can control the choice they made to take a drink when they have already admitted to themselves and the world that drinking is their excuses for despicable behaviour.

Every time anyone uses alcohol or drugs as an excuse for behaviours in a court of law, the court should order them to never take another drink. It is logical to expect that if an adult is going to say they are not capable of controlling their behaviour when they drink that they should then be expected to control their behaviour while they are sober and choose not to drink. If they find that impossible, they clearly required court-mandated rehab.

There is no form of abuse that should be tolerated in our homes or society. Human beings are completely capable of controlling their behaviours if they choose to. Most human beings will rise to reasonable expectations. It is reasonable that each and every man, woman and child on this planet be entitled to live a life free from fear and abuse.

Each and every one of us must set the expectations for our own lives, as it is not possible to control the actions of others.

It is possible to choose what you will and will not accept or tolerate in your life. I was not responsible for my husband's cocaine habit. This mother was not responsible for her husband's abuse. We are both responsible for the decisions we make for our children and ourselves. I sincerely hope that this mother and all women in similar circumstances love themselves enough to choose not to accept abuse.

Leaving Jason on a moments notice not knowing were we were going or how I was going to care for Daniel and Laura on my own, I may not have known where we were going. I did know where we would not go. I would not go back and would not allow my children to go back. Sometimes in life, all you have is what you know you will not do!

There were lines that I had drawn in the sand for my life even as a child. Telling myself I would never be on welfare and would never let anybody abuse me as my father had beaten my mother. I would never allow my children to live the life I endured as a child.

Having no idea at the time how to possibly keep these promises to myself. I did know that by drawing the line in the sand for my life crossing that line would never be an option.

19

BLESSINGS &
NEGOTIATIONS

During the month that we lived in this transition house, I would travel each day to my hometown for my job. Once again at a point in my life were I was totally stressed, working only six hours a day and making only $6.50 an hour, how was it possible for me to afford to live on my own with my children? Jason would be expected to pay child support, given the cost of his current drug habit and his state of mind there was the distinct possibility that we would never actually see any of his money.

As this was a small town, the story of my situation was making the restaurant rumour mill almost before it happened. I was blessed with help from sources, which were completely unexpected. There was a wonderful woman who owned one of the local Real Estate Companies. I had met this woman several times. She was a regular customer at the restaurant; she was also the mother of a boy who was in swim club. Her son was several years older than my children. We did not know each other well we had spoken both in the restaurant and while watching our children swim.

This wonderful lady asked if she could speak to me. We sat together in the restaurant. She said she heard that I was going through a difficult time and that I was living in a transition house. Explaining the situation to her stating that I was not sure what I was going to do and that I was sure we could not go back.

She told me that the first thing she thought I needed was a good lawyer. At this point divorce had not been considered. Stating that what I needed was a place to live and a job that paid more money and that at this point was not yet considering divorce. I didn't think I needed a lawyer.

She explained that the lawyer was not required for a divorce. I did require a lawyer to be sure that my children and I were protected financially. She was explaining how I was entitled to half of the house and support for my children.

At this point, my life was running on automatic pilot, leaving with nothing but my children, a car and my purse, The need to find a better job and a place to live was constantly running through my mind. Moreover, the one-month deadline for leaving the transition house was fast approaching.

The woman I was talking to had been through a divorce, she was a very wise and caring person. She explained to me that because I had the children and was living in a transition house I would be able to get a temporary order to live in my house until it sold and that Jason would have to find somewhere else to stay. I had not yet contemplated the whole picture, selling our house, us being permanently apart.

I had been with Jason for more than half my lifetime and it was all falling apart in what seemed like over night. Acknowledging that she may be right and perhaps we could temporarily move back home, however I did not have a lawyer and there was not enough money to pay rent or the mortgage. Paying for legal advice would be impossible.

Our conversation continued as she said the most amazing thing. First, she explained that she had a lawyer. Her lawyer was a woman and she had already spoken to her about me. Her lawyer had already agreed to take my case. It would be possible for me to pay her later after we sold the house. Shocked, thankful and relieved that this woman who was only a casual acquaintance had already done so much to help me. I thanked her and arranged to see her lawyer.

Asking her why she had done so much to help me. I had no idea what the answer would be. Perhaps this woman felt sorry for me or she liked helping out charity cases.

Her answer surprised me and gave me yet another way of looking at myself. She answered that she wanted to help me because she had always admired me. I was not sure what I was hearing, never imagining that I could be someone that others would look up to. It never occurred to me that I was someone that others would even notice.

This woman who owned her own company, dressed in business suites and lived in a world I imagined to be full of uncaring rich people wants to help me, not out of pity she actually saw me as someone she admired.

She told me that she had admired me for caring for children. She had seen me with Alex. She knew that I was a mother; a foster mother and she knew that Richard and James were living with me, plus I had operated a day care. She said she didn't know how I did it, and that she would give anything to have the patience that I had with children.

Until this conversation, it had not occurred to me that my current life was unusual. I loved it and it felt so natural to me to have a house full of children. Taking in children who had no place to go was so personally important to me, it was on my mental list of things I had to do it was never considered to be anything special. It never occurred to me that anyone would even notice let alone admire me for such a thing.

I made an appointment with this woman's lawyer and was able to arrange leaving the transition house and moving back into our home until it sold. The month that we spent in the transition house driving back and forth to work, dealing with lawyers etc. was a month of stress on top of stress on top of stress. Again living with a permanent pit in my stomach unable to eat I was hospitalized.

I required surgery for another cyst on my ovary. This time the cyst had been bleeding and emergency surgery was required, returning to the transition house after the surgery and returning to work with the stitches still in my belly. Telling myself if I could not pay the bills on my whole paycheque what would I do if I missed days at work.

During this time that my family was living in crises mode, I was again formulating a plan for my future. Having to come up with a new blueprint of where we would go from here. We now had a temporary place to stay. Once we sold the house I imagined that I would once again be renting. There would likely be enough money for the down payment from the sale of the house, however my wages would hardly qualify for a mortgage.

This was something I did not want to do. I had worked so hard at finding us a home and had worked so hard at creating, what I thought would be the perfect environment to raise our children without having to move. It was all falling apart and my kids were only half grown.

This same wonderful woman who had helped me find a lawyer offered to list and sell my house without charging the regular real estate commission. This would leave more money for my children and me.

Telling myself from the moment, we left that I needed a job that paid more money and a place I could afford for my children to live. A place to live was temporarily looked after increasing my income was next. Doing the math and coming up with the amount of money required each month to barely get by. Calculating that I required a minimum of $9.00 per hour full time to survive on my own with the kids, I was currently making only $6.50 part time.

Knowing the owner of the restaurant for several years as she was a friend before I worked for her. She knew my situation, informing her that I would have to look for another job and would give her as much notice as possible once I found something. She asked me what I thought I would do.

The answer was that I had no idea. My office skills were now more than ten years old typewriters were being replaced by computers. My job at the department store included some computer experience; at the time, I worked for them computers still used key punch cards, my office skills would need to be upgraded in order for me to return to this type of work.

Even if upgrading my office skills were possible, it may be difficult if not impossible to earn the money required and remain in this small town. There were not many jobs available. The ones that were available usually had a long line of applicants and low wages. My friend and boss asked me what wage I required, telling her that after doing the math $9.00 an hour if it was full time would be the minimum requirement.

Arriving at work the next day as usual, my boss took me aside and asked if I would be willing to stay on as her manager if she could offer me full time work and $8.50 an hour. She added, "we may be able to look at it again in a few months." Of course, I jumped at opportunity to say yes.

Once again questioning my life, asking myself if she was doing this as a favour to me, was she offering me more money and a full time job out of friendship or pity. I would have never asked for this kind of an increase. It may look like nothing today but at the time paying someone $8.50, an hour to work in a small town restaurant was definitely not the norm.

My relationship with my real estate friend was helping me to see that I may actually have some value. I was at least now willing to ask myself if maybe the reason my friend and boss offered me more money and full time hours was that I was a good employee, a good manager and perhaps she thought she didn't want to loose me. Questioning myself as to the possibility that she may have believed I was worth it.

Amongst the chaotic details of getting through each day a tiny part of me was beginning to feel that it might be possible that I was actually worth something. Always knowing that I was worth something to my children, all children look at their parents as being their whole world. I believed I had been a good wife. My definition of a good wife was totally distorted but I believed I was a good wife. This was different.

This was personal. I was actually beginning to feel like maybe, myself, Rose as a person was worth something to others. I now had two occasions where people were telling me that I actually mattered. Being offered a raise and asking me to stay made me feel good. It made me feel that at least for now I was not worth less than. I was worth more.

Throughout this month long Transition House stay the necessities required for my children were beginning to come together. I kept the appointment with the lawyer. This would also be a great learning experience. Our first appointment dealt with the details of my being able to return to our home with the children until it sold. The lawyer would contact Jason and explain the situation.

Jason was advised to retain a lawyer, which he did, the remaining appointments required with this lawyer would teach me valuable tools that I was later able to pass on to others. This lawyers practice was primarily family law. Divorce and custody were her specialty. I had absolutely no knowledge of the legal system. Knowing that David at times had a Legal Aide lawyer was the extent of my lawyer knowledge. This woman was not only an expert at what she does she also cared.

On one of our appointments after Jason had retained a lawyer, my lawyer commented on the lawyer my husband chose. Jason also had no knowledge of lawyers or the legal system.

Her comment was, "oh good this guy is primarily a real estate lawyer, he usually calls me for advice when he handles a family matter." Although it may seem like an insignificant point the knowledge that I now had that it was important to retain the correct lawyer for the job would in future prove very valuable.

As we discussed the particulars of my situation, it was becoming obvious to my lawyer that I was in a mental place of feeling responsible for looking after Jason. In the same mental place I had always been. Putting my children and my husband's needs first, Even under these circumstances I felt determined to be sure that Jason was looked after and was concerned that I was being fair to the man that I had spent the last eighteen years with.

Stuck in the mental place that I had always been in where I was responsible for it all. WE had been together for eighteen years, WE had two children together; WE had built a family and a home TOGETHER. There had been eighteen years of WE, yet I chose to take responsibility for it all. As WE were now separating, I had the mind set that some how I would take some; leave Jason what I felt he needed and I would be completely responsible for the children. Of course, in my mind, I somehow felt Jason needed more than I did.

My lawyer could see what I could not. She explained to me that I had to look out for and protect my children's interest. Daniel and Laura were the most important things in my life. Believing I was absolutely looking out for their best interest. I stated that I was asking for custody of my children and because of

Jason's new drug habit that I wanted his visitations supervised only until his life-style changed.

The picture playing in my head was that we would live separately; I would take the kids and would do what I had always done. I would work harder and do more. Only now, I would financially have to support us on my own. This had already been accepted as the new picture of my future. It would be a struggle but we would get by.

Unable to see that my lawyer's definition of look out for and protect my children's interest was completely different from mine. My lawyer was very patiently trying to make me see that she wanted me to look out for our financial future.

We had several different conversations involving child support, spousal support that she said I was entitled to after being married for sixteen years. There were also the proceeds from the sale of the house. I would talk with my lawyer and think I had everything straight in my mind, and would then talk to Jason and negotiate away most of the items my lawyer had reviewed with me. This went on and on.

In my lawyer's office listening to her logic and agreeing with her as to what was best for my children and myself; I would then talk with Jason. The emotional attachment I had for this man that I still deeply loved would find me wanting him to have more. I was telling my lawyer and myself that he deserved to have something after eighteen years. Somehow, I could not see that I also deserved to have something after eighteen years.

My idea of having something was I had Daniel and Laura. With negotiations going nowhere in my lawyer's office once again adjusting the previous plans she had set out. This day would be different. After listening to my newly negotiated items, she told me that she could not in good faith allow me to accept this settlement. It was her next statement for which I will always be grateful.

She said to me, "I see a picture of your future. I see you working hard, constantly struggling, being poor and you and your children doing without." My response in my head was, "duh"! That is the picture of my future. I have already accepted that! Some how we will be all right, I had been telling myself I maybe poor again as I was as a child but I would do what ever it took to make sure my children knew they were loved and that they would always have enough.

My lawyer continued to explain to me that if I negotiated away what my children and I were entitled to that was the future she saw for me. This was the only future I saw for me! Until this moment in the conversation I had no idea that she had been desperately trying since the first day, I walked into her office to tell me that there were other options for my future. Telling me, I was entitled to full child support and spousal support and half of the proceeds from the house.

All that I could see was Jason struggling to live on his own because he was forced to pay so much to me. The picture engrained in my mind engrained in my soul was that I was somehow completely responsible for my children. Although I did not consciously know it, I had been playing the tapes of my mother in my head that were telling me that if I asked for something, if I asked for anything I was greedy. How dare I ask for something for myself?

Until this day, until this moment in my life I did not see that asking for more for me was in fact asking for more for Daniel and Laura. I believed that all my children needed was me and that I would have to do whatever it took to take care of them and myself.

My lawyer had drawn me a portrait of my future. A picture that was the exact duplicate of the picture I had drawn for myself. Some how when she explained what she saw she was seeing a picture that did not have to be. She was seeing a picture that she was trying desperately to change. Until this moment in time I had been seeing a picture of the way, I believed it was and until this moment I had been willing to accept my picture as my new reality.

Looking at both pictures, I was starting to see her interpretation of my future as something in which I had a choice. I may not have been able to see all of what my lawyer was seeing as she was trying to protect my financial future. I was able to see that in her office on that day that I was not the one who should be doing the negotiations.

I made the decision that day to allow my lawyer to negotiate on my behalf. I told her that I was too emotionally attached to the situation to be objective; it would be better if I did not talk to Jason about this until the negotiations were complete. I trusted her to act in my best interest.

Jason objected to paying full child support. I was concerned that with his new drug habit. If he was expected to pay what he considered to be, too much he may not pay at all. My lawyer negotiated for less child support and I would receive two thirds of the proceeds from the sale of the house. I would also have sole custody of the children. I did not ask for or receive spousal support. Jason never missed a child support payment. He paid child support and remained in his children's lives. We were at the hospital together when our first grandson was born.

My new real estate friend not only sold our home without charging commission. She found me a temporary basement suite to rent while she was looking for a place I could afford to buy. We found a townhouse for sale only a few blocks away from where our house was. It was out of my reach financially. My real estate friend spoke to the credit union on my behalf and they agreed to give me a mortgage. Richard and James had been living independently during this period. Richard was going to move back in with me and I was able to use his income to help me qualify for the mortgage.

In my world believing I had to do it all on my own. In my world where I made myself responsible for every detail I was now beginning to see that there were people who were not only willing to help but also actually wanted to help me. Beginning to acknowledge that It was possible to ask for something or to accept help without being considered greedy or a burden, although not yet comfortable with this realization. I was willing to try to see the picture I had painted of my world through the eyes of others.

Thank you to my real estate friend, my friend, boss, and my lawyer for all they have done. I especially thank you for teaching me so much about myself.

During this time of negotiations, Jason and I were also negotiating on the emotional issues. Having lived with Jason for more than half my lifetime, Jason was only a year older than I was; he too had spent half of his lifetime together with me.

We had emotional conversations about our situations. Jason was saying we could work things out. He was saying that we did not need to separate. He wanted us to work out our problems on our own. I was telling him that our problems were due to his drug use. Even after leaving with his children, as we were negotiating with lawyers Jason still could not see that he had a drug problem.

Our personal negotiations were not progressing, together in our living room the day before I was to leave the transition house. Jason had found a temporary apartment to rent and was moving his things. Doing my best to put the house together, knowing coming home with their father gone and household furniture missing would be upsetting for Daniel and Laura.

We were both in an upset, emotional state. Jason was again saying that he wanted us to work things out. He was telling me that he loved me. This time he said he would do whatever it took. He offered to go to counselling, saying we could go to counselling together.

I loved this man will all my heart. I told him I was willing to do what ever it took. Telling him that I loved him, agreeing to go to counselling with him, stating that he had to stop using drugs and stop drinking. Agreeing that if he made the appointment I would go anywhere with him and would not leave him to deal with his problems alone. I was willing to do what ever it took to help the man I loved take back his life.

Jason said he would do what ever he needed to do. He also said that he wanted me to come back first. He wanted us to move back in and do this together. The minute the words came out of Jason's mouth I felt my inner brick wall go up. It was like being in an emotional time warp. Able to see the words come out of his mouth, looking at my husband the man I loved; I was hearing my father's voice.

I was hearing the same, "I'm sorry, I'll change, I'll never do it again, I'll quit drinking for good this time" speech that I had heard my father tell my mother a thousand times. I could see the, "I will give you just one more chance answer." I could see the next time my mother would be laying on the floor waiting for an ambulance.

I was no longer mentally in the room, literally feeling the emotions draining from my body. A few minutes before I was feeling love, I was feeling sympathy and caring for my husband. We were both negotiating in tears.

The minute Jason said I would have to come back first every bit of me, every part of my body and soul was saying this is the line in the sand that you drew as a child. This is the line you will not cross! This was one of the lines I had drawn for physical survival.

Listening to my husband say, he wanted me to move back home with him and we would work it out together. I was seeing the picture in my mind of me leaving again in a panic looking for a place to stay. I would not go there! I would not do this! I would not put my children through this! Once was already too much.

Telling Jason that I loved him, telling him that I was willing to go to counselling and was willing to stand by him. I also told him that this was his problem. He was the one with the drug problem. He was the one with the alcohol problem. I was willing to help him but I could not do this for him. If he made the appointment, I said I would be there.

Stating that I would only consider coming back to live with him after I was sure he no longer had a drug or alcohol problem. Telling Jason that whether it took six weeks, six months or six years it would be up to him to decide if he wanted his life back or whether he would find himself sitting on a couch somewhere stoned playing Nintendo or watching television.

Jason never made a counselling appointment. I never came back. I am grateful that without knowing it, through their disturbed actions, my parents had taught me the importance of drawing the correct lines in the sand for my life. Once again, I may not know where I am going or what I will do when I arrive. I absolutely know where I will not go and what I will not do. Sometimes in life that is all you have and all you really need to know to survive.

20

I'M SPECIAL

Six months or more had gone by since leaving the transition house. We had moved to a temporary basement suite after the house sold until I was able to purchase and move into my townhouse. Daniel and Laura were still able to attend the same school throughout our ordeal. Jason was renting an apartment in the same town so the children were able to see him on a regular basis.

Richard moved into the townhouse with me. James had been living in his own place. I know he would have liked to come back and live with me. He was too proud to ask and he did not want to be a burden when I offered. James did move into and share the apartment with Jason for about six months due to his financial situation.

Life was a little less hectic. My stress levels were lowering and I was now concentrating on my future. Telling myself in the past that I did not want a career, I wanted a family. Knowing at the time when I was working for five years in the offices at the department store that it was only temporary until I could quit and be a stay at home mom. Today I was looking at having to work to support my children and myself for the long term.

Looking at options for myself, perhaps upgrading my office skills, which would allow me to work for a little more money at what was easier work. For the first time in my life I was contemplating wanted more education and a real career. Telling myself, I wanted to be able to work at something I liked and something that made a real difference.

While not in a position to quit my job and go to school. I was just considering future options. I started reading the brochures from the local College and various literatures about student loans, grants and assistance for single parents. The College in the next town the same town I had driven each day to the transition house offered University transfer courses. A student could take their first two years of a four-year University program at the college for far less money and then transfer to a University for the final two years, several of the courses were offered in the evening.

Particularly interested in the Social Worker program, I was considering being able to take my first two years part time at the College and perhaps when my children were grown or in their teens it would be possible to finish the last two years. This would mean having a career as a Social Worker once my children were grown.

There was a part of me that was drawn to wanting to expand and maybe one day actually have a career. There was also a part of me that kept asking myself if I could actually take a college course and pass? My school experiences were almost non-existent. My high school years I went through the motions of being in class.

Always completing enough to pass, without being involved or attached to any of it; graduating grade twelve only because I wanted to please Jason. I had no career ambitions; my mother told me at eleven-years-old that if I could work I did not need school. The idea that I was even considering taking a college course had me asking myself if it were even possible or was I really too stupid?

Reading a pamphlet from the college one day, there was a section on subsidies. One caught my eye. This program helped to finance single parents who wanted to return to school or upgrade their skills. Picking up the phone, I made an appointment.

I wasn't sure if I was college material, if there was a program that would help with the cost I was at least willing to see what they had to offer. I did my homework, and arrived at the appointment with all the pertinent information regarding the Social Services Program at the College that I wanted to take. What a disappointment this would be!

Meeting with the Program Co-ordinator I expected to discuss financial options for single parents. After the polite introductions, she asked me what I thought I would like to do. Explaining that I was interested in the Social Service Program at the College, and was hoping to take my first two years of a Social Work Degree locally, I realized that it would require having to transfer to a University in order to complete the last two years. I was meeting with her to see if there was financial assistance available to help pay for the first two years.

Fully aware of what I had just said; I may have been nervous but I am sure I spoke clearly and explained myself in understandable terms. I have no idea what this woman heard. The first question she asked me after my explanation was if I was sure I would not be more interested in becoming a dental hygienists. They were in demand right now. I very politely told her that I had no interest in dentistry.

She then proceeded to tell me that they had several programs available to assist me in advancing my education. I only had to be on Unemployment Benefits or on Social Assistance and they would be happy to help.

I told her that I had a full time job, it did not pay much and it did not pay enough for me to be able to advance my education. I explained that I was a single mother that was looking for a way to improve my education so I would not have to work in a restaurant for the rest of my life. I had no plans of quitting my job and living on Unemployment or Welfare.

She then stated that if I wanted help to pay for school the requirement was that I not only have to not be employed, I would have to live on Unemployment or Welfare for six months before I would be eligible to apply for this program. I left this appointment feeling disappointed and disgusted. It made no sense to me that a program advertised as being for single parents to improve their education and living conditions did not include single parents who worked for a living.

I continued to read each college pamphlet that arrived in the mail. A few months had passed since my disappointing interview. The spring booklet from the college arrived. It was February or March. The opening article was a reminder that now was the time to book college entrance exams. This was the exam that a student must pass to insure they have the minimum reading and writing skills to complete a course. The test was being booked in the next month or so for students intending to register for courses the following September.

Talking myself into making an appointment to take the test, there was not much point in my continuing to consider taking college courses towards a new career if I was not smart enough to go to college. Booking the appointment, I passed the test.

I felt inspired and a little more competent after passing the entrance exam. I decided I would consider taking only one night course. Taking one course at a time would be affordable. It would take a long time to finish, but I was working towards a long-term goal and may as well start where I could. Registering for Human Services, which was one of the courses required for the Social Services Program. The course would start in September.

Daniel and Laura were slowly adjusting to our new life; the daily details were being looked after. I received a phone call from a Social Worker. She was calling regarding Alex. Alex had returned to his aunt. His aunt unfortunately was again dealing with a serious health issue and was living in Alberta at this time.

The call I received was from Alberta Social Service. Due to his aunt's health problems, Alex was again in foster care. At the time of this phone call he had been in five Alberta foster homes and as many schools in a three month period. Most foster homes were not able to cope with his severe behaviour issues. Alex had been permanently expelled from school and was only in the first grade.

This Social Worker was calling to ask if I would consider taking Alex back. She was calling as Alex had asked to come back and live with me. I told her I would take him. Social Services in my hometown arranged for him to return to live with me. Alex was now seven-years-old and was repeating first grade.

Alex would live with me for the next seven years. At age fourteen, he returned to live with his mother. This young boy who came into my life at five-years-old had extreme behaviour problems due to a combination of fetal alcohol syndrome and the environment he lived in before age five. He had a mother who loved him. Alex also had a mother much like the young seventeen-year-old mother of my first foster child in Bella Bella.

Alex's mother was not a fetal alcohol syndrome child herself. She did come from an abusive dysfunctional family and had been surviving on her own struggling to raise herself since she was about eleven-years-old. This young mother told me that she loved her son enough to know that she was not capable at this time of raising a child. She wanted what was best for Alex. She thanked me for caring for him. I told her how proud I was of her for making such a difficult decision. For choosing to put her sons interest first.

In the seven years, I cared for her son this young mother made amazing strides in her own life. At the time her son returned to live with her, she was self sufficient, employed and better able to care for him.

I cared for Alex for seven plus years. I knew he was considered an extreme behaviour problem child even before I met him. Knowing in my heart that I gave this child all I had to give. Somehow of all the children I have had the privilege to care for, Alex was the only child I feel that I failed. This was the one child that I was never really able to reach.

I have cared for several children over about a fifteen-year period, some for a few weeks, some for a few months and some for a few years. I may not have changed their lives; I sincerely hope that for whatever time they were with me that they were able to feel wanted and cared for. In seven years of caring for Alex, I am not so sure I achieved any real emotional connection. It may have been that he was so severely emotionally handicapped that he was not able to let me in.

Knowing that I cared for Alex's physical needs and knowing I was always there, I desperately tried to reach this child on a meaningful emotional level. I gave Alex what I was capable of giving and Alex received what he was capable of receiving. Somehow, it feels like not enough.

Alex returned to live with me; he was now seven-years-old and due to his circumstances was repeating the first grade. The social worker informed me that due to his aunt's health issues he was placed in foster care in Alberta. As I have already mentioned Alex had been shuffled through five foster homes and as many schools in the three-month period between leaving his aunt and returning to me. The foster homes were not able to cope with his extreme behaviour issues. Alex was asked to leave the last school he attended and not return.

This boy at seven-years-old was at times violent; he was still going to the bathroom in his pants even at school. His aunt told me that his room had a very bad odour, after months of trying to detect the source of the odour; she discovered that he had been peeing in a boot in his closet for months.

When Alex lived with me, he would often mess his pants. I taught him how to use the washing machine. Explaining that he could just clean himself up and wash his clothes and no one would know. I did not want this boy teased or want him to feel bad. Alex chose not to take me up on this solution. Over the next three or four years I would often find his full messed underwear in various hiding places including stuffed down heating vents.

His behaviours at school would be at times violent. Alex had a real need for attention and negative attention was all that he knew. At seven-years-old, he functioned emotionally at the level of a two-or-three-year-old. He was able to reason and learn. I believe Alex was capable of learning at close to his age level. Alex was considered by the schools to be special needs and a behavioural problem, he was not expected to behave and learn at his appropriate age level. Alex's world was accepting him as a problem, different, not capable. That is what his school world allowed him to be. At home with me would be the exception.

Contacting the school and explaining Alex's circumstances before his arrival, I did my best to explain that I felt this young boy needed expectations. Explaining that his circumstances have not given Alex much of a chance to relate to other children, at seven, Alex emotionally functioned as a two-year-old. He wanted to play with other children he had no knowledge of what it meant to play together. He was more comfortable playing beside another child.

Interaction was not something Alex understood. He often mistook normal play by other children as something he feared. If a child picked up a toy he thought he wanted to play with or if another boy bumped him as boys often do he would either run and cry or lash out and punch or hit. In Alex's world, even the smallest things were understood as a threat.

At home, completely aware of Alex's circumstances, I understood that he required patience and understanding. I also understood that he needed expectations. I expected Alex to behave and function as a seven-year-old. If he fell short of my expectations which he often did. I would explain to him what was expected and offer him suggestions and ideas as to how he could have handled what ever the situation may have been in a seven-year-old manner. Alex may not have been able to obtain being a fully functioning seven-year-old. I knew if I expected him to be seven he would at least aspire to be a capable seven-year-old boy. By excusing his behaviours and permitting him to live at a two-or-three-year-old level, he would only aspire to be a dysfunctional three-year-old.

Alex's first day of school at what was now school number five or six in a short time period. In Alberta, he was expected to repeat first grade. The BC school system felt it was better to place him in second grade with children his own age. Alex was placed in a grade one/two split class, which seemed to be appropriate. His grade level from this day forward would follow his age rather than his abilities. His teacher was aware of his history. Dropping him off for the day, the expectations of both the teacher and her new student would set the tone for their future. The teacher would inform me of the day's events.

The first sentence out of this young boys mouth on his first day at this new school was, "I'm special I do not have to do what everyone else is doing!"

The exact words from the teacher I do not know. They did not matter. She was a very caring, loving teacher. Having explained Alex's history to her in advance, I had tried to explain that I believed it was in Alex's best interest that she have expectations for him to aspire to. I cannot speak for this teacher; I believe she had a picture of teaching this child, which included lots of patience and understanding. I also believe her picture included sympathy rather than empathy. It was sympathy, which allowed this caring teacher to accept Alex's definition of himself as being, "special."

Empathy is the ability to see another person's world from their side, to understand a person's circumstance with out feeling sorry for this person. Empathy rather than sympathy would have allowed this teacher to show the same caring, patience towards Alex. Empathy would have also allowed her to try to understand what Alex had endured in his seven short years. The difference is, in feeling sympathy rather than empathy for Alex this teacher was also able to allow Alex to use his past as an excuse for his present and his future.

Empathy would have acknowledge this young boys past, would have offered the same patience, caring and understanding that Alex so desperately needed and would have also allowed this caring teacher to make empowering decisions for Alex which, would allow Alex to see himself as capable in spite of his circumstances rather than to see himself as a product or victim of his circumstances.

At seven-years-old functioning at the emotional level of a toddler it was clear to me that Alex had repeated to the world, this child was repeating to his new teacher exactly what his world had taught him, "I'm special, I do not have to do what everyone else is doing!" How sad it is, that we have taught so many in our world that to be someone special is also to be less than.

I often wonder how different this grade two-class experience would have been, and every other class to follow if this wonderful caring teacher had had the experience and the tools for this difficult situation.

I believe what Alex needed to hear after he announced to his teacher on his first day that he was special was, "Your right dear, you are special, and this is your lucky day, because this is a school where all the children are special. Since we are all special we can all do everything together."

This simple statement would have acknowledged what Alex had been taught about himself. This simple statement did not make being special being less than. It simply would have told Alex that he was welcome and that he was equal. This could have been the start of a simply wonderful educational experience for Alex who needed both education and wonder in his life.

LIFE KEEP IT SIMPLE MAKE IT MAGNIFCENT!

The most important educational tool available to us all requires no special funding and no special classes; it is simply to have GREAT EXPECTATIONS!!

Sadly, the remainder of Alex's education would be anything but wonderful. Alex lived in a world from birth to four-or-five-years-old where his emotional and physical needs were not met. At seven-years-old, he had lived in more than eight homes. It is not difficult to understand why this child was unable to trust or become attached to anyone. This was a world I had lived in myself as a child. It was in my similar world that I learned to become invisible. I could see that Alex was living alone in his mind. His physical body was present he tried to keep his emotional mental self-buried deep inside. In my childhood world I wanted not be seen. This child was different Alex was emotionally buried. On the outside, he craved attention. His body was going through the motions while his mind was emotionally detached.

As Alex would grow and the school year was progressing, I was beginning to see the pattern for his future education unfold. His behaviour at school ranged from as the teacher was teaching the class he would walk over to the windowsill which doubled as a bookshelf and one by one knock the books off the shelf onto the floor. He would put his hands in the containers of counting beads and make as much noise as possible rattling the beads. He would often have to leave the room to change his clothes after messing himself in class. If Alex was asked to stop a behaviour or was upset at anything, he would lash out hitting the teacher and other students. Alex's attempt at grade two was becoming a battle of wills. Alex was determined to attract as much attention as possible, his teacher spent the remainder of the year trying to keep Alex entertained and happy so he would not get angry and cause a problem.

This was a battle they were both loosing; the teacher was not able to teach a child who would not be taught. She was also loosing out on time that needed to be spent on the other students in her class. The students were loosing out on what could have been an exciting enjoyable school year as their school day was constantly disrupted by the behaviour of one small boy.

I was loosing this child! Alex was loosing himself to a world where he felt empowered and in control at school. He could behave in any number of inappropriate ways and in return was rewarded, with everything from computer time, to play time, anything to pacify him in an attempt to modify his behaviour.

At home, Alex was expected to behave and function in a civilized manor; he was expected to participate in what ever the activity may be. Alex was expected to ask for what he wanted and to explain what he did not want. Violent behaviour, temper tantrums, throwing things was not accepted. They also were not happening. Alex was capable of functioning as a reasonable human being at home, yet he was completely out of control at school.

The only explanation I have to offer is that Alex's behaviours mirrored his expectations. At seven-years-old, a part of this little boy believed he was expected to be quote: "special" at school and he was. He was expected to be a capable, functioning seven-year-old at home and he was. He rose to both expectations as required. It does not take a childcare professional to figure out which world Alex would grow to prefer.

There was a small stream of school psychologists, teacher's aides and psychiatrist who would offer opinions and suggestions for Alex's welfare. There were endless meetings and discussions. I was never able to convince any of them that the behaviours they were seeing at school were not happening at home. The school psychologists strongly recommended that I take Alex to see a child psychiatrist. After several phone calls and a few months waiting time, I finally had an appointment with a psychiatrist. The initial appointment was for me alone without the child. The psychiatrist wanted to go over Alex's history, his reports from school and his current behaviours at home without the child being present.

After reviewing the school reports and asking me numerous questions, this professional psychiatrist that I had waited months to see concluded that he could not take Alex on as a patient because his behaviours were too severe. Not a very comforting thought that I was trying to help and trying to raise a seven-year-old child who was considered too severe for professional psychiatric help.

I would like to share some unrelated school incidents, which I believe could have benefited from a different way of thinking.

The first situation involves Daniel. Both of my children were able to read before they entered kindergarten. Throughout elementary school, Daniel and Laura were top students. I often received compliments from the teachers on my children's abilities and behaviour.

I would like to share parent teacher interviews for each of my children with you. The first interview was with Daniel's grade six teacher. As I have said, Daniel was always a top student. The interview started with the teacher complementing Daniel's abilities. He then stated that he had only one problem.

Explaining that when it came to math class he could not get my son to settle down and do his work. His teacher continued with Daniel would be looking out the window or playing with a pencil etc. he would wait until the last fifteen minutes of the class before starting his work. Asking this teacher, "so are you telling me that his work is not complete?" The teacher answered, "no his work is complete he manages to get it all done." I then asked, "so are you telling me that he rushes through it and it is all wrong?" He responded with, "no, he has it all right." I then asked, "So what is the problem?" The teacher repeats, "The problem is that I can't get Daniel to settle down and start his work unit ¾ through the class." Asking in frustration, "If Daniel is able to complete the work and have it done correctly in fifteen minutes why would he take a full hour to do it?" Stating I believed that if he gave Daniel an-hours worth of work that was more advanced math Daniel would likely require a full hour to complete it and would therefore begin his math at the beginning of math class.

This seemed like such a simple solution to me. This teacher was looking at me as though I were speaking in a foreign language. He then stated that he could not expect Daniel to do more than he expected of the other students. My reply was, "then you will continue to have the same problem."

The conversation changed to English class. This teacher was commenting on Daniels writing ability. He was stating that he felt my son was a gifted writer, and was specifically speaking of a short story Daniel had turned in as an English project. My response to this teacher was, "I wanted to talk to you about that."

You gave Daniel an "A+" for that story. The teacher than commented that he had wondered if perhaps I had helped Daniel write it?

Relaying to the teacher, this particular story had been the source of an argument between Daniel and me. This was a project the students had a week or two to complete. The night before this story was due Daniel remembers at ten o'clock in the evening that he had to have his story completed by morning. Daniel was a very intelligent young man, I am sure that he had this story completed in his mind for the past week and a half and had not taken the time to write it down. It was ten o'clock in the evening when he recalled that this had to be completed. Sitting at the kitchen table Daniel begins to write. An hour later, he is finished. Glancing at Daniel's paper work, I was not happy. Stating that he had two weeks to complete this story and he waited until the last minute to scribble it out on paper. My comment to Daniel was, "your teacher is going to take one look at this and know that you scribbled it out at the last minute." Daniel's comment to me was, "oh mom; you don't know what your talking about."

Daniel was right. I didn't know what I was talking about. He not only received and "A" for his efforts he received an "A+" I do not recall a lot about my school experiences. I am quite sure an "A" would have required the story to be interesting, the writing to be neat and everything on the page to be properly punctuated and double spaced for easy reading.

Daniel was a good student; handwriting was not one of his better subjects. The page I was looking at was a mess. This teacher's comment was that he gave Daniel an "A+" for his creativity. It was a good story. My question was, "If you give Daniel and "A+" for a story that may have been creative but was scribbled out on a piece of paper at the last minute, where is the incentive for Daniel to take the time to produce neat accurate complete work that he could be proud of?" The teacher did not have an answer. Explaining that I expected that Daniel would receive a "C+" or maybe a "B" for his work with the comment that the story was terrific. If he had taken a little more time with the presentation, he would have received an "A." An "A+" should be reserved for work that has all of these components done exceptionally well.

Leaving this interview, I found myself wondering about the grade that a child may have received who had worked hard for two weeks on a neatly written well-presented story that may have been less interesting to the teacher. It is important that we appreciate our children and that we acknowledge their creativity. It is also essential that we teach them to see the whole picture. Daniel's creativity may not be as appreciated in the working world if he has never learned how to present his creative ideas in a professional, acceptable manor.

Laura's teacher interview was when she was in fifth grade. She was a good student with a report card for English showing an "A." In her classroom, looking through her notebooks, her English notes caught my attention. Reading a story that Laura wrote and had received and excellent mark for, it required my reading the first page three times and I was still not sure what the words said. Consulting with her teacher as to what this story was supposed to say. The answer was unbelievable.

Laura's fifth grade teacher said to me, "Oh' it is difficult to read because of her spelling. She is spelling the words the way she thinks they are spelled." Asking, "doesn't anyone correct her spelling?" Her teacher replied. "We don't correct spelling, we want the children to enjoy writing so we just allow them to write without corrections."

These words were unbelievable. As a mother I was viewing my daughters "A" in English on her report card as an indication that she was able to read, write, punctuate a sentence and spell. As Daniel had so clearly stated, "mom you don't know what you are talking about!" My expectations of what my children were learning in school, my understanding of the report cards that they were bringing home was clearly out of touch with the current classroom reality.

In fifth grade, Laura could not write a sentence in a story that was readable. If her teacher were not correcting her spelling, how would she learn how to spell? Having a creative idea in her head that she was trying to share requires the ability to spell the words she was using to communicate correctly.

It is our responsibility as parents and teachers to provide our children with the tools they require to be successful adults. It is important that we appreciate our children's creativity and provide a positive image for every child. It is also essential that our children be taught the realities of life.

As young adults, as these children pursue further education or career opportunities they will not find employers or University Professors willing to give them top salaries or top grades for incomplete or inaccurate work. A resume which is scribbled out or which contains words that are misspelled and unreadable is not likely to attract a top job in any field.

It is so much kinder to teach our children well; with realistic expectations while they are in school, than it is to send them into the adult world unprepared only to watch them fail.

There is one more elementary school story I would like to share. Daniel was in seventh grade this was his last year of elementary school before starting high school. Jason and I had been living apart for about a year. As with any child going through a divorce Daniel was feeling the stress of the world that he knew turning upside down.

The grade seven year had begun. Daniel was excited and had been discussing his expectations for what high school might be like next year. The first report card of the year was a surprise. Daniel had always had "A's" and "B's" this report card was showing a decline in his grades.

As we discussed the decline in his grades, Daniel was telling me not to worry about it. He said he had a lot of other things on his mind besides school. Daniel had always been close to his father. Jason was only a few blocks away it was not the same for Daniel or Laura as having there father at home every night.

Telling Daniel that I understood he may not be as focused on his schoolwork, and letting him know that I understood that he missed his father and that he wished we had never had to move. Also commenting to Daniel that this was his last year in elementary school and that he wanted to be sure to keep his grades up so he would be able to go to high school next year, knowing this was something that Daniel was looking forward to.

Daniel stated, "You don't have to have good grades to go to high school," to which I replied, "yes you do; you have to be sure that you pass grade seven." Once again, I (Mom) had no idea what I was talking about!

Daniel continued to explain that Bobby in his class had already failed a grade and that Bobby was failing almost everything in grade seven but he was going to high school. Asking Daniel, "how do you know that Bobby will be going to high school and he won't be repeating grade seven?" Daniel simply replied, "he can't fail, you are only allowed to fail one grade in elementary school, besides, Bobby will be turning thirteen-years-old and thirteen-year-olds are too old for elementary school they have to go to high school." Daniel would turn thirteen in July and would start high school in September.

Daniel was telling me that he had already concluded that he would be thirteen and therefore no matter what his grade seven marks may be, he would be going to high school.

Trying to explain to Daniel that it was import to him, it was important to his future that he keeps his grades up, telling my son that I understood that his world had been turned upside down. I wanted Daniel to understand that although our current circumstances were affecting him, they were not caused by him and were not about him. Daniel needed to absolutely understand that his father's issues and mine could not be used as an excuse for his choices.

Letting Daniel know that I loved him; also wanting him to understand that if he chose to fail in school, he would only have himself to blame. School may be more difficult under these circumstances. If it were possible to change any of this for him, I would, telling Daniel that he may have to try harder for a while. Whatever he chose, whatever he would become as an adult it was up to him.

I wanted Daniel to understand that he had a father and a mother who loved him, he had a home and whatever he may need. It was not perfect. If Daniel chose to fail at school or at life, it would have nothing to do with his father or me. This was Daniels life; He was the only one who would have to live with the decisions he made. He was the only one in control of whether he saw himself as a success or a failure. Daniels life and his future were up to him and for him alone to determine.

21

MOVING ON

The school year progressed and work continued, dealing with life's daily details and caring for the four children now living at home. Both excited and apprehensive about taking my first college course in September. I would attend classes two evenings a week and spend every spare moment on my breaks at work and at home completing the required assignments and term paper.

Absolutely loving this Human Services Course, the subject matter felt so natural and comfortable to me. I was involved in the materials and had forgotten my concerns about whether I was capable of passing a college course. Turning in my term paper, I received an "A+" on my paper and an "A" for the course. There was no longer any doubt as to whether I may be too stupid to go to college.

The next two semesters I would continue with one night course at a time. Human Services was followed by Communications followed by Psychology 101 these were all required coursed for the Social Services Program. I passed them all.

The Communications Course would be a challenge. Feeling confident in my ability to communicate on paper, I was not at all confident or comfortable speaking in class. Terrified of standing at the front of the class and speaking, the requirements for this class were to complete a term paper and present your paper to the class. Completing my term paper, this took about three months and included various interviews and research. The Subject of my paper was alcohol use by native youths in British Columbia.

The instructor for this class was a man I did not care for. The Human Services instructor I liked and felt a connection with him and the materials. Commenting to myself many times during this communication class as to why this instructor was teaching communications when he did not seem to be a good communicator. This instructor would often make negative remarks to students or about students. My personal opinion of him was I was not sure he liked much of anything or anyone in his class. This was not a man who instilled confidence in a student who was terrified to present their work in class.

The course was concluding. The last three or four evenings would be presentations by students of the papers they had work on for the term. The papers had been turned in and graded. Grades would not be disclosed until well after the class had concluded. The oral presentation was also a part of the grade.

Spending an entire class listening to presentations and the instructor's comments after each student had completed their talk. Knowing I was scheduled to present my paper during the next class.

I knew the material as I wrote the paper, telling myself I could do this, telling myself that I had notes to refer to if I was to forget something. The time to present my work had arrived. Being so nervous, I was not sure even after my presentation was complete if I had missed anything or whether I had made any sense out of the materials being presented.

The comment from the teacher was a recommendation that I move around more as I was speaking. Relieved that it was over and relieved that his only criticism was that I did not move around enough, it would not have been possible for me to move. Being so terrified I am sure I was glued to the floor on the spot where I was standing.

On the last day of the class as the students were leaving the instructor was returning our marked papers. There were comments written across each cover. The comment on my report was: You have a dynamic speaking style. You spoke from the heart and it showed. I could not believe what I was reading. So sure that my presentation had been barely adequate and that it was obvious to everyone including the instructor that I was frozen in fear with my mouth barely moving. This instructor who I personally did not care for and believed was too negative showed me a picture of myself that I liked. I left his class on the last day feeling capable and confident.

On my own now for about two years, I enrolled in my third college course, had also enrolled in, and completed the Crises Intervention Program at the college. After completing the Crises Program, I was now qualified to volunteer for the teen and crises lines. These were the 24-hour telephone lines an adult or teen could call if they were feeling suicidal or experiencing situations where they needed someone to talk to. I volunteered for the Crises line for two years.

During this two-year period, Laura had developed problems with her joints and her muscles. Both of my children had been in swim club for several years. Laura who was now nine-or-ten-years-old swam her first race two lengths of the pool at age four. At age eight, she was the BC Summer Swim Champion for her age group. She was a very fit and athletic child. By age nine Laura was making regular visits to an orthopaedic specialist. The Specialist was telling me that her muscles had tested weaker than the average girl her age. This was a major concern. Laura should have muscle strength much greater than the average child her age due to her seven-day week swim training.

After several test and what seemed to be increasing muscle failure over the past year the specialist explained to me that he did not know the exact cause of my daughter's problem. He said that he had other patients that he was treating for the same problem. He could not explain why but he stated that this seemed to be a problem for people living in the BC Fraser Valley. Laura was born in the Fraser Valley and with the exception of the time we lived in Bella Bella had lived here all of her life. This specialist told me that his recommendation to his other patients was that they move. He had kept in touch with his patients that had moved and all but one had improved after leaving the Valley.

The one patient who did not improve had other health issues that could explain her condition. This specialist said to me, "If she was my daughter I would move. If you do not move she may be in a wheel chair in a couple of years." I made the decision in his office that we would have to move.

A few months before the Specialist had suggested we move I met a man I was just beginning to know. A friend of his who was a regular customer introduced this man to me at the restaurant. His friend told me that this man had been divorced about two years before we met. My first question to this friend who was trying to play matchmaker was, "what's wrong with him? Why did his wife leave?" His friend told me there was nothing wrong with him. He was a nice guy; after their children had grown, they just drifted apart as a couple and that was why they were divorced.

After several invitations to meet for coffee, I finally said yes. We had gone out on a few occasions over the past few months. I was telling this new acquaintance Bill that I did not know where I was going but I had to move. Although we had not known each other for very long Bill said that if I was moving he wanted to come with me, it was time for a change in his life. I considered his suggestion over the next few months as we were seeing more of each other. Bill was willing to sell his house and buy a property in the country if I was willing to be his partner. I would keep my townhouse and rent it out.

Talking to myself about how I would manage to move Laura to a different area, find a place to live, find a new job to support us all. Where would we go and how would I do it all on my own with four children? There were no answers only questions. I knew moving was not a choice it was a necessity for Laura. Making the decision to try this new relationship and move together after months of considering what I believed to be my options.

I knew my decision was based on logic and economics not on the emotional part of this new relationship. Weighing my options, move on my own to what ever town I found to be suitable, rent a house, find a job and go back to struggling. Expecting small town wages would be part of my new job what ever it would be.

Option 2: take a chance on this new relationship. Maybe it would become something special. Allow Bill to buy the property he said he wanted in the country somewhere and live a life where I would have to work but we would be sharing the bills and I would not have to worry about putting groceries on the table. I chose option number two.

We began the search for a new town and a new place to live. Discussing some possibilities with my doctor, I wanted to choose an area that would perhaps be beneficial for both Laura's condition and Daniel's asthma. We had planned to find a new town and a new home before the school year began in September.

We chose a small town in the BC Southern Interior. This was a much dryer climate than the Fraser Valley and could possibly benefit both children. We made a couple of trips to this town to look for property and found a Five-bedroom farmhouse on ten acres of land. The property also contained a three-bedroom mobile home, which rented for extra income.

Bill bought the property. I rented out my townhouse and intended to keep it as a future investment or as a place to return to if need be. We arranged to move for July 1st after the school year was complete. Richard, found a roommate and decided to keep his job and remain in his hometown.

Embarking on a new adventure, I moved three children to a new town with a new partner living on ten acres of land including cows and chickens, which were part of the purchase.

In the time since leaving Jason my world had changed, I had changed. I was looking at my world and myself in a new way and had developed some confidence in myself. Beginning to realize that I had worth, instead of looking at this new relationship wondering what I would have to do so Bill would not leave. I had actually been wondering how long I would be willing to stay.

The summer months were spent unpacking, organizing the house and getting to know our new town and each other. The family who lived on the acreage across the street had three boys. The youngest was the same age as Daniel.

Daniel was now fourteen-years-old and would be starting grade nine in high school. Laura had just turned eleven and Alex was now ten-years-old. The new school year was about to begin. Contemplating how I could possibly make the transition to a new school and a new teacher a positive experience for Alex. Alex was being enrolled in the fifth grade although he was working at a grade one level or lower. His school experience up to this point had not allowed for much learning to take place. I was hoping a new school might somehow be able to change this.

22

NON-NEGOTIABLE EXPECTATIONS

The schools were open for registration the last two weeks of August. Enrolling Laura in grade six, Daniel was enrolled in the high school. I made an appointment with the school Principal to discuss Alex, providing letters and information from his previous school. I wanted to make this transition as easy as possible on both Alex and his new teacher. With hopes that this school, experience for Alex would include some actual education.

After meeting with the school, Principal and explaining some of Alex's history and his previous school behaviours this new Principal and I were discussing what I felt would be best for Alex. Explaining that Alex did not have the same extreme behavioural problems at home, as he was having at school. The Principal suggested that we place Alex in a grade three/four split class, which would perhaps be an easier adjustment than a grade five class. Alex could attend a three/four split this year a five/six split class next year and would then be placed in a grade seven class for his final year of elementary school. This would allow Alex to leave elementary school at the appropriate age. The teacher for the three/four split class was a wonderful woman with a lot of patience.

Meeting with this teacher and the Principal again before classes would begin in September, I liked this lady; she was an older woman who loved the children she was teaching. She was patient and kind with a permanent smile and a jolly disposition. After discussing Alex with her, she asked me if I was working. Stating that we had just moved to the community and that I was not working at this time but I had planned to look for work. She suggested that it might be an easier transition for Alex if I were to be in the classroom with him for the first few days.

This would allow her to get to know Alex and she asked me to give her tips on how I handled Alex at home. This was a wonderful Idea and perhaps an opportunity for a new educational experience for Alex.

We agreed that we would start with me being in the classroom for the morning. This would allow time for me to assist the teacher, while allowing the teacher to observe any changes in Alex during the afternoon when I was not present. My few days would turn in to six months, attending classes with Alex every day for the first six months in his new school.

The first day of school had arrived with me attending class with Alex. Sitting in a chair at the back of the room where I could observe for this first day. Alex put his coat in the coatroom took his new school supplies and sat at an available seat. The teacher introduced herself. Her name was Mrs. Wilson, she asked the children to take out a pencil and to write their name on each of their books and on their other supplies. She continued with explaining where the supplies would be kept in the classroom.

As the children were labelling their supplies Mrs. Wilson would call each child by name and say welcome. Most of the children were familiar with the teacher and the classroom. As this was a grade three/four split class most of the grade four students had been in Mrs. Wilson's class for grade three. There were a few new children. With each new child, the teacher would spend a few minutes asking where they had moved from and asking a few details about their previous school etc.

Alex was sitting at his desk writing his name on his items, as was every other child in the room. When Mrs. Wilson asked Alex where he was from, he simple answered that he had moved from Fraser School. There was nothing outstanding; there was nothing different about Alex's answers or his behaviour.

As the morning progressed, the teacher handed out worksheets for the students to complete. She explained that as they were completing their work she would ask each child to read a few lines from a page in the book she was holding. She would come to each child's desk and he or she could read this page quietly to her. She just wanted to know how well each child could read.

Each child was quietly reading this page in turn. Alex had been completing his work sheet. When Mrs. Wilson asked him to read the page Alex said," I don't want to read." Mrs. Wilson asked again. She said, "I would like you to read only a few lines." Alex repeated, "I don't want to read." Mrs. Wilson said, "that's okay" and continued with the next student.

When recess arrived, I spoke to Mrs. Wilson, explaining to her, that Alex could read. He reads at a grade one or two level but he was capable of reading. She replied to me that she did not want to make Alex do anything he did not want to do. I tried to make her see that with Alex this was not an option.

Describing how at home with Alex I often had to make decisions for him. He was capable of making some decision. Providing her with an example I stated that Alex could choose whether he wanted to wear the blue outfit or the green outfit. Alex was not yet capable of choosing what he would wear to school with out some guidelines. Alex would make inappropriate choices such as putting on shorts when it was snowing out side.

Trying to make her understand that if she wanted Alex to read she would have to be clear to Alex that she knew he was capable of reading and that when it was reading time he did not get to choose. He could perhaps choose the book he could not choose whether he would read.

Although this teacher clearly cared for her students, she clearly loved teaching, she had asked me to be in the class room to give her suggestions and ideas as to how to deal with Alex, her reply to my explanation was that she could not insist that a child do something that he did not want to do.

My expectations of a new educational experience for Alex were beginning to fade and this was only the morning of the first day of school. I had expected that Alex would behave in an acceptable manner on this first day of school, as he knew I was in the classroom. I had seen this child act reasonably at home and at the swimming pool. As both Laura and Daniel were in swim club, I asked Alex if he would like to try it. The alternative was that Alex would spend hours at the pool watching other children swim. He wanted to learn to swim. Alex not only learned to swim he was able to conduct himself in a civilized manor at swim practice and at weekend swim meets.

Knowing that Mrs. Wilson was unaware, that Alex had already set the tone for their relationship. Alex said he did not want to read and had received the answer he was hoping for. On his first day of his new school again Alex knew that he was special he did not have to do what the other children were doing. It did not require words Alex had learned at ten-years-old the subtleties of controlling his environment. Living in two different worlds, one at home and one at school Alex was becoming a competent con artist. He was and expert and getting exactly what he thought he wanted out of his school experience.

The first day at school was only a half-day Alex came home with me at lunch-time. The second day returning to the classroom; Mrs Wilson and I had discussed that during my time in class depending on Alex's needs I would help the students with their work, help to grade papers, what ever assistance was required. As I was not expecting to be in class for more than a few days we both wanted Alex to experience a normal school day without interaction with me unless it was required. The second morning was as uneventful as the first with me leaving the class at lunchtime as we had arranged.

Returning for the third morning Alex appeared to be adjusting to his new environment. The children left the classroom for recess Mrs. Wilson described the previous afternoon. She began by saying that she could not believe the change in Alex's behaviour when I was not in the classroom. She had watched him for two mornings with the exception of not wanting to read function in a reasonable manner. The previous afternoon Alex was not willing to co-operate or participate in class. Alex was displaying the behaviours that Mrs. Wilson had read about in the reports from his previous school.

Continuing to assist Mrs. Wilson for the next six months, Alex continued to function in the mornings and be disruptive in the afternoons. I do not recall the reason, we were about two months into the school year and I was not able to attend the morning class. Mrs Wilson had asked if it would be possible for me to attend the afternoon class for this one day.

Arriving for the afternoon class, Mrs. Wilson explained that the class was going outside to play soccer. I was no athlete although I was sure that I could remember enough soccer rules from Daniel's soccer practices when he was seven to handle a grade three/four soccer match.

The class ran out the door and took up positions on the soccer field. Mrs. Wilson's class played soccer twice a week in the afternoon. The children took up which, ever position Mrs. Wilson delegated. I was the designated goalie. Alex was on the field and played his assigned position. The children seemed to enjoy the game. It was a beautiful sunny fall day. Alex seemed to be enjoying the game. Mrs. Wilson blew her whistle to signal game over. The children ran off the field and headed back to class.

Being a little older and a little slower than fourth graders, Mrs. Wilson and I walked back to class. She said to me, "wow, I wish you could be here every afternoon." I wasn't sure what she was referring to. I didn't think my soccer skills were that impressive. She continued to say that this was the first time all year that Alex had participated in gym class. My response was, "why?" to which she replied, "Because Alex doesn't like gym."

I had tried on so many occasions with so many different situations to show and explain to Mrs. Wilson that Alex was a very capable ten-year-old. Alex will do what he is expected to do. I did not know how to make it any easier to understand. Perhaps I was not explaining myself well enough. I knew what I was trying to communicate. I did not seem to be able to make Mrs. Wilson or anyone for that matter understand that Alex simply needed consistent expectations.

Desperately trying verbally and through examples to show others in Alex's world that if they expected Alex to do something, if they made it clear to Alex that whatever the situation was he did not have a choice Alex would rise to his expectations.

As we walked across the grassy field once again explaining, how I saw Alex. Repeating to Mrs. Wilson that it was obvious to me that as we had just watched Alex run out onto the soccer field and play soccer, we had watched this boy play and watched as he appeared to be enjoying the game it was clear to me that Alex did like gym and Alex was very capable of playing soccer.

I thought I was making it clear to Mrs. Wilson that Alex was not the one who should be making the decision as to whether or not he participated in gym class. Alex should be told that he was not only capable but that he was expected to participate in gym class and in all classes at school.

Alex played soccer this day because he knew that on the day that I was on the soccer field-playing soccer was not going to be a choice. He never said a word, he never said he didn't like gym class; he never said he didn't want to play. Alex saw me on the soccer field and he knew that on this day, he was expected to be a capable ten-year-old boy and he was.

I do not understand the apprehension of others especially teachers to have expectations which are not negotiable. Alex was not traumatized; Alex was not having a temper tantrum he did not even say that he did not want to play.

Alex did play soccer for the first time in two months and he appeared to be enjoying it. As parents and educators, we need to be aware that it is possible we may be killing our children with kindness. I believe that our children deserve better. Alex was a fetal alcohol syndrome child with legitimate emotional issues. This child had issues to deal with that were created for him before his birth. There is no amount of kindness and understanding that will ever change that part of Alex's life.

I wanted Alex to know that even though he may have difficulties that he could have a wonderful life. I wanted Alex to be aware of all that he was capable of. I did not want Alex to define himself by what he believed to be his limitations.

Sincerely believing that if Alex lived in a world with constant clear expectations as a child as difficult as it may seem at times, Alex would one day see that he had far more successes than failures. Alex needed to be able as an adult to look back on his childhood experiences and be able to draw on the tools he had learned.

If Alex was able to tell himself that he could achieve what ever he set out to do as long as he had the expectations for himself that he could do it. I knew as an adult that he would be able to take care of himself.

It is possible to be kind, caring and at the same time have non-negotiable expectations when required. I know because I have done it and have seen the results in Alex. Sadly, Alex had made the decision at seven-years-old that he preferred to live in the world, which saw him as special. I was struggling to keep him in my world this was a struggle I would not win.

This would be the only day that Alex participated in gym class at school. As the school year, progressed Alex did not take gym because he did not like it, he did not take music because he did not like it. Alex did not take art because he did not like it. Alex was shrinking! In an environment that was meant to educate and expand a child's knowledge Alex was permitted to choose what he would and would not learn.

Continuing to be in the classroom daily, I would often mark papers or would sit with some of the children who required extra help. I spent a lot of time with one boy. Something about Tommy stood out, Tommy was a well-spoken very energetic child with a grin that lit up the room. I saw a lot of Daniel in Tommy. He was eager, intelligent and full of enthusiasm. Mrs. Wilson had explained to me that Tommy was a child who required extra help. Tommy was in forth grade and had Mrs. Wilson as his third grade teacher.

Mrs. Wilson saw Tommy as a hyperactive child who could not settle down and do his work. I saw Tommy as a very bright boy with capabilities far beyond this fourth grade class.

Mrs. Wilson believed that Tommy did not complete his work because he was just too fidgety he was just too inattentive to complete a project. I saw Tommy as a child who was bored as he was far too advanced for this class. Watching Tommy I was thinking of Daniel in sixth grade playing with his pencil and looking out the window in math class.

Tommy was one of the students who would regularly sit with me. Mrs. Wilson commented to me one day that she did not know what it was that I did but when Tommy was with me, he always completed so much more and that Tommy was asking to sit with me. I was still not able to communicate to Mrs. Wilson that I did with Tommy what I had always done with Alex I simply had great expectations.

Mrs. Wilson was giving instructions to the class on one of the first days that I had worked with Tommy at the beginning of the school year. There were eight lines written on the black board. The instructions to the class were to copy these eight lines into their notebooks before it was time for recess.

The last line of the instructions was directed at Tommy, Mrs. Wilson said, "Tommy you try to do two lines okay."

I cringed with this last statement. I know that Mrs. Wilson believed that she was doing what was best for Tommy. She believed that Tommy was not capable of copying all eight sentences in the time allotted and was giving Tommy a goal she believed would be obtainable, mistakenly believing that this would in turn allow Tommy to feel good about himself and his accomplishments. She was trying to show Tommy that he could be successful by lowering her expectations to what she believed to be his achievable level.

What I heard when Mrs. Wilson said, "Tommy you try to do two" was that Tommy was not capable of writing eight lines. In trying to give Tommy a reasonable goal so, he could feel good about himself when he achieved it. Mrs. Wilson was in fact telling Tommy that she believed she had already predetermined that he was not capable. Mrs. Wilson was telling Tommy that she saw him as less than.

When the instructions were complete Tommy asked Mrs. Wilson if he could sit with me. I had a table, which I would use to assist four of five students at a time. Tommy came and sat with me. Tommy was a bundle of energy; he was excited as he sat down. He was talking a mile a minute. Tommy always had something to tell you about his day. I listened to his story and included my feed back on what ever his story might have been. As Tommy paused in his story telling I would remind him why we were sitting at the table. I said, "Remember Tommy we are trying to do lines before recess." Tommy opened his book. I said to Tommy, "you know what Tommy, I think you are smart enough and quick enough to do five lines before recess" to which Tommy excitedly replied; "I think I can do all eight!"

Replying I said, "well lets see if you can do five or eight we can make it contest. Lets see who is right. I say you can do five." Tommy repeated, "I know I can do eight!" Tommy began eagerly writing his lines. He had completed about a line and a half when he began to tell me another story. Listening to his story and again at an appropriate pause reminded Tommy that he was in a contest with a deadline. Tommy would begin writing again. We repeated this pattern of story telling and line writing until the recess bell rang. We were both wrong Tommy did six lines. I said to Tommy, "Look at that you did six lines, I guess we were both wrong." Tommy replied, "That's pretty good next time I will do eight."

I would like to tell you about another child in this class. This young girl was struggling in both reading and math. One of my duties in the classroom was to mark the children's homework. Correcting math papers, this girl's paper stood out. This was basic subtraction. There were maybe twenty subtraction questions on the page. This girl had all but two of the questions wrong; this child also received extra help in reading. Setting the paper aside wanting to point it out to Mrs. Wilson I had assumed that this girl required someone to sit with her and explain what it was she had done wrong. I showed the page to Mrs. Wilson expecting that she would say that she would have to show this child where she was making her mistakes. Expecting that she may ask me to sit with her and help her with math. I was surprised and disappointed with the instructions I received. Mrs. Wilson said, "just tick the ones that are right and put a smiley face on the bottom of the page. We wouldn't want to devastate her by telling her they are all wrong."

We wouldn't want to devastate her by telling her that she got them all wrong! What about the damage to this child's ego and to her future if she leaves elementary school without basic maths skills? I was asking myself if her future employer would be willing to put a smiley face on her paycheque if her work was not adequate.

It is possible to let this child know that she has made an error in math and teach her how to do her math correctly without it being a devastating blow to her self-esteem. Had the education system always been this out of touch with what I considered reality or was this definition of education something that was new to me?

I recalled a grade ten English class of my own high school years. I had become an expert at being invisible, showing up to each class, doing my work and never saying a word. I had always done what was expected and had always passed. I did not want to bring attention to myself by not turning in homework or having failing grades. This particular term I had not followed my usual habits. After meeting Jason, I was spending time with him out of class and was spending my time in class daydreaming about him.

The term report cards were being prepared. It was English class the teacher was calling each student up one at a time and filling their marks in on their report card. This teacher had a ledger book with spaces for each assignment mark for the term. He would look at the students name and assign a grade.

I had not turned in a single assignment for this class. Panicking inside, realizing that there would be no marks beside my name. The teacher called my name, handing him my report card, he glanced down at this book at my name and filled in a "C+" on my report card. I was both thrilled and amazed. There was nothing to base this grade on; and no marks beside my name to correspond with the work I had turned in for the term. This teacher simply looked at my name and gave the same mark he had always given me for this class. Concluding that if I showed up to class, was not a problem this teacher assumed that I was worth a "C+", he likely didn't even know which student I was.

Contemplating this little girl's future as it related to her math and reading abilities I recalled a young man that had worked for me one summer in the restaurant. This young man was hired for the summer; this was his first job as he had just graduated from high school. One of this employee's duties was to run the cash register. This was a time when not all cash registers would tell you what change to return. The till in this restaurant did not have this capability.

Watching as this young man struggled to make change. This was a busy fast pace restaurant and speed was an important part of the job. I took this young man aside and asked what the problem might be. This was his first time running a till and he was not familiar with counting back change. Explaining that the easiest way to count back change was to add rather than subtract, giving him an example. If the customer gives you a two dollar bill, we still had one and two dollar bills at this time, and his bill is a dollar fifty rather than subtracting a dollar fifty from two dollars it is easier to add. Stating that you start at a dollar fifty add a quarter, which would now be a dollar seventy-five and one more quarter would equal two dollars.

It did not take me long to realize that the real problem was that this young man who had graduated from grade twelve only a few weeks ago did not have the skills to do simple math. I tried to work with him with the same principle of adding, giving him a bill, we would practice. As his math, skills were becoming apparent I found him a job to do, which did not include running the till. I had broken making change down to the simplest of terms I made the decision to change his job description after realizing that when asked if I give you a quarter and what I am buying cost ten cents how much change do I get back. He was not able to give me an answer.

As parents and educators, it is important that we teach our children that they are valuable; it is critical that our children see themselves as being capable. We are fooling ourselves and handicapping our children's futures when we leave reality out of our definition of education. There are no amount of smiley faces, pats on the back or shinny stickers that will give a student the confidence to go forward in the world unless these items are a part of and not in place of a complete education. This young girl and this high school graduate are both fully aware of their capabilities and their shortfalls.

Had someone included patient proper math instructions with the smiley faces perhaps this young man would have entered the adult world with the ability to make change from a quarter. How much confidence do you think he has in himself as an adult when he wants to buy a simple chocolate bar and does not have the skills to determine if he has received the correct change? This young man has entered the adult world where he is expected to earn a living, pay bills and balance a cheque book after twelve years of school he has a diploma to hang on his wall yet he is not capable of making change from a quarter. This is not my definition of education. Our children, all children deserve better!

As the school year progressed, another one of my classroom duties was to teach cooking class. The teacher's lounge had a stove with an oven. Mrs. Wilson would send a group of six or seven students with me and I would teach the children how to make cookies. Cooking class was once a week and the children rotated so each one had a chance to learn the fine art of cookie making. I would teach the children how to follow the recipe and each child would have a chance to add an ingredient, stir the bowl or place the cookies on the pan. As the cookies were baking in the oven, the students would spend the time copying the recipe into their notebooks.

It was during the note taking part of one class that the children were asking questions. One grade four girl I worked with on only a few occasions. In this particular class, Julie wanted to talk. She began by asking me if I was Alex's mother. I answered that I was Alex's foster mother. Julies next question was, "Alex has a lot of problems doesn't he?" she followed her question with the statement, "I mean he is a nice boy but he has a lot of problems." I agreed with Julie that Alex had a lot of problems and that he was nice boy.

Julie's next question took me by surprise, she asked, "but you still love him don't you? I mean you still care about him." I answered Julie that yes, I did love Alex and I did care about him. One of the other students then asked, "how come he lives with you?" I told the children that Alex lived with me because his mother was not able to look after him right now. Tommy spoke up he said, "Well you know that I am adopted" he continued with, "my real mom loved me but she couldn't take care of me either so I am adopted."

One of the other grade four boys added, "well I live with my grandma, my dad lives in Russia and I don't have a mom so my sister and me live with my grandma." Julie then added, "well I live with my mom on school days and I live with my dad on the weekends. At first I didn't like it but I'm getting used to it now." I assumed by Julie's statement that her parents had recently separated. I commented to the children, it was interesting to know that they each had different living arrangements. I continued with, "see we are all different but in some ways we are all the same." Julie commented, "yah even Alex."

I could tell by the excitement and the interest in the room that it was important to each of these children to be able to tell their own story. It was important to them to know that they were not the only kids in the classroom or in the school who had alternative living arrangements. I was thinking to myself that it was too bad Alex had not been present for this cooking class. It may have helped him to realize that many of his classmates were living in home situations that were similar to his.

I had not mentioned to Julie or to the other children that I knew the reason she had such an interest in Alex. A few days before this cooking class in the afternoon, Alex had been acting out in class. The classroom had one computer. Each child had a personal computer time. This particular afternoon it was Julie's time to be on the computer. Alex decided that he wanted to use the computer. It was Julie's computer time. Alex would have a turn when it was his scheduled time. Julie objected to Alex wanting to use her computer time. Alex got angry and punched Julie square in the teeth.

I received a phone call from Mrs. Wilson explaining Alex's behaviour the day that it happened. She asked me what I thought she should do about it. Replying that I thought she should take away Alex's computer privileges until he could demonstrate that he could behave properly and explained to Mrs. Wilson that she had to make it clear to Alex that hitting was not acceptable at any time for any reason.

Mrs. Wilson replied, "I can't take away his computer time, it is one of the few things that Alex likes." My response was, "that is precisely why you should take it away. Alex has to learn that what he did was wrong and that if he wanted to have a turn on the computer he would have to earn it."

Not knowing what Mrs. Wilson's response to Alex was at the time this incident occurred, as I was not there. I do know that Alex continued to have his computer time. Alex also continued to lash out and hit students when he was upset. Alex seemed to reserve his anger for hitting the girls. I was not sure if this was perhaps because ten-year-old boys were more likely to hit back.

The school year was progressing life at home was reasonably settled. It was approaching early spring and I had not yet found a job. My Unemployment Insurance claim would soon be running out. I would have to find full time employment soon. I informed Mrs. Wilson that I would have to leave my classroom duties in the near future.

We agreed that I should start coming to school less often, perhaps only two or three days a week. This would allow Alex some time to adjust to me being permanently away. As predicted the more time I spent away the more Alex's behaviours escalated. I did find a full time job and was no longer able to be at the school.

Mrs. Wilson would often call in the evening to fill me in on Alex's behaviours, especially if she had a difficult day. The school year was more than half over. Alex was not participating in any subject he did not like. Alex was once again in a classroom where he was being entertained and pacified so he would not get angry and cause a problem.

Alex was now allowed extra computer time as this seemed to be something that he enjoyed and would sit quietly to do. Not once but twice Mrs. Wilson reported to me that the school had to send the computer out for repair because Alex had tampered with it and broken it. This classroom computer used floppy disc. Alex would peel the edges of these discs up so that they would not be usable. The classroom was without a computer for a week or more each time Alex would do something to break it. Although Mrs. Wilson would report the incident to me and even report the cost of the repairs she still refused to take away Alex's computer time.

I returned to school several weeks after starting work. I would come in once and a while for a morning if I happened to have a weekday off. The first thing that I noticed was Alex was wearing his coat in the classroom and he had his backpack sitting under his desk at his feet. On the first day of school and every day after that that I was there all the students hung their coats in the coat room and placed their backpacks on the appropriate shelf.

Questioning Mrs Wilson about Alex and his coat, She replied, "he always wears his coat he says that he is cold." I asked her about his backpack she relied, "He keeps it there because he says he is hungry so I let him eat something in class." Asking why Alex did not eat his snack at recess and his lunch at the appropriate time as he had previously done. She replied, "Alex spends his recess and his lunch hour on the computer. He says he does not have time to eat so I let him eat in class."

It seemed to be impossible to make Mrs. Wilson understand that this was not in Alex's best interest. Alex was able to complete half a year without being cold or hungry in class. To allow Alex to stay in at recess and lunch time to use the computer was taking away from time that he desperately needed to learn to socialize with the other children.

It was logical to me that if Alex was too busy on the computer to eat at the appropriate times that he needed to be told that he was not permitted to be on the computer at recess or lunchtime until he had finished eating. If he chose not to eat, he would have to wait until he was home after school and would not be permitted to eat during class time.

I knew Alex; he wanted to wear his coat in class to prove to Mrs. Wilson and to himself that he was special. He once again wanted to be the centre of attention for all the wrong reasons. Alex's world was again accepting him and allowing him to be special rather than capable. This would be the beginning of an escalation in Alex's negative behaviours.

The phone rang it was Mrs. Wilson with a report on yet another eventful day for Alex. Once again, Alex had been angry and hit a student, this time he had also punched Mrs. Wilson in the stomach. Alex had hit his teacher at his previous school on several occasions. This was the first time that he had directed his anger a Mrs. Wilson.

Her question to me on the phone was, "does Alex hit you at home?" I replied with, "if Alex ever hit me it would be the last thing he ever does." Mrs. Wilson was clearly shocked by my answer; there was silence on the other end of the phone. I continued with Alex has never hit me and he never will. Alex knows his boundaries at home. He may not know what would happen if he hit me because he has never hit me. He does know that I would not be happy and that I would not accept his behaviour.

There was a picture in my mind of Mrs. Wilson viewing me as being a violent person after this statement. I pictured her listening to my statement and thinking now I know where Alex gets it. I was not saying that if Alex every hit me I would hit him back or worse. I was trying once again to make her understand that if you draw boundaries for Alex and Alex knows your boundaries are non-negotiable that he will not cross those boundaries. Alex will behave in whatever manner he believes is acceptable at the time.

There is an old saying: "If you give me an inch I will take a mile." This statement reflects Alex's thinking. Alex will test each new situation and each new person in his world. He will adapt his behaviour according to the results of his test. Alex had tested Mrs. Wilson on the first day of school when he refused to read. She allowed him to decide what he would and would not do in her classroom. When I was no longer present in the room Alex would set the tone for his day to Mrs. Wilson's standards, which were much more appealing to him than mine.

The school year was coming to a close. I had not been in the classroom for the last couple of months and was at the school to meet with Mrs. Wilson and the

Principal regarding Alex's placement for the next year. Walking down the hallway as school was letting out for the day, Julie saw me, she came running up to me and gave me a big hug. She said, "I missed you, where have you been? You were the best teacher we ever had. We could tell you anything."

This was the best compliment that I every received. Thank you Julie.

23

YOU ARE WHO YOU SAY YOU ARE

My first year in this new town and in our new home included more than my classroom experiences with Alex. Laura had been doing remarkably well with her health issues. In the two years before her specialist recommended that we move Laura had used crutches to walk on several occasions. There were times when her knees would be so swollen and full of fluid that she was unable to walk at all. The last few months before we moved Laura was on crutches most of the time. There were times when the specialist would say that if the medication she was taking did no relieve the swelling he would have to remove the fluid from her knees.

Laura had required crutches only two or three time in the first half of this year. It appeared that the move was making a remarkable difference to her joints and her muscle strength. Daniel was also showing improvement with his asthma. He still required an inhaler I had not been in the emergency room with him for treatments for a few months. There were times living in the Fraser Valley when Daniel would be in the emergency room so often that the doctors had left a standing order for his treatment. Daniel had been hospitalized for the first three months of the eighth grade due to fluid in his lungs and complications from asthma.

It appeared that I had made the correct decision when choosing the location for our new home. It was early spring Laura was in her first year at her new school an in the sixth grade. It was March or April. Laura had not been feeling well. After several doctor appointments, test, and finally an ultra sound Laura was diagnosed with what was believed to be a large cysts in her abdomen and was scheduled for surgery. I was pacing the floor waiting for the surgery to be complete. The nurse arrived to say that Laura was now in the recovery room. I had asked how the surgery had gone the nurse only answered that I would have to speak to the doctor.

A short time later, the nurse returned to say that the doctor was on the phone and wanted to speak to me. The doctor explained that they had not completed Laura's surgery. I asked "why? What was wrong?" The surgeon explained that they believed they were going to remove a large cyst about the size of an orange. When they went in, it was not a cyst at all. He continued to explain that what they had found was in fact a tumour.

The doctor continued to explain that this tumour was so large and so solid that he believed Laura may have been growing it since birth. I asked why they had not removed the tumour. He explained that I had only signed consent to remove a cyst. In order to remove the complete tumour they would also have to remove Laura's complete left ovary. As she was only eleven-years-old, this was not a surgery they could have completed without my knowledge and consent. I signed the consent for the surgery. Laura would come home and return in a few weeks.

The second surgery went well. The doctors removed the complete tumour. We would have to wait a couple of weeks for lab test to determine if the tumour had been cancerous. Those two weeks seemed like an eternity. I was not a religious person but I was asking God to take care of my daughter and I thanked God with all my heart when the results returned and the tumour was benign.

A few months after our move, Daniel introduced me to one of his new friends. Daniel was fourteen his new friend was seventeen. Nick was small for his age Daniel was six feet tall Nick was maybe five feet four or five inches tall with a very slight build. There was something about this young man that I immediately liked. He was one of those kids that you took one look at and said what a cute kid.

Nick would be over often. I learned from Daniel that Nick was a kid who had lived on his own on the streets since he was twelve-years-old. He was from a large family with not one but two alcoholic parents. Nick looked after himself. He worked for different farmers at whatever work they had available. Daniel met him through another friend. Nick had been sleeping on this other friends couch for the past month or so. It was late November Daniel was telling me that Nick was looking for a place to stay, as the friend that he had been staying with was moving.

Nick had a job at this time for one of the local farmers. It was the time of the year where he would not have much work until spring. Daniel was asking if Nick could stay with us. We had a five-bedroom house with not one but two full rec. rooms downstairs. Nick was offering to pay rent. He didn't make much; he was hoping we would agree to allow him to help on our ten acres if he was short for the rent.

Nick moved in and would live with us for the next four years. This young man would become part of our family. It did not take long after he moved in to understand why at seventeen Nick was a friend of Daniel's who was several years younger. Nick was very much like Richard. His ability to reason and to understand was much younger than the age on his birth certificate. As I got to know Nick, I believed he was functioning at a twelve-or-thirteen-year old level.

It would be several years later as an adult when Nick was having legal problems that the court ordered him to be evaluated. I was in the courtroom when the assessment report was read, The report concluded that Nick function well below his age level possibly due to alcohol use by his mother before he was born and by his own alcohol and drug use as a teen and now a young adult. Nick was one of the kids that I took in that I would grow to love as one of my own.

As the year progressed, Bill and I were adjusting to life together. I had been with Jason for eighteen years; Jason was my first and only real relationship. Living on my own for about two years before being introduced to Bill, I knew that I had opted for a new relationship for financial survival.

Bill and I had been getting to know each other for the few months before we moved, I genuinely liked this man. I did not know him well enough to love him and was not sure I would ever love anyone as much as I loved Jason. Positive that I would not set the tone for a new relationship out of fear that he would leave me. The time spent living on my own; I was beginning to enjoy doing things for myself and was enjoying the classes I was taking. Gaining confidence in myself and feeling that I was worth something; I Rose was feeling capable and was beginning to feel equal to and not less than.

It was not perfect but I was enjoying the parts of my life that I was giving back to me. Willing to give a new relationship with Bill a try that it may grow into something wonderful for both of us I was not willing to give up the part of me that I was just beginning to discover. I was beginning to like being me.

Bill seemed like a genuinely nice guy. We enjoyed being together he was enjoying his new acreage life. Bill had three grown children. I met both of his sons who were attending different universities and his youngest child his daughter who was twenty. All three of his children had been to our new home on different occasions.

Feeling at home in this new town, I continued to follow the real estate listings although Bill had already purchased a home. Housing prices were very appealing in this town. Discussing it with Bill, we decided that we would look for an investment rental property while prices were low. I still had my townhouse, which could be sold for a down payment; Bill had some cash saved that could also be used.

We found a suitable house in the town limits. It was an older home on a double lot, which would make a good rental investment. Remembering my real estate friend who had helped me buy my townhouse, I learned a lot from this special lady. She taught me a lot about life and a lot about real estate.

One of the real estate conversations we had was about purchasing property. The best thing my friend every taught me was that if at all possible you want to use somebody else's money. She explained that it was possible to buy a property with no money down. It was possible to buy a property using the banks money. She would laugh and say, "why not? They have more money than you or I do." She also taught me that the biggest problem people have is that they are intimidated by the banks. Most people don't realize that they have nothing to loose if they would only ask.

This special lady said to me, "When you arrive at the bank they don't know who you are." "They will believe that you are who you say you are." She was not telling me to go to the bank and pretend to be a business executive or lie about who I was or my assets. She was telling me that most people walk into the bank thinking inside that they hope the bank will say yes. They walk into the bank with the picture in their mind that they are already less than, they see themselves as being needy and are hoping for the bank to meet their needs.

The picture the person sitting behind the desk at the bank sees is a needy person who wants something and who is not sure that they have the assets or ability to obtain what they believe they need.

Her explanation continued with, "when I go into the bank to apply for a mortgage, I walk in with confidence. I walk in as though I already have the money. I want the bank to see that I am choosing to use their money and as they are in the business of lending money, it is in both of our best interest that I use theirs. The person behind the desk at the bank is seeing a picture of a good investment rather than a picture of potential risk."

Our conversation ended with, "I know this works because I have done it. You should try it some time!"

I made an appointment with the local Credit Union. I had also learned from my friends experience that a Credit Union was more flexile than a bank. Talking to myself for a few days before my appointment, there was so much good advice running through my mind. Telling myself that I had nothing to loose, I was looking for a mortgage for an investment property. If the bank said no I had lost nothing. Repeating to myself that I could do this,

The conversation with myself went something like this. "I will put on my best business attire and walk into my appointment with confidence. I will show the bank my available assets and explain that I would like to keep them. I will simply state that I am purchasing this home as an investment property. I have the money for a down payment, which, I do not wish to spend and will state that I would like to purchase this property with their money. I have nothing to loose if they say no and I gain a house if they say yes."

My appointment was a success. I can honestly say, "I know this works because I have done it. You should try it some time!" NEVER FORGET: YOU ARE WHO YOU SAY YOU ARE!!!

Six or eight months after our move I was beginning to see a different side to Bill. There were occasions where he would get angry which seemed to have no logical explanation. It didn't seem to matter who he was with when his mood would change; he would be angry and say some pretty nasty things to who ever he happened to be with.

He would be talking to a neighbour or to a person in a store or a restaurant and I would see his mood change, he would make a rude comment and storm out. I was beginning to make mental notes that I was seeing a side to Bill that I did not like, a side that could possibly be violent.

Telling myself on more than one occasion, "now I know why your wife left you because you have a temper." A year had gone by, school was out for the summer. The more behaviours I observed in Bill that I did not like the more I withdrew from our relationship. We were tolerating each other we were not enjoying each other. Bill made the decision that he would return to the Fraser Valley and work for a while. He would work away for the next year.

It was early fall, the new school year had begun. Bill was living away. I was working and taking care of the acreage with Nick for my farm help. Nick was a great kid and an excellent worker. I would give Nick a list of items that needed to be completed and knew it would all be done well and quickly. Nick was one of those kids who did everything in overdrive. He was always rushing or running somewhere and he was always smiling.

Getting to know him, I would learn that Nick came from a large family where the children did their best to look after each other due to both parents drinking problems. Most of his siblings including himself tolerated home as long as they could and ended up on the streets. Much like my childhood, education for their children was not one of Nick's parents' priorities. Nick had more time away from school in his elementary years than he spent in class.

Missing school in his early elementary years for Nick resulted in his not being able to read or write. At seventeen-years-old he was not able to read a simple job application form or write enough to fill in his name, address and telephone information without help. I helped him fill out several application forms for employment and for Social Assistance.

In one conversation, Nick was telling me about applying for a carpentry job. Nick was a competent worker. He was explaining that he knew how to build; he could not keep a carpentry job because he could not read a blue print. He was able to understand the drawings. He was not able to read the notes, which accompanied the drawings.

Throughout Nicks school years as he missed so many classes he was behind at a very early age. Once he fell behind and could not read he was considered the problem child in the class who did not want to settle down and do his work. His frustration in school often ended up with him being involved in fights with other students or arguments with the teachers. Shuffled into high school, which he quit as he was completely frustrated and felt as though he was not only a problem but also that he was stupid.

With help from Daniel, Laura and me, Nick would learn how to read and write at a first or second grade level over the next four years.

24

TREASURES IN THE TRASH

Part of the move with Alex included transferring his file to the local Social Services Office. This was a small town with only two Social Workers one Financial Intake Worker and one or two office staff members. This town also employed a Youth Street Worker. The Youth Worker did not work for Social Services; he did work with Social Services.

John was a wonderful man who had a way of connecting with teens that was honest, sincere, and realistic. All the kids in town knew John and liked him. Daniel was introduced to John through Nick shortly after we arrived in town. Small towns have a unique way of communicating; the rumour mill seems to start even before an event happens. The kids in town were all aware of the new guy when Daniel arrived. They were also aware that Bill had returned to the coast.

I had one or two occasions to meet John. We had discussed Nick's situation and we had discussed Alex. It was early fall maybe October; Bill had been gone for a couple of months. John called and asked if he could come to the house as he had something he wanted to discuss.

Sitting at the kitchen table drinking coffee, John said he had a kid he wanted to tell me about. Anthony was sixteen-years-old and was in foster care. Anthony had fetal alcohol syndrome and was born a drug-addicted baby. His family still lived in town; both his mother and father were drug users and alcoholics. Anthony and been in and out of foster care most of his life. There were several attempts at Anthony returning home, which always-ended in disaster with him returned to foster care.

John was explaining that Anthony was about to have his seventeenth birthday. In the foster care system, this would mean that he could choose to remain in foster care for one more year until he turns eighteen or at seventeen, he could choose to be considered an adult and move out on his own. Anthony wanted to be out of the system and on his own. John was concerned that he lacked the adult skills required to live independently.

Social Services would continue to fund Anthony, as he was very special needs and borderline employable. Anthony was attending school he was enrolled in the alternative school and was working on a modified grade ten program. John was here to ask if I would consider taking Anthony in.

John knew how well I related to Nick and he knew Daniel and Laura. He also saw me with Alex and was aware of Alex's issues, as was most of the town. John had suggested to Anthony that perhaps it would be easier for him to adjust if he was to live on his own but with a family that would be there to assist him if he needed help to learn how to cook, or clean his room or how to manage the cheque that he would receive each month.

Social assistance would pay for Anthony's room and board directly.

Anthony would receive the remainder of his cheque, which would have to last for the month for all his other needs. John knew that Bill was no longer living here and he felt that perhaps I could use the extra income and that I would have the extra room.

I would have said yes without knowing Anthony's life story. Promising myself never to be the one explaining why I could not take a child who needed a place to stay. Telling John that I would be looking forward to meeting Anthony and if he chose to stay, I would love to have a new room mate.

Anthony stayed for more than a year. There would be eight more teens or young adults I would have the pleasure of rooming with over the next three years. Sharing my home with five girls and three more boys during the three remaining years on these ten acres. I would like to share some of their stories with you. Most children stayed for only a few months Anthony, Nick and one other boy stayed for a year or more.

I would like to begin by sharing the stories of the four girls. Two young native sisters, a fifteen-year-old who had been living on the streets for more than a year, a sixteen-year-old single mom with her six-month-old baby daughter and a fourteen-year-old American runaway. I had the privilege of sharing a short part of each of these unbelievable lives.

I will start with the two young native sisters who stayed for about three months. The older sister was Laura's age and a friend of Laura's from school. Nick and Anthony were living with me at the time. With Alex, Daniel and Laura I was sharing my home with seven children. As Laura and the older sister were friends, I had met the girl's mother several times. We did not know each other well but I liked this single mom and we considered each other friends. As with many parents our conversations often included our children. It was common knowledge at this time that Alex, Anthony and Nick were all living with me. I believe it was knowing that I was able to cope with children with problems that allowed this mother and friend to share her circumstances with me.

We had shared coffee and conversations on several occasions. This time was different; this visit had a purpose. This mom who was about my age maybe a year or two older was dealing with some serious issues. The conversation began with this friend acknowledging that she knew her older daughter was having problems at school. The conversation continued with an explanation of some of her daughter's history. This young girl; had been molested by her father up to age seven-or-eight. Her father always told her if she every told anyone what he did that he would kill himself.

Her daughter was no longer able to deal with her fathers abuse and she told her mother what had been happening to her. Her mother believed her and called police. This young girl was maybe nine-years-old when her father took his own life. This mother did everything she could to help her daughter to believe that she made the right choice. She told her daughter that she was not to blame for her fathers abuse or for his death.

Her daughter logically knew it was not her fault. Emotionally at nine-years-old and still on this day this mother believed that her daughter blamed herself. This was not an easy story for this mother to tell. She was telling me about her daughter's history, as she wanted me to understand her daughter's current behaviours.

This mom and I had similar personalities, not knowing much of her own history; I knew it had similarities to mine. This mom had gone through life the hard way. She also had the most amazing attitude and a very realistic way of looking at and dealing with life. We had very similar ways of looking at children and all people who the world seemed to view as problems.

We had many great conversations about what we saw as our realities of life. The thing I liked the most about her was she was so honest. She was not a person who made excuses for mistakes or blamed the world or anyone for her life or her problems. She knew who she was, she knew her strengths and her limitations and she dealt with it all honestly and up front. She was not looking for sympathy or for someone to solve her problems for her. She was simply explaining the realities of life for her daughter and herself and was asking for temporary help for both. I very much admired this lady.

The reason for her visit was to ask if I would be willing to take both of her daughters for an unknown period of time. I will not share the details of this mother's situation other than to tell you that she required a home for her daughters while she was awaiting trial for attempted murder. Her daughters were aware that they would have to go into foster care and had asked to stay with me. The girls lived with me for three or four months. My friend was acquitted.

The fifteen-year-old girl I would like to tell you about also asked to stay with me. The girls that I am writing about stayed with me at different times. Other than the two sisters, I only ever had one girl living with me at a time. This young girl was on a Social Services Program similar to the program, which supported Anthony.

At the time one of the criteria to be underage and be considered an adult by Social Services was to be able to prove to Social Services that you have survived on the streets as a minor for more than a year. Many youths considered for this program would be between the ages of fourteen and eighteen who had been placed in foster care and were kicked out or ran away.

Children who have lived on the street for a period of time although they are minors and should be placed in foster care do not adjust well to house rules and bed times. They often run away and are back on the streets. This was a program designed to help support children until the age of eighteen with funds for room and board and if they could find it the opportunity to live as an adult in a home with some available guidance as to how to function in the adult world responsibly with little or no resources.

At fifteen, this young girl had survived on the streets for more than the required time. She was a wonderful young lady. Daniel, Laura and I still keep in touch with her today.

The next two stories I would like to share are different yet they are both sad examples of what we all lose as human beings when life is lived with our eyes closed. Realistic expectations, logic, common sense and love are all necessary ingredients for life if it is to be lived, "happily ever after."

This story involves the circumstances of the sixteen-year-old single mom who stayed with me for a few months with her six-month-old daughter. This young girl had two parents; her parents had been married since before she was born and were still together at this time. Her parents lived in the town forty-five minutes away.

Her parents were not poor. Her parents were not ill. This sixteen-year-old girl had the family that any one of the children that I cared for over the years would have dreamt about. This young girl had the family that I dreamt about as a child. Two parents, not poor, not alcoholics, not drug addicts, not physically or mentally ill; I was not sure that this type of family actually existed other than in fairy tails or on television. Yet, this young girl had a real life all together complete family. Why was she living with me and learning how to care for her beautiful baby daughter from a stranger?

At sixteen, this beautiful young girl was tossed out with the trash when she told her parents that she was pregnant. This was not the 1950's, when family or society did not accept a pregnant teenager. This was 1994; although she had two capable parents who I assumed loved their daughter the day before she got pregnant, this young mother delivered her baby alone in a home for unwed mothers in Kelowna BC. I did not know that in 1994 homes for unwed mothers even existed. Much like the transition house where I stayed with my family, this home had a time limit that a new mother could stay. At sixteen this new mother packed up her belongings at the home for unwed mothers cradled her baby daughter in her arms and headed to the closest town to her home. She new a few people in town and was hoping someone would help her find a place to live that she could afford on a Social Assistance cheque. Daniel brought her home to me. I told her she was welcome to stay as long as she needed. She stayed for about six months until she found a roommate and was able to move into town.

The day that she told her parents that she was expecting a baby they told her she was on her own. She got herself into this mess and they were not about to get her out. How is it possible to raise a child for sixteen years and just throw her away because she made a mistake? How is it possible for a mother to hear that her daughter is carrying her first grandchild and to throw them both away because the timing or the circumstances are not perfect?

What lesson do these parents think that they are teaching their child? Any parent who has lost a child knows that there is no greater loss. These parents lost a child and a grandchild by choice. There is simply no amount of explaining or logic; there is no lesson so important that it is worth the grief that these parents have inflicted on their daughter, their granddaughter and themselves.

I wonder had their daughter been struck by a car and killed on her way home to tell them that she was pregnant if they would have grieved her death or been happy for their loss once they discovered she was pregnant. I believe that they would not only have grieved her death but they would have also been telling God that they would do anything if they could only have her back. Why is it that they cannot see that in choosing to treat her as though she were dead they are choosing a lifetime of grief for them all?

These parents who cared enough to raise their daughter to age sixteen are so caught up in their anger at the timing of events that they have closed their eyes and are refusing to see anything but their own disappointments. The picture that they had in their minds for their daughter's future was unexpectedly shattered.

They chose to pick up the picture and throw it away. They could have made the decision to pick up the pieces and carefully put them back together. The picture may not look as bright through the cracked pieces there will come a day when the broken parts will be replaced and the picture will be as good or better then the original.

With their eyes closed, seeing only disappointment in their minds they have no opportunity to see the beauty in their granddaughter's eyes or the smile on her face as grandma pushes her on a swing. These are pictures they had of a granddaughter who would arrive at a more convenient time being carried by her married daddy.

These parents determined that if they could not have the exact perfect picture that they painted in their minds for sixteen years then they would choose to have no picture at all.

I do not have the words to explain the emptiness inside that I have felt as an unwanted child. I do not have the words to describe the hole in my very soul after loosing a child. For anyone to choose to inflict such life altering circumstances on themselves and their children is beyond my comprehension.

I ask myself how different this young mother's experiences could have been. How different the remainder of her parents' lives could have been; had they only made the decision to see their daughter and their expectant grandchild with their eyes and their hearts open. Had these parents been able to tell themselves that although they were disappointed and did not approve of their daughters situation they believed there is no circumstance in life that cannot be overcome, this unexpected event could have been a blessing.

Had this been my daughter I would have told her that I loved her. I would have told her that the choices she has already made while they may not have been ideal have already been made and it is not possible under any circumstance to go back and change them.

As it is not possible to go back, it is only possible to go forward. I would have told her that having her first child no matter what the circumstances is a gift if she chooses it to be. Had this been my daughter I would have let her know that I would be there for her. I would have told my daughter that children are a precious gift. There is no circumstance, which makes the gift less precious. I would have told my daughter I know this; because she was a gift to me; and carrying my first grandchild only made her more beautiful no matter what the timing.

Had this been my daughter I would have wanted her to know that having her first baby at sixteen would not be easy, her life will change I would want her to know that I believed she was capable of making decisions for her future and that she was not alone.

I have not kept in touch with this young girl. I did hear a few years later from someone who knew her; that this beautiful sixteen year old girl who had the family that some dream about growing up; now had three children from three different fathers and a drug habit.

She was thrown out with the trash; she believed that was what she had become. Her future life matched her beliefs. I grieve for this young life; I grieve for her three babies being raised by a mother who sees herself as trash and who medicates her life with her drug of choice.

There is one more story of a throw away child I would like to share. This young girl was fourteen-years-old and was an American citizen. She had crossed the border into Canada and was living on the streets. At fourteen, this young girl ran away from her foster home in Washington State and hitchhiked to Canada. She was passing through this town on he way to Vancouver.

Katie had been on her hitchhiking trip for some time when Nick met her sleeping in the local park. Nick associated with Katie for a week or more before he told me about her. He was concerned because he knew that she was sick. He did not know what to do to help her. I told Nick to bring her home. Katie was a tiny blond girl. She introduced herself to me and said that she was seventeen. Looking at this little girl, who looked thin, un-kept and ill she looked like she was twelve-years-old. Telling myself she maybe a young looking fifteen but this girl was not seventeen-years-old.

I offered Katie a temporary place to stay and asked her if she would see a doctor if I was to make an appointment. She agreed. I called John and asked him to come over for coffee, telling him there was a child I wanted him to meet and that I needed his assistance. Knowing that Katie needed medical attention, I wanted to be sure to handle this situation correctly as I also knew she was not a Canadian Citizen and would not have medical coverage.

John met Katie sitting at my kitchen table. Katie told us both that she was seventeen-years-old and that she had runaway from her foster home. Katie told us her story of two alcoholic abusive parents and a life, which up to this point consisted of being shuffled back and forth between her parent's home and several foster homes. She made it clear that she did not intend to return to foster care.

Katie was telling us that she knew she only had to survive on her own until she was considered an adult by the courts. She explained that there were circumstances in Washington State when a minor can be considered an adult and is permitted to live on their own. She also said she only had to wait until she was eighteen. At this time in Washington State the legal age was twenty-one. She wanted us to believe that she had less than a year to wait before being legally declared an adult.

John and I talked for some time about Katie after she left the room. John looked at me and said, "There is no way that girl is seventeen-years-old, she is fourteen maybe." We both agreed this was a very young girl, we also both agreed that it was obvious that this child needed medical attention. If Katie were willing, it would be safer for her to stay with me than to sleep in a park. John said that he worked closely with one of the health nurses in town and that he would contact her, explain Katie's situation and see if there was a way to have her treated by a doctor.

John and I also discussed Katie's story. John was able to use his Social Services connections to see if he could find Katie's American Social Worker and verify her history. John would also be able to contact the Boarder and the American authorities to see if anyone had filed a missing child report. If Katie had a family that was looking for her we wanted to be sure that we did all we could to contact them.

It was obvious to both John and me that this child would have to return to Washington State. If we handled this situation correctly, Katie could be returned willingly. If she were forced to return, she would only run away again. We both wanted Katie to receive the medical attention she needed and to convince her that it was in her best interest to let John help her return to her home City on agreeable terms. We did not want Katie to resume her interest in continuing her trip to Vancouver.

I could see Katie standing in line with the other underage hookers on Vancouver's Infamous East Side. If Katie chose to continue her travels, it may be the end of her trip and her life.

John arranged for Katie to see a local Doctor; no questions asked and no fees exchanged. Katie was ill from a sexually transmitted disease that had gone untreated for an extended period of time. According to the Doctor, she had been sick for some time.

As we got to know each other, Katie would share some of her experiences. This had not been her first attempt at living on the streets. It was likely that she had contracted her illness from any number of men she had spent the night with over the past few years. Katie explained that it was easier to sleep with someone and be allowed to stay the night than it was to sleep in a doorway or a park when it was cold outside.

Katie wanted me to know that she was not a hooker. She wanted me to know that she would never sell herself for money. She would however give herself away in exchange for a warm bed for the night. Her comment was, "especially in the winter." I was looking at this young girl thinking that she looked so young. The stories she was telling made me believe she was giving herself away before she had turned twelve.

It was not difficult for me to believe Katie's stories of giving herself away in exchange for a warm place to stay. I had known several kids in my early teens that did the same thing. The neighbourhoods I lived in were full to overflowing with left over children. There was a common understanding among young girls who desperately wanted to hold on to a fragment of pride; it was somehow acceptable to give yourself away in exchange for survival. To sell yourself for the same purpose made you dirty. These children gave themselves away out of desperation and the determination not to be labelled a hooker.

John was making progress with his American contacts. He had learned that Katie did indeed come from the background she had described. Her foster care experiences consisted of several different homes over most of her lifetime; including one home where her foster father had molested her. Katie had talked to her current Social Worker about being considered by the courts to be an adult; it was this Social Worker who told Katie that she would have to be eighteen to apply. Her Social Worker confirmed that Katie was only fourteen-years-old.

John had many discussions with Katie and by telephone with her Social Worker. Katie had agreed that she would be willing to try foster care again if John would help her Social Worker find her a foster home that she liked. Her Social Worker had agreed that if it were at all possible Katie might be able to choose.

The wheels of bureaucracy turn slowly, even more slowly when you are dealing with two different systems in two different countries. More than a month had passed since John and I had sat with Katie for the first time at my kitchen table.

John did not work for Social Services he did work with Social Services. This allowed him more flexibility in the decisions he made when dealing with street kids. As the negotiations and the planning to return Katie to an agreeable foster home were underway, John was receiving tips from the local Social Service Office. He arrived for coffee one afternoon to pass on the latest tips from one of the Social Workers.

John had been advised that he should not be spending his time on a kid that was an American. There were no policies in place to deal with such a matter, he was also reminded this kid was a runaway and should be sent back to Washington State. The tip that was meant for me was that John should let me know that I could be arrested for aiding and abetting a minor. John should warn me that I could be in trouble if this girl had parents who were looking for her.

John tried to explain that he had contacted the American Authorities and that he had been in regular contact with Katie's Social Worker. He also explained that he was trying to arrange for Katie to return voluntarily so she would perhaps not run away again. John was completely frustrated at being told that he should watch his back and that he could be jeopardizing his job if he was not careful. He felt he should pass on the part of the message that was intended for me,

I thanked John for the tip. He already knew what kind of response I would have for this Social Worker who could not find the correct Policy to fit Katie's needs; and felt compelled to advise that we should not be wasting our time on a kid that didn't match the proper criteria.

As John had delivered the message, he had the unfortunate pleasure of listening to my reply to this Social Worker who was so dedicated to the care and well being of children.

Stating that both John and I knew that Katie did not have parents who were looking for her, this was one of the first items on John's checklist on Katie's first day. Had she had parents who cared and were looking for her I would think that they would be grateful that someone cared enough to pick their sick daughter out of a park and care for her until arrangements could be made for her safe return. If you want to arrest me for caring for this child go right ahead! It will no stop me from caring for Katie or any other kid requiring help.

Had Katie not been ill and not been fortunate enough to sleep in a park where she met Nick; she would have continued her trip to Vancouver. There are countless underage boys and girls on Vancouver's East side, most are not Americans and would surely fit into some Social Workers correct policy or criteria. Yet, they are still there! No one is threatening to arrest anyone for child neglect; yet, I am threatened for being willing to help the one that was on her way. If only we had a policy to cover stupidity!

A few weeks after this message was delivered the RCMP showed up at my door. They were there to escort Katie back to the Boarder. I called John and told him what was happening. John arrived and tried to explain to the officer that arrangements were being made for Katie to return. The RCMP officer knew

John, he knew the situation and he said there was nothing he could do. Katie was returned.

Six or eight months after Katie was returned I received a phone call from John. He was telling me that Katie had shown up at his door. She was hurt. I met John at the local hospital.

Katie had once again run away, she had been beaten up by some local teens and was in need of medical attention. Katie was treated and again returned by the RCMP to the American Boarder. I have not heard from Katie since that day.

This next story is about a young man who shared my home. Kevin came from a local family. Kevin was born with signs of both fetal alcohol syndrome and drug use by his mother. Both Anthony and Kevin had the appearance of being special needs. Anthony's physical appearance was more noticeable; Kevin had the look that you knew something was not right but it was difficult to determine what it might be.

Kevin's parents still lived in town; both of his parents had drug and alcohol problems. Kevin was coming to see me about a place to stay as he had just returned from a six week stay at a drug and alcohol rehab centre in Kelowna BC. Kevin was twenty-two-years-old although he functioned at a much younger level.

Kevin arrived in the early evening. We were sitting at the kitchen table completing the introductions. On this particular evening, we had other adult company. Laura was being a good host and asked Kevin who she knew was an adult if he would like a beer. It was a hot summer evening and the other adults were drinking beer.

Before Kevin had a chance to answer I explained to Laura in front of Kevin that it was nice of her to offer but that it was not appropriate to offer someone who has just come out of drug and alcohol rehab a beer. Kevin replied to my comment. His first sentence was, "oh, that's ok; I have learned how to control my drinking." I do not remember exactly what his next few sentences were. Kevin was giving me the standard I do not have a problem any more speech. He had been speaking for a few minutes; I had been listening to his words. I had heard this speech a million times in my lifetime.

At an appropriate break in the conversation, I asked Kevin a question. I asked Kevin, "So are you trying to convince you or me?" He was looking at me as though he did not understand the question. I asked Kevin again, "are you trying to convince me that you do not have a drinking problem, or are you trying to convince yourself that you do not have a drinking problem?" No answer from Kevin, I continued with, "You do not have to convince me of anything, I don't even know you. You are an adult; I am not going to tell you what to do. If you want to have a beer than choose to have a beer. It is up to you, it is your choice. You do not have to be honest with me, you do have to be honest with yourself."

"It is obvious to both of us that you have a drinking problem. No one spends time in rehab if they do not have a problem. If you choose to have a beer then have a beer; but at least tell yourself that you are having a beer because you have a drinking problem and you cannot say no. Do not sit here and try to convince both of us that you have your problems under control. Make a choice based on what is real for you. If you choose to be a drunk, it is not going to affect me. Whatever you choose; you are the only one who has to live with the consequences."

I could see the change in Kevin's face. He had been smiling and fairly outgoing through our initial introductions. He was sitting at the end of the table his body language had changed from slightly nervous and excited to dead calm. Kevin spoke in what was now a very soft voice. He spoke words that were both sad and unbelievable. He said something I have never forgotten.

This twenty-two-year-old, six-foot husky man looked at me and softly said, "wow; you are the first person who ever talked to me like I was a real person." I think that was about the saddest statement I had ever heard. I looked Kevin in the eyes and said, "Well you are a real person." This was the start of what would be a yearlong friendship.

How is it possible to be twenty-two-years-old and feel as though you are not a real person? Kevin had just spent six weeks in a drug and alcohol treatment centre with professional staff. How is it possible to treat anyone for anything if you have not yet made him feel as though he were a real person?

The words I spoke to Kevin were not some profound, mystical teachings. I simply spoke the truth, telling Kevin what I saw as his reality, simply communicating that what he did with his life was his choice. I simply asked Kevin to choose.

In a world full of caring experts, specialists and philosophers; in a world full of those who choose to lead, those who choose to guide and those who choose to teach; how is it that one can spend twenty two years in classrooms, medical facilities and communities and not feel acknowledged as a real person.

LIFE KEEP IT SIMPLE MAKE IT MAGNIFICENT

Why is it when gifted with a perfect Rose there are those who choose to see only the thorns?

25

I QUIT

I have shared some of the special circumstances I was privileged to be a part of during my four years in my new home. The second school year was now into its second or third month. Attending school with Alex only a few times since I began my full time job, I met with the school Principal and Mrs. Wilson at the end of the school year to discuss Alex's placement for what was now a split grade five/six class.

Mrs. Wilson agreed to take Alex for a second year. This would mean that she would now teach a grade five/six class and would allow Alex to continue with the same teacher. The school wanted to avoid having to deal with a transition for Alex to a new teacher, new students and a new classroom. It was agreed that if Mrs. Wilson was willing to have Alex in her class for one more year that the school would provide Alex with a teacher's aide. Alex's behaviours were severe enough to warrant the funding for a teacher's aide for this particular student.

There was a teacher's aide who worked in the school. This teacher would work in different classrooms with different students. In Alex's classroom for grade three/four, this teacher's aide taught the math class. I have been in the classroom with this teacher-teaching math. Math was one of the subjects in which Alex actually participated. After watching this teacher's aide in the classroom, I knew why Alex did math without being a problem.

This woman was tall, and heavyset. It was clear by watching her with the children that she loved her work, it was also clear that this was a teacher who knew her students. I watched her with Tommy and I watched her with Alex. I watched her remind them both that this was math time and we were doing math now. This was a teacher with a caring gentle side. This was also a teacher with non-negotiable expectations. When she told Alex to put his things away because we were doing math now, she meant it. Alex knew she meant it and he never challenged her.

During our year-end meeting, I suggested that this teacher's aide would be a good fit for Alex. She knew Alex; Alex knew her and knew her expectations. The principal explained that this teacher's aide was not eligible for the position. It had something to do with union rules as to who would be hired for this available position. I did not understand the logic in bringing in a stranger to deal with Alex when there was a qualified person already here, in keeping with the correct policy; an aide was hired for Alex.

It was a Tuesday evening, October or November early into the new school year. I received a call from Mrs. Wilson. She called to tell me that Alex was welcome to come to school for Wednesday but that I would have to keep him home for Thursday and Friday; I of course asked why? She explained that she was not going to be in the classroom for Thursday and Friday.

The students would have a substitute teacher. She was concerned that Alex would not adjust well to a new teacher and it would be better if he were not in class. My first question was, "where is Alex's aide?" Mrs. Wilson answered, "oh she will be there," to which I replied, "If his aide will be there then why can Alex not be in class?" Mrs. Wilson answered, "Well she is not used to Alex yet, she is afraid of him."

I had recommended the current teachers aide for Alex because she had the experience and the personality to be a benefit to Alex and in turn would have benefited the entire class with Alex requiring less of Mrs. Wilson's time and attention. Union rules prevailed and the aide that fit the rules was hired to assist Alex. The aide, whose only purpose for holding a job in this classroom was because of Alex, was a tiny, soft-spoken woman who was afraid of Alex.

This arrangement was a benefit to no one. This arrangement was the worst possible choice for Alex. Alex could read this teachers aide like a book. He knew from the moment that they met that he was in complete control. Alex was now eleven-years-old and had become an expert at reading and using each person and each circumstance in his world.

I was angry at this telephone call and stated that if Alex had a paid aide in the classroom there should be no reason why he could not attend school. I had to work and Alex could not be home alone.

Alex did not display the out of control behaviours at home that he was becoming expert and using at school. He was however showing other disturbing behaviours. In the four years that we lived on this acreage Alex had on three separate occasions tried to light fires, arson in not an unusual behaviour for a child with severe emotional problems.

There were two occasions I found Alex had made piles of sticks and paper to resemble a campfire. One such pile was in the rec. room hidden behind a deep freezer. The second was under the basement stairs. Each pile contained several paper matches, which Alex had tried to strike and was unable to light. The most frightening place that Alex built several such campfire piles was inside of an old wooden well house on our property.

This well house was built from tinder dry wood. There were shelves on the inside meant for storage. Each shelf had a small ridge on the outside, which made the shelf more like a mini bin. Alex had dozens of piles of sticks and paper inside of this shed. On each shelf that was within his reach, he had attempted to light these piles. Each mini bon-fire pile was littered with dozens of matches, which Alex had unsuccessfully attempted to strike.

I found Alex inside of this shed with the door closed trying to light his camp-fires. He had no concept that if one of those matches had actually lit; this tinder dry building would have gone up with Alex inside. Thank God, this child did not have the skills to strike a paper match.

A week or so after this phone call to ask me to keep Alex out of class, I received another phone call from the school. This call was from the Principal. He was calling to ask if I would come for an after school meeting regarding Alex. In the past year and a bit I could not count how many meetings I attended involving strategies for Alex. I had attended school every day for the first six months and had offered countless tips and advice; none of which appeared to be heard.

Once again agreeing to attend a meeting, I assumed that as this phone call was so soon after me being asked to keep Alex out of class that this meeting was related to this issue. Assuming this meeting would include Alex's new aide and perhaps some advise I could offer her as she was said to be afraid of Alex.

I was wrong; you know what they say; "never assume anything." At some point in this phone conversation, I mentioned Alex's new aide. The Principal commented that she would not be attending the meeting. Of course asking, "why not?" He answered, that as the meeting was to be after three o'clock and she was paid only until 3 o'clock she would not be attending. I replied that as the only reason for her to be employed in this school at this time was to deal with Alex and she is admitting that she is afraid of him and therefore is unable to successfully deal with him; one would think that she would not only need to be at this meeting but that she would also want to be there.

The phone call ended with the Principal stating that he would ask her if she was willing to attend. He called back the next day to tell me that she was not going to attend the meeting to which I replied, "Then neither am I!" The Principal actually had to ask me why I was now not willing to attend.

Very clearly explaining that I failed to see the point in attending yet another meeting to discuss the same subject. It is blatantly obvious that you do not intend to listen to what I have to say regarding Alex.

I recommended a competent aide for Alex. The school found reasons why this was not possible. The system chose to hire an aide who does not have the skills to deal with Alex's needs. This new aide; then is paid to attend school for two days when the child she is hired to assist is not permitted in the classroom. You now want to meet to discuss Alex once again and the one person whose only job is to assist him in the classroom will not be at the meeting. I see no point in my attending or in us having yet another meeting.

As this school year, progressed Alex was once again in a classroom where he was entertained and pacified. His new aide actually took him out for ice cream one day so the rest of the class could have a break from his constant interruptions. There were several occasions when Laura was called out of her grade seven classroom and asked if she would help in dealing with Alex when he was out of control.

After learning from Laura that she had been asked to leave her classroom to deal with Alex. I made it clear to the Principal and to Mrs. Wilson that it was not appropriate for Laura to be asked to deal with Alex whose behaviours were so out of control that a school full of professional adults was unable to deal with him.

It was becoming clear to me and to Alex that he was winning this game of wills. His behaviours at school were escalating and Alex was getting older. One more year and he would be too old for elementary school and expected to adjust to high school. This was a child who was eleven-years-old; the school regarded him as being in grade six, Alex was working on grade one and two work or realistically he was working on no work at all. The next two years would be an escalation of the first two. The next two years would be the last two years that Alex ever attended any school anywhere.

It was early spring April or May Bill had been gone for some time. He was returning and wanted to try to make our relationship work. Nick and Anthony had been living with me for some time. Bill wanted to try fitting back into my life including all five kids currently living with me. The next year would be fairly uneventful; Bill was on his best behaviour. Our relationship was what it had been when we first met and were getting to know each other. It would take close to a year before I would see a repeat of Bills mood swings and temper.

Bills behaviours began to surface once again. He was feeling comfortable enough in our relationship to now be his true self. I was telling myself that he no longer felt that he had to be on his best dating behaviour. Bill was comfortable enough that he was now starting to treat me as he had treated his wife. This was the real Bill. I was telling myself his wife left because Bill had a temper. As Bills behaviours escalated, I again retreated from our relationship. We made the decision that our relationship was not going to continue. We agreed to sell the acreage and the rental property and we would go our separate ways. It would take a full year or more before the acreage sold.

Late one afternoon Bills daughter pulled into the driveway for an unexpected visit. I was outside when she drove up. All three of his children had been aware that we had been apart and then back together. The first thing his daughter noticed was the, "For Sale" sign on the front lawn.

Bill was in the far section of one of the hay fields when his daughter arrived. She asked me if we were splitting up again referring to the sign. I did not want to say anything negative about her father to her. I did want to explain the situation before Bill walked across the field, telling her that we were selling and were planning to go our separate ways. She naturally asked, "why?" I answered, "I hate to say this; but the bottom line is, Bill is violent."

Surprised at her response, She simply said, "yah; I know, that's what made my mother leave." I had been telling myself that this was something I believed I was seeing in Bill. I had also told myself that everyone who knew Bill, including his own children were telling the same story of why he and his wife of more than twenty years had split up. The story was always that after the children grew up they had just drifted apart. Everyone made the same statement about Bill being such a nice guy.

I cannot speak as to what his children were thinking. I believe his children wanted their father to be happy. Perhaps his daughter was hoping that this relationship would be different for Bill. Perhaps she had been asking herself if part of the problem was her mother. Whatever the reason for no one wanting to tell me the truth about Bills marriage and his temper; I now knew that I had made the right decision to end this relationship. Had his daughter made this statement before I moved in with Bill this relationship would have ended on the day that I knew. Bill once again returned to the coast to work and did not return.

Alex would complete the remainder of his grade five/six year, his grade seven year and one year of high school before the acreage sold and we moved. This allowed Daniel to complete his grade twelve year.

As the school year once again was concluding I was meeting with the school to discuss Alex's placement for grade seven. This would mean a change of teacher for Alex. Laura would be starting her first year of high school. There were two grade seven teachers in this school. One was the teacher that Laura had for her grade six year. She was a good teacher. She did not have the happy bouncy personality of Mrs. Wilson she was much like the teacher's aide that taught math in Mrs. Wilson's class. She had very distinct expectations from her students, which were non negotiable.

The second grade seven teacher was a very soft-spoken man. Mr. Jackson had been Laura's grade seven teacher. I have stated earlier that Laura was always a good student. Her grades were top of the class. Her grade six teacher liked Laura so much she asked to have her in her grade seven class. Laura chose to change to Mr. Jackson.

I received a phone call from the school. It was late May or early June of Laura's grade seven year. This was not a call about Alex. This was a call from Mr. Jackson about Laura. He was calling to tell me that Laura had decided that she was not particularly interested in class at this time.

He continued to say that he knew she was a top student and there were only a few weeks left in the school year. As Laura was not interested, was not participating in class and was spending her time talking he had allowed Laura to take a break, go for a walk and miss classes. He was considering allowing Laura to miss classes for the remainder of the school year and was calling to ask how I felt about this situation.

Stating that I felt he should tell Laura that she is to sit down, stop talking and do her work. Mr Jackson replied; that it was not his job to make a student do something that they did not want to do. Mrs. Wilson spoke this same statement on Alex's first day of school.

It is difficult to understand why educated professional adults are not able to see that there are some choices, which are appropriate for children to make and there are some choices, which must be non negotiable. It is inappropriate and severe child neglect to allow or expect that children should choose what and when they would learn.

There are reasons why we define the differences between adults and children. Children simply do not possess the tools to make appropriate decisions to be successfully self-sufficient. The entire purpose of childhood is to explore, learn and acquire the tools required to be a capable adult.

Teaching children the appropriate skills to survive, physically, intellectually, financially and spiritually is not optional. Educated, progressive societies pass laws that make attending school for children mandatory. There must be more to educating our children than the requirement that they simply show up in class and turn another year older.

It is absolutely the job of parents and professional educators (teachers) to expect children to do something that they do not want to do. With out this expectation there are children who would never make it out of the sand box.

The expectation that our children spend twelve plus years in a classroom; does nothing to prepare them to succeed in the adult world without the inclusion of NON-NEGOTIABLE & GREAT EXPECTATIONS.

I made it clear to Mr. Jackson that if he was not able to tell Laura that she was expected to participate in the remainder of the school year; I would tell her. I expected that he would not allow her to wander the halls for the next few weeks of the school year.

This conversation with Mr. Jackson was running through my mind during the meeting with the principal to discuss Alex's grade seven placement. Explaining to the principal that I believed Laura's grade six teacher would be a more appropriate fit for Alex. The Principal replied that Alex had already said that he wanted to be in Mr. Jackson class. It was obvious to me why Alex made this choice.

If Mr. Jackson was not able to control Laura a top student who until recently had not displayed any problems in seven years of school; Alex had him pegged as someone he could control. Alex also knew that the alternative teacher had non-negotiable expectations.

Relaying the story of my phone call with Mr. Jackson regarding Laura to the Principal and stating that I felt Alex would walk all over Mr. Jackson and that is why he is asking to be in his class. The Principal replied with how he felt it might benefit Alex to have a teacher who was a man. I could tell by the way this conversation was going that the school intended on placing Alex with his teacher of choice.

It was the last week of the five/six school year; picking up the phone, it was a call from Mrs. Wilson. She was calling to discuss Alex's placement for grade seven. A minute or two into the conversation I knew that the Principal had asked Mrs. Wilson to call and give me a list of reasons or excuses for why the teacher I had recommended would not be a good fit for Alex. Mrs. Wilson was stating the advantages of a male teacher for Alex. She was telling me that the classroom that I preferred already had a problem child and putting the two in the same room would not be a good idea. I stopped listening after the first couple of excuses.

Stating to Mrs. Wilson that I knew she was calling to give me a list of excuses for why the teacher I had requested would not fit. After spending the last two years talking to people who were not willing to listen; it was clear to me that the school intended on placing Alex with the teacher of his choice in the mistaken belief that this will somehow make Alex happy and less of a problem.

Making it absolutely clear to Mrs. Wilson that if, the school was choosing to again ignore my recommendations I had had enough, simply stating that I quit! If the school chose to place Alex with Mr. Jackson for his grade seven year I would not be willing to spend one more year attending meetings, being called on a regular basis to deal with whatever the problem of the day is. Stating that for the time that Alex is at school the school would be responsible for him, do not call me! If Alex burns down the entire school, it is your problem. I will deal with Alex after 3p.m.

26

SUICIDE OR HOMICIDE

We had a fairly uneventful summer. September arrived and the new school year was underway. Five or six weeks into the school year, I found the usual meet the teacher notice in Alex's backpack. The notice had a portion for the parents to sign and return to the school with information as to when they would like their appointment to meet their child's teacher.

Already having met Mr. Jackson and stating in June that if Alex was placed in his class I was not intending to be involved in this school year. I ignored the notice to meet and greet the teacher.

The school secretary called a few days later. She was calling to see when I would like to book my appointment with Alex's teacher. My reply was, "I don't want an appointment."

The Secretary of course asked, "why not." I explained to her that I stated at the end of the school year; if they intended to ignore my input concerning Alex that the school would be on there own this year. I had no intention of coming to this or any other meeting this year.

It took only two months before Alex was no longer in Mr. Jackson's classroom; as I had predicted, Mr. Jackson was not able to control Alex and Alex's behaviours in school had been escalating now for two years. The solution the school came up with was; that Alex would sit alone in what they called the nurses room. This was a small room with a cot used for children who were not feeling well; Alex would be given a computer and could work alone all day.

The past two years Alex's computer experiences consisted of playing games and mutilating the floppy disc. Not much of an educational experience for what was now a grade seven student. The school is fully expecting that this child will attend high school next year. Alex had reading and writing skills, which were maybe second grade level and absolutely no social or behaviour skills. After completing, the remainder of the grade seven year alone with his computer he would be considered to have passed grade seven and will be sent off to high school. Alex will have his thirteenth birthday two months before the high school year begins. As Daniel had informed me when he was in his grade seven year; school policy states that thirteen year olds are too old and too big to be in elementary school.

Late November and the first report cards arrive. Reading Alex's report card thinking to myself; "you people have know idea how manipulated you are by this child. You also have know idea what Alex is really capable of." Alex is a third of the way through his seventh year in elementary school plus one year of kindergarten.

The only skill that he is able to take with him into a world that will soon have adult expectations; is the ability to manipulate and con people into giving him what he mistakenly believes he wants.

Alex's first report card of the seventh grade read: Alex is doing very well. Alex has been completing his work on the computer, which he enjoys. Alex loves animals and has been looking up facts on how to care for his guinea pig.

A grade seven student is preparing for high school by looking up facts on the care of his guinea pig that he just loves. Alex never told his teacher that the guinea pig that he is researching so diligently; the guinea pig that Alex is so fond of had been dead long before the school year even began. Alex was told not to take his guinea pig outside, he did not listen, he took it outside and forgot it for a few days and it died of exposure.

As I read this report card, I was not sure if I should laugh or cry. I had cared for Alex from age five and then again at age seven through now age twelve-and-a-half. I had lost Alex. Alex was completely absorbed into his world of, "I'm special." Alex was living the life he was allowed to choose for himself. I absolutely knew that he was capable of so much more. I was not able to convince Alex or anyone else of what I saw in him.

Alex's world was full of caring, loving, educated, capable, intelligent people. Each one believing the choices that they were making on his behalf were in his best interest. Some how not one person was able to see that as they were all so busy choosing the correct program, the correct teacher the psychologically correct words to not shatter his self-esteem. They were all so busy researching how to correctly care for Alex that not one person simply did what needed to be done. Alex was somehow left out of the real picture. Had Alex spent more time caring for his guinea pig than researching its care; the guinea pig would have survived.

The tools required for keeping Alex in my world of realistic, non-negotiable, great expectations were available to all who tried so hard to assist Alex. How sad it is that of all those who were so willing to opened the tool box not one was willing to pick up a tool and actually use it.

As the school year progressed, the elementary school was beginning to have discussions with the high school regarding Alex's placement. Both schools believed it would be in Alex's best interest for him to be evaluated by the district school psychologist and a psychiatrist before deciding on his final placement. These evaluations would be completed at the local health centre. Both specialist were from out of town and would use the health centre offices for local appointment.

The school psychologist echoed my concerns about Alex being able to adjust to high school. She was concerned that his learning skills were nowhere near high school level. She also had concerns regarding Alex's ability to fit in with high school students. Alex was small for his age; he would easily fit into a grade five or six class and not stand out. Her recommendations were that his learning skills, size and lack of social skills should be considered before deciding to place him in high school.

The psychiatrist met with Alex, I would have a separate appointment once his evaluation was complete. In the psychiatrist office, he was relating some of his findings and concerns. He was confirming what I already knew about Alex. He stated that he felt Alex was capable of functioning close to his age intellectually. His school progress certainly did not show this ability. He also stated that he believed that Alex functioned emotionally at a level below age two, likely, due to his early childhood experiences and his emotional needs as an infant not being met. The specialist believed that Alex was emotionally shut down, He was emotionally a two-year-old or younger.

As our meeting progressed, he was asking me my thoughts and opinions about Alex. I agreed with both of his findings. I knew that under the right circumstances Alex could function close to his age level. I also knew that this child was emotionally non-existent, explaining that I believed that Alex was not capable of any real emotions. He seemed to have no real attachments to anyone or anything. He did not even have a favourite toy or teddy bear.

I also explained that I had seen Alex on numerous occasions at school turn on and off anger and temper tantrums. This child was capable of being in a total rage, punching, crying and the instant he gets what he wants he can turn it off. It is all a well-choreographed act with no real emotions attached. At twelve years, old Alex still had the social skills of a toddler. He was able to play beside some one at times. He was not able to interact with other children. Alex still found most normal children's behaviour to be a threat to him. He showed no remorse and seemed to have absolutely no ability to see the consequences of his actions.

On Alex's twelfth birthday Laura, Daniel and Anthony took him swimming. Alex did not have any friends his age; it was not possible to have anything but a family birthday party. They returned home early. I asked what had happened. Knowing with Alex anything was possible. Alex had been thrown out of the pool and told to go home. At twelve-years-old, Alex was holding a younger kids head under water. The lifeguard had to pull him off.

Alex was not so dysfunctional that he did not know that if you hold someone's head under water that they could drown. Had this not been a small town with everyone aware that Alex was quote, "special" he would have been arrested.

Alex's explanation for his actions was: The kid was playing with coloured rings that are provided by the pool. The rings are weighted so they sink; you toss the ring and then swim to the bottom to retrieve it. Alex decided in his head that he wanted to play with the rings. He did not ask to play; he did not simply retrieve a ring. He chose to hold the boy who was playing with the rings he wanted underwater.

Alex's behaviours had been escalating over the past two years. He was attempting to light fires. This was a kid who could punch a little girl square in the teeth, with the teacher watching and two hours later still deny that he did it, to the point of screaming and calling the teacher who saw him do it a liar.

Stating my concerns to this psychiatrist that I believed it was possible that Alex may be a Sociopath. To which he replied, "now you sound like a hysterical mother." I was neither hysterical nor his mother. I was realistically concerned for Alex's future. Arson, assault and attempted drowning are considered criminal offences and are signs of some serious problems at any age.

Although this psychiatrist dismissed my concerns as hysteria, he continued to tell me his concerns for Alex. He stated that whatever the reason Alex has his emotions shut down. Cases, which are this severe, when the child enters puberty, often end up in homicide or suicide. He went on to explain that the child becomes so angry that he kills someone else or he becomes so depressed that he kills himself.

Relaying my opinion to the psychiatrist, that I believed with Alex it would be homicide. With the recommended formal evaluations completed and the paper work filed. The school concluded that Alex would attend high school next year in the special needs classroom. His classmates were a handful of students, some requiring wheel chairs. In my heart, I knew this was not the place for Alex.

The year progressed as I contemplated my future. Where would I go and what would I do once the properties were sold? Slowly selling of the farm animals, I was not sure how long it would take to sell and fewer animals to care for made my life easier. I had been offered a business partnership, which I had been considering. This would mean moving to another small town. I was hoping that the sale would take long enough to allow Daniel to complete his last year of high school. Fortunately, it timed out perfectly.

Still employed full time, Alex, Laura and Daniel were all attending the high school. I had received some of the regular calls regarding Alex from the school over the year. It was February maybe March when I received a phone call at work. It was a teacher from the high school. This teacher said that he needed me to come to the school right away. I of course asked, "why? What happened?"

He replied Alex was completely out of control; he had punched a student, punched a teacher and had thrown desks around the room. The next statement was that this teacher had no idea where Alex was at this time. He either had taken off or was hiding somewhere in the school. He continued to say that Alex's behaviour was so out of control that he would not be allowed to return to school until he received psychiatric help. He stated that he had called Social Services and left several messages with Alex's Social Worker stating that Alex needed psychiatric care and would not be permitted back in school.

Arriving at the high school, I was met by a teacher who said he was Alex's guidance councillor. They found Alex; he was sitting in the councillors' office. Walking into the room, Alex was sitting in a chair. I simply stated to Alex," assault is against the law and you are not twelve years old anymore." I could not believe the sentence that came out of this guidance councillor who was standing behind me. He actually said to me, "let's not make this negative now." I turned to him and asked, "Since when is assault not negative?" Turning to Alex who now had a smirk on his face. Alex was enjoying watching this councillor make this somehow seem like it was my fault. The councillor stated that he thought we should sit down and discuss what happened and find out what made Alex so angry.

My reply was; "that I did not care what made him angry, there was no excuse for his behaviour! I had to leave work in the middle of the day because Alex was so out of control, and was told that he is not permitted to return to school unless he receives psychiatric help. Alex does not need to discuss what made him angry. Alex needs a good dose of reality. He needs to know that hitting a student, hitting a teacher is assault and it is against the law! Had this been any other thirteen-year-old student you would be calling a cop not wanting to sit down and have a chat."

Taking Alex home and sending him to his room, I was not sure whom I was angrier with Alex for his actions or the ridiculous guidance councillor who somehow believed that I was turning a perfectly good assault case into a negative situation.

Spending the remainder of the afternoon trying to contact Alex's Social Worker, I knew the school had left several messages. Alex was not allowed to return to school. I had to return to work in the morning and Alex could not be left home alone even at thirteen-years-old. Anthony had stayed home with Alex when he was not permitted to go to elementary school for the two days with the substitute. I told myself then that I would not do this again. Anthony needed to be in class and was not a designated babysitter.

Needing to talk to the Social Worker about what was involved in acquiring psychiatric help for Alex and if there were any resources available for someone to care for Alex during the day while I had to work. I did not receive a call back from Social Services. The phone rang that evening; it was the school councillor. He was asking to talk to Alex. I told him that Alex was in his room for the night. He stated he wanted to talk to him; he wanted to be sure that Alex was not upset. Once again, I could not believe what I was hearing. Thinking to myself, that someone needs to shake this guy and wake him up. I stated to this concerned councillor that I believed after Alex's behaviour today he should be upset.

Repeating that Alex needed to know that what he did was wrong and that he would not be permitted to come out of his room to talk on the phone. I asked the councillor if the school had heard anything from Social Services. He stated that the school had left several messages stating what the problem was and that they had had no response.

Spending the evening thinking of what my options were. I had to be at work in the morning. Alex could not be left alone and keeping another child out of class to watch Alex was not appropriate. It was not possible for me to take him to work with me.

There were a million thoughts running through my mind, knowing that Alex was becoming increasingly out of control. Also knowing that as he got older this could one day become a situation that I was not able to control, telling myself many times over the past six years that realistically Alex would be a child all of his life. As hard as I tried, I could not see a future for Alex where he would be capable of independent adult living. The psychiatrist's words of homicide or suicide in adolescence were running through my mind.

Mixed into all of the above thoughts was the fact that when this property sold I was seriously contemplating moving to another town and being a partner in my own business. If Alex were this out of control, how would he ever adjust to a new town, new people a new school, new students and a new teacher? How would I adjust? I was beginning to doubt my ability to start over again with Alex in a new situation. I was beginning to doubt my abilities to deal with Alex's escalating behaviours when he was sixteen, seventeen or eighteen. How long would Alex be accepted in a new high school.

I went to bed that night not knowing what I would do in the morning. Contemplated calling work and saying I would not come in. This was not an affordable solution on a regular basis.

Not sure when or how the decision was made to take this next step, I was up in the morning got dressed for work. Getting Alex up, we drove to the Social Services office. I had to be at work by 9 a.m. The Social Services Office opened at 8:30a.m. Walking into the office with Alex, telling him to sit in the waiting room, I asked the receptionist who knew me well if the Social Worker was in. She replied that she was not sure if he was in yet. Telling her that I had to be at work I asked her to tell the Social Worker that I had left him a present. Leaving Alex in the waiting room, I went to work.

After working for about half an hour, the phone rang. It was Alex's Social Worker. He was yelling into the phone. I heard the words, "you can't expect to just dump your problems on me." I hung up the phone. The phone rang again. I do not recall what the words were to this second conversation. I said, "I had to go, as I had to work, stating that after leaving several messages for him yesterday. Knowing that the school had left messages explaining the situation, neither the school nor I had received a response. I continued with; he had an office full of help and I had only me. Not only had he not return my phone calls or the schools phone calls he did not even have the courtesy to have his secretary call and offer to make me an appointment." With this statement, I again hung up the phone.

Fifteen minutes or so later the phone rang for a third time. Once again, it was Alex's social worker. He was not yelling he was actually quite polite. He simply asked if he could make an appointment with me after work to discuss Alex. I agreed to meet him at 5:30 p.m. Opting not to tell him that work was finished by 3 o'clock. Knowing that the Social Service office was closed at 4:30p.m. I decided this time it was his turn to wait.

Arriving at the office at 5:30 p.m. I was greeted by a very polite Social Worker. His first statement to me was, "I don't think I have ever had anyone leave me such a present." His next statement was to ask the question, "So what is it that I can do to help you?" We discussed the incident at the school. This worker had a complete file, had spoken to the school and the teachers involved, it was amazing how he was able to accomplish so much in just one day. We discussed the fact that Alex was in need of psychiatric help and that the school was insisting that he not return until he had been evaluated and a plan was in place for his education.

I asked about a youth psychiatric assessment facility in Vancouver. He stated that he believed this would be the best facility to evaluate Alex, he also stated this was not a facility that you could access quickly. The wait time to have a child admitted for a two-week evaluation was about three months. We agreed that we would start the process to have Alex admitted. The most pressing question for this social worker was whether I intended to take Alex home with me.

I could see the apprehension when he asked me the question, stating that I was willing to take Alex home; and that I required assistance with his care if he could not attend school. I agreed to keep Alex until he was accepted for an evaluation. I made it perfectly clear that I was not willing to wait indefinitely. I stated that if this application were to be shuffled around with no real results that I would be returning with Alex.

It was now early May. Alex was still on the waiting list. Contemplating how long it would take for the property to sell and telling myself that it would be ideal if I were able to relocate during the summer months.

There were serious concerns about relocating with Alex. Was I even capable of dealing with his needs? I had been telling myself for some time, only not wanting to admit, that I had failed Alex. Believing that I would never give up on a child I was having serious doubts about my own ability to deal with a new set of teachers and professionals. Feeling emotionally burnt out in dealing with Alex.

Lying on my back contemplating my future, thoughts of my new business venture and a new town were running through my mind. I was also realizing how much I was going to miss this place. Anthony had already moved on. Nick was planning to stay until I moved. Laura of course would move with me. Daniel was considering temporarily moving to the coast with his father. There would be far more job opportunities for him in a City.

I had grown to love this acreage life, caring for the animals, the deer in the field every evening. The fresh cut hay and sitting on the porch in the evening watching the bats fly between the barn and the yard light catching what seemed to be an endless supply of moths. Telling myself how wonderful this place had been I began thinking of who would take my place here, if I were meant to move on then someone out there was meant to be here.

As I have stated I was not a religious person. Finding myself on this occasion to be what I considered praying. I was simply saying thank you to God for finding me this beautiful place and saying thank you for Bill. It had not turned out to be what either one of us had hoped. Bill did provide me with the means to care for my family when I needed to move.

Thanking God for Alex and telling him how sorry, I was that I had failed. Questioning if perhaps I was only ever meant to be a temporary solution in life for Alex as Bill had been for me.

I found myself saying to God, that if I were meant to leave this beautiful place, could he please find someone who would love this place as much as I did to take my place. I was asking God to find someone who would appreciate everything, including the bats. I could not imagine someone living here and calling in a pest control company to clean out the barn rafters.

In anticipation of interested parties looking at the acreage I had been taking extra care to be sure that the grass was mowed and everything was looking its best. The Real Estate agent would call before bringing anyone over to view the house. As hectic as life can sometimes be I had been looking at the lawn for the last few days thinking that it really required to be mowed. There was a lovely crop of fresh dandelions, which were in full bloom. There had been no phone calls and no interested house hunters for quite some time.

Making a mental note of when I would be able to attend to the lawn. It had been about three weeks since I lay on my bed seeking help to find the perfect replacement for myself on this acreage. Arriving in the driveway to find my Real Estate agent and one other empty vehicle. I had not yet had time to trim the dandelions. My agent apologized for not giving me notice. He had an out of town client who was interested, who was not going to be in town very long.

Not only had I not mowed the lawn I had been out all day and had no idea what my house would look like. How many dirty dishes were waiting to be put in the dishwasher and I was sure that I had not vacuumed for at least a couple of days.

There was nothing to be done at this point except to apologize for whatever mess there may be and for the dandelions on the lawn. As our conversation was ending a tall slim man in his early, thirties emerged from the rented mobile on the property. The realtor had a key. The renters were also not home and had not been given notice to spit-polish the accommodations for guests.

Saying hello and apologizing for the dandelions, I loved the response I got. This bubbly enthusiastic man said, "don't apologize, I love dandelions." He proceeded to tell me that dandelions were the perfect home for a particular type of bee; I knew this was a person who would not only appreciate but would truly love this place. As our tour continued I commented that my favourite evening pass time was to watch the bats swoop to catch the moths in the yard light. He excitedly commented, "wow! You have bats." As I was giving him the tour of my goat barn, which was now minus the goats he commented that he had plans to turn this area into a pottery studio.

This wonderful enthusiastic man who loved dandelions and bats also had a wife and three children. He made an offer and I accepted. As he had children in school, he requested that he not take possession until after the end of the school year. It could not have been more perfect.

The day had been bright and sunny, in the late afternoon after these new owners had left it poured buckets outside. Sitting on the porch after the rain had stopped, looking out over the field to admire the deer, I saw not one but two majestic hawks soaring in the sky. Somehow, I felt that God was showing me that it was my time to soar. I silently said thank you. Thank you for it all.

Possession date for the new owner was July 1, 1996. We would move out and move on. Alex was admitted for his evaluation. As difficult as it was, I made the decision that I would not take Alex back.

Social Services contacted Alex's mother. Alex was now fourteen-years-old. His mother had a much different life style. She had a job and was not only able but was willing to try to have Alex live with her.

Alex never did return to school anywhere. He moved in with his mother were he is still living today.

Meeting with his mother shortly after my move to Alberta years later. Alex was now in his early twenties and was doing well; I could tell she had some concerns. The conversation some how turned to Alex's school experiences.

Telling his mother about the psychiatrist homicide or suicide comment, She very calmly and quietly said, "With Alex I think it will be suicide." My reply was, "I always thought it would be homicide."

Three years later speaking to his mother again, Alex was doing well he had a job. I told his mother the last time that we met that I always felt that I had failed Alex. His mother wanted me to know that although Alex did not talk much about his life. He did tell his mother that he was bad on purpose. He told his mother that he always believed that if he was bad enough I wouldn't want him and I would send him back to her, which is were he always wanted to be.

Alex was right; it took seven years. I was at my breaking point with Alex. I did not have it in me to start over in a new town, a new school, with a new teacher and Alex. His behaviours had escalated to a level, which I was no longer willing or able to deal with, so I did send him back. Goodbye Alex, I love you!

There was one more item to deal with before packing up and leaving town. The rental house property was still for sale. The prospect of leaving town and being an absentee landlord was not sitting well with me. Not wanting the stress of having to return to deal with whatever issues may arise.

Again talking to myself, asking myself if I knew anyone who wanted to buy a house. The answer came to me right away. A family who had rented the house for a while, she really liked the house. They moved across town for what they believed was an opportunity to rent to own a house. This deal had not worked out as expected.

Knowing this family did not have a lot of money I kept telling myself that this makes no sense. I have a house that I need to sell. They want to buy a house but lack the resources. There has to be away that we can accommodate both of our needs.

As the school year was nearing and end I was even more determined to sell this house before leaving town. I stopped thinking about it and picked up the phone. We had not spoken more than a couple of times since she had moved out of the house.

Starting the conversation with the usual how are you, haven't talked to you for a while, and stating that I was calling for a reason. I asked if she was at all interested in the house she used to rent, telling her that I was moving out of town and that the house was for sale.

She answered that yes she was interested but that they did not have the money to buy a house. I asked if she thought she would qualify for any kind of a mortgage. She answered that she was not sure, as she had never applied for a mortgage. I suggested that she apply at the Credit Union to see how much of a mortgage she would qualify for.

If she qualified for close to, what the house was worth I would be willing to loan her the down payment out of the proceeds from the sale of the acreage. She would not be able to tell the Credit Union that she was borrowing the down payment. Advising her to tell them that it was a gift if she qualified, we would arrange for the sale to take place after I was paid from the acreage and would have the money to loan her.

This was a win-win situation for both of us. I could sell my house and leave town with no worries and this family would be able to purchase their first home, which until today they had believed was out of their reach.

The Credit Union agreed to give her a mortgage, and I supplied the money for the down payment, which was paid back over the next two years; I was now on my way to a new town, a new business venture with only one child. Laura and I were beginning a new life together.

27

AINT LOVE GRAND!

Laura and I arrived in our new town. Investing my money in a new business venture with a partner, I made a few trips to this small town during the time I was waiting for the properties to sell and loved it. The main street was only a few blocks long. The town population was about 1500 people. The surrounding farmland and area totalled about 3000 people. There was one grocery store, a drug store, a credit union and a medical clinic. The City was only a forty-five minute drive away if you required anything more.

This small town would be my home for the next eight years. The first year and a half was spent concentrated on building my new business. A year into this new venture I determined that my plans required an adjustments. The expenses were quickly out numbering the income, which is very often the case when you are building a new business. As my resources were slowly dwindling, I concluded that it would be necessary for me to take a second job. I planned on working for a year or two until my business income was capable of sustaining both the business and by personal expenses.

Once again finding myself in a situation where I required employment in a small town with slim employment opportunities. Telling myself that I did not require a large income, I did require an extra income and it was only temporary. Any job available would be over and above the work required for my business. The work would have to be local, as I did not have forty-five minutes each way to spend driving to the City for employment.

There was a job opening at the local hotel for a cook. Knowing this was a job I could do and do well, which was close to home. I completed the interview and got the job. Working the 5:30a.m. to 2:30p.m. shift five days a week. Choosing to work the weekend shifts allowed me Mondays and Tuesdays, and each afternoon and evening to deal with my own business. I would keep this job for the next two years.

I had been in town a little more than a year and was busy keeping up with two jobs. Laura had started working part time in the kitchen, mostly on weekends and evenings. A part of me was beginning to feel that I wanted more. I wanted something to do that would be for me. Something that I enjoyed and that would allow me to meet people other than through the hotel.

An article in the local newspaper caught my eye. It was about the local Food Bank. The President of the Food Bank was stating that the need had been steadily increasing and that the Food Bank was in need of volunteers. The information for attending the next meeting was printed in the article. I thought about this article a few times over the next week, as I had always been involved in the community where I lived.

I had been the Treasurer for the Swim Club, volunteered on the soccer field; had been the Registrar for the District Foster Parents Association and a Crises Line volunteer before moving to the BC interior. Caring for several children in my home, managing, caring for the farm animals, and volunteering for the Pregnancy Out Reach Program in the town that I had just left. I had always had a job on top of my extra activities and was missing this personal involvement.

There was a college in the City, I considered continuing the courses I had enjoyed. Keeping up with two jobs the drive back and forth and the amount of time required to spend on studies in order to do top work did not seem like a realistic project at this time.

The Food Bank meeting was approaching, I made the decision to attend the meeting to see if this was something I would enjoy being a part of. Volunteering for the Food Bank as much as possible until I was able to leave my cooking job I loved it. With only one job and being self-employed enabled me to spend more time with the Food Bank. Elected Treasurer for two years, I would serve as the Food Bank President for the four following years. Laura and I spent countless hours shopping, stocking shelves, fund raising and serving clients. At eighteen-years-old, Laura served as Food Bank Secretary for one year.

During the first year and a half of living in this new town my mother, who was living in Vancouver became seriously ill and required surgery. She was in intensive care in a Vancouver hospital. One of my younger sisters who I was just beginning to know after more than fifteen years without any contact was at the hospital with me to see our mother.

Mom was in her early seventies; we were discussing her being able to care for herself in Vancouver. Bernice and my youngest sister were living in Alberta. I had spoken to Bernice once or twice over the past twenty years. My younger sister was much the same. None of us knew each other or much about each other's lives. I had no idea where David was living although I believed he was in Vancouver. The sister at the hospital with me lived on the outskirts of the same small town where I was now living.

My sister asked my mother to move in with her until she was well enough to return to Vancouver. My mother agreed. A year or so later my mother would move to this same small town. She is now in her eighties and has had a heart attack and open-heart surgery since her move. My mother had a house in the town limits for a few years. Since her last heart surgery, she has lived in a mobile on my sister's acreage.

My adult relationship with my mother was difficult. The memories of my childhood never completely went away. A part of me believed that my mother did not love or want any of her children. A part of me wanted to believe that she had done the best she could with what she was able to give at the time. Not seeing my mother much over the years, She did come to the house to see Daniel a week or so after, he was born. She never made the trip to see Laura. Laura was a few months old when the job situation was looking grim for Jason. We were in Vancouver as Jason was looking for work. We stopped in at mom's place, as she had never seen Laura. Jason asked if she had a newspaper, as he wanted to check the job ads. Mom handed him a pile of *National Enquirers*.

Mom did come to visit one time when I lived on the acreage in my last town. Living two hours away from Vancouver if she did visit it was not often and it was only for the day. This was different, we lived far enough away that this visit was expected to be for a week. I spent many years until my early forties literally hating my mother. I did not speak of her or my childhood often. There were times in a conversation if mothers were mentioned that I literally would say, "I hate my mother."

I had a friend who would visit me on the acreage on a regular basis; this friend's daughter was two years older than Laura. Her daughter and Laura spent a lot of time together and we became good friends. This was one of the few people I talked to about my mother. This friend was sitting at the kitchen table drinking coffee with me when my mother arrived for her visit.

Knowing that I had been tense for about a week just thinking about my mother's arrival. I had know Idea how much our current relationship affected me. I had not been a child and had not lived with my mother for more than twenty-five years.

Although we did not see each other, my mother would call on the telephone or would write letters. I discovered only a few years ago that she also wrote letters to Bernice. Her letters would arrive at different times for no apparent reason.

They did not seem to connect to any particular event. What ever my mother was thinking at the time for whatever reason, she would write a letter and mail it.

I later learned that the content of my letters and Bernice's letters were not much different. The letters usually started with a list of everything that was wrong with me. How horrible I was. For some unknown reason my mother was disgusted at the idea that Alex lived with me. She often wrote to say that I was a horrible person and that Alex belonged with his mother. She seemed to like to repeat the phrase, "I don't know what is wrong with you. You have nothing but hate in your heart! All of my kids have nothing but hate!" She would write this phrase in her letters or she would yell it to me over the telephone on so many occasions that I could not begin to count them.

My mother would tell me that I had no business taking care of Alex; she would say that children belong with their mothers. I don't know if she felt some kind of guilt. I was her child and had spent most of my childhood being looked after by people who were not my mother. She would occasionally send a letter in the mail addressed to Alex. I never gave him any of these letters, although I did read them. They usually consisted of her telling him that he should be with his mother. At times, they contained references to his father who he had never met. I burned these letters.

Although my mother was sure that Alex belonged with his mother and that, I was full of hate for keeping him. When she learned that I had actually sent him away and that he was again living with his mother, She telephoned me. Picking up the telephone to say hello, she was screaming into the phone those same words. "I don't know what's wrong with you, you have nothing but hate in your heart!" She was disgusted that I had sent Alex back.

Sharing coffee with my friend, a week after my mother's visit to the acreage was complete. My friend shared her observations from the day that my mother arrived. She told me that she could not believe the change in me when my mother arrived in the driveway. She had not even come in the house. My friend observed that I was a completely different person. This was not a change for the better.

Asking myself why do I allow myself to go through this. If contact with my mother is having such a negative affect on my life, why am I still allowing her in my life?

Although my mother was capable of saying some pretty nasty things to me, I was never able to do or say anything to her that would hurt her. Listening to her ranting over what ever she believed I was responsible for on countless occasion, never saying a negative word to her. I would tell myself that I didn't want to hurt her feelings.

I had accepted that she really was not capable of understanding how much hurt she was causing. Telling myself on many occasions that if I wrote it all out in black and white she still would not understand, what would be the point of me doing or saying anything to deliberately hurt her? I was not mentally ill. I knew better, I could not bring myself to hurt anyone deliberately including my abusive mother.

Although I would not do anything to hurt my mother, I had no desire to have contact with her. It was a great relief when call display was available for my home phone. I could now screen my calls. My mother had a thing about leaving a message on voice mail. Her name would come up ten or twenty times before, she would finally leave a message. The message would usually be something like, "are you alright? You never answer your phone, I thought maybe you were sick or dead, call me its mom." If she left a message, I always returned her call.

After her stay in intensive care, I was concerned about my mother's age and her health, and was apprehensive about her moving to this small town. Ideally, as she did not drive, it would be the perfect place for her. Her house was not more than a few short blocks walk to the main street in town. This would be the first time since I was a child that I had lived in the same town as my mother, and I was not sure what her or my expectations would be of this new situation.

In anticipation of her move, I had done a lot of thinking about my mother and our relationship. I was not willing to allow this move to change me into the tense negative person my friend had witnessed when my mother visited for only a week. It was not possible to change the circumstances. My mother was moving to this small town. Concluding that as she was aging and not in the best of health, she had expectations of being looked after by her children. Remembering our past non-relationship could there possibly be a way to make this work for both of us without it being a negative drain on my life.

Talking to myself constantly for the few months prior to her move, I concluded that I was capable of accepting my mother for who she was today. Had she been an elderly neighbour who was not well and required help to pick up groceries or a ride to the drug store I would not hesitate to say yes. This was the relationship I intended to attempt on her arrival, Simply refusing to allow any negative comments to affect me, it was possible for me to choose to ignore the negative and have a minimal relationship with my mother as if she were a new neighbour I was getting to know.

On one of my first visits to my mothers new, home she had company sitting with her at the kitchen table. I do not recall if this was the minister from the church stopping by to invite her to attend or the local health nurse. Introducing myself, sitting and listening to the conversation, my mother's life seemed to be grouped into different themes at different times. She had a few years where life was all about medical articles from the *National Enquirer* and horoscopes. At this stage in her life, her interest seemed to be in the television news and politics.

Listening to this conversation, coming to the realization that I had made the right decisions in accepting my mother for who she was today. My mother was telling her new visitor how she could have gone into politics. She was telling the story of how she had been asked to run for office but had to turn it down. Her story continued with she turned down this offer because she knew how hard a life of politics could be on her family, "Political life is hard on children you know." she stated.

Somehow, in this political conversation the subject was now hockey. I do not recall if the sports section of the news was on the television, but my mother was now telling her audience of one, how her son David had always wanted to play hockey. She continued with, "I just couldn't do it. You know; if your kid plays hockey you have to get them to the rink early in the morning. I just couldn't do it because I had to go to work."

Listening to these stories and the intensity in the voice of my mother the storyteller, I was asking myself what world did she live in? Did she really believe the stories she was telling? I could not imagine David asking for a glass of water, let alone to play hockey. He would have been knocked across the room for even thinking such a thing. I could just imagine the life long comments about how ungrateful and greedy he would have been expecting that someone would spend money on him for hockey. Acknowledging to myself that this story she was telling was pure fiction; perhaps she was talking about David this way out of some sense of guilt.

Whatever the reason as I drove home the thoughts running through my mind were of the person my mother was today. Had she always been this delusional? Had I just spent more than forty years hating this woman for something she does not even recall?

This would be the beginning of a new and very different relationship with my mother. Completely accepting my mother for who she was today, lifted forty years of hate and grief off my shoulders. There was no one left to hate. There was nothing left to grieve. The mother I hated for so long in my head did not even exist. My memories of my childhood, my memories of a mother who did not care and did not love me were replaced by the realization that it no longer mattered. Whether my mother's actions were deliberate or unintentional even she does not know. To hate this woman sitting at the table relaying stories of what she believes was her life would be ludicrous. I chose to love her for who she was today. Today was what we had. Today was what was real for both of us. I would see her with today's eyes, not yesterdays!

My new relationship with my mother was becoming enjoyable. She still had times when she would call to tell my how horrible I was. Listening and never mentioning it the next time, I would see her. I actually found myself picking up the phone to call her and see how she was doing. We would spend occasional evenings together playing cards. My mother decided that she would like to accept the Reverends invitation to attend church services. I never thought I would see a picture of Laura my mother and myself attending church. Yet, there we were and we were all enjoying it.

My mother actually got a small dog. Watching her with this little thing, this was a complete transformation for my mother. She commented to me one day that she had no idea that animals had feelings. I could see that this was something she actually cared about.

Every pet we had ever had as children she at some point would give away. You knew as a child not to get attached to a pet. I never understood why she would give us a kitten or a dog. We had several dogs and cats over the years. You never knew when they would be gone. She would just look at the dog one day, decide that she didn't want it and call the pound.

I was now seeing my mother as a very lonely person. Her feeling for this little dog seemed to be the first real attachment or feelings she had for anything in life including her children. It was wonderful to see her actually showing emotions other than hate and disgust for something.

Aware of my involvement my mother would often make comments about me wasting my time at the Food Bank. The more I got to know my mother and the more time that I spent with her I was seeing an amazing change in her.

One day watching me preparing for a fundraiser for the Food Bank, organizing a local bazaar with items donated to be sold and the proceeds going to the Food Bank, my mother asked if we could use a quilt for the fundraiser?

My mother made and donated a quilt for a Food Bank raffle. She had her picture on the front page of the local paper with a thank you. This was an amazing transformation. My mother was actually giving back to the community and she was enjoying it. Over the next few years, she would donate several quilts; she baked homemade bread and donated her basement space for Food Bank storage at Christmas time.

Seniors who used them as lap blankets while sitting in their wheelchairs purchased her smaller quilts. My mother donated many lap quilts to the local seniors home. She also by request made and sent several to hospitals and nursing homes in Vancouver and still does this today. Her sewing machine is a source of comfort and has allowed her to feel appreciated, which I know she enjoys.

Between running my business, working full time and volunteering for the food bank there was not a lot of time spent on social event. I was getting to know my younger sister who I had had little or no contact with for more than fifteen years. My sister enjoyed playing bingo. She invited me to go to the City for an evening of bingo. She was playing a table full of cards at the same time. Not familiar with bingo I was struggling to keep up only playing one or two cards. Watching the crowd of dedicated bingo players, telling myself that I was definitely not cut out to be a regular player.

The bingo evening had just begun, I recognized a man sitting at a table two rows in front of me. He recognized me and nodded a hello. This was someone that I had seen in the restaurant. He was a semi regular customer and often arrived dressed in leather carrying a helmet. It was obvious that he drove a motorcycle. Although I had never spoken to him, I knew that the regular customers called him Mercedes. He also drove a Mercedes and had several older collector models that the regular guys liked to discuss over coffee.

There was a break in the bingo calling and Mercedes came over to my table to say hello. He introduced himself as Stefon and said that he recognized me from the restaurant. I said hello and asked if he would like to join us as he had been sitting alone. He accepted my invitation. Stefon had a thick accent that I was not able to recognize. Asking where he was from, he stated that he was originally from Austria and had lived in Germany for several years. It was clear that Stefon was not a regular bingo player, it took both of us to play and although my sister was playing several cards at once she would reach over and dab the ones we had both missed.

Over the next few weeks, I would see Stefon in the restaurant, we would say hello or spend a few minutes talking to each other. As he was paying his bill, he said he was thinking of going to bingo again on the weekend and asked if I would be interested in joining him. Thanking him for the offer, I said I had other plans.

I had not given any thought to a personal relationship for quite some time. My relationship with Bill had been virtually non-existent for more than a year before the properties sold. I had been in this new town for more than a year.

Meeting Stefon had me contemplating whether I was willing to consider any type of a personal relationship. My relationship with Jason although it had been built out of love was completely dysfunctional.

I had negotiated with myself and agreed to a relationship with Bill out of financial need and the hope that what started out as a close friendship would possible grow into something more. Contemplating Stefon I was not willing to negotiate a relationship ever again.

I had grown too much to ever repeat the dysfunction that I shared with Jason. There were times over the past few years that I would complement myself for being able to cope with the kids, the farm and the finances all on my own. As difficult as it was at times I was thriving on the mental freedom, and was finding myself at times adopting a negative attitude towards men. I had gone from believing my only purpose in life was to look after Jason's every need to making comments at times like; "what would anyone want a man for anyway?" At the time that I met Stefon, there was a part of me that was not sure that I ever wanted another man in my life.

Anticipating that Stefon would again at some point ask me to attend bingo or some other social event, questioning to myself, whether I was willing to consider a social relationship with Stefon or anyone at this time? Saying no again may be the last time he asked, saying yes, even to go out for coffee would be telling Stefon that I was willing to consider getting to know him better. Spending the next week or so talking to myself; going back and forth. At times I was trying to talk myself into trying another relationship and at times, telling myself that I was not willing to go down this road again with anyone.

There was no definitive answer. There was a part of me that wanted to remain independent and in control of my life. There was a part of me that was willing to admit it would be nice to have some one to share my life with. I concluded that it was time for me to take some of my own advice. I had told countless kids over the years that if they did nothing else they had to be honest with themselves. I was honestly not sure if I was ready for a new relationship and was completely committed to maintaining the independent lifestyle that I had grown to love.

As we chatted in the coffee shop Stefon once again asked if I would like to go out with him on the upcoming weekend, this time I said yes. We were talking over dinner at a restaurant, which had a spectacular view of the City as it was lit up at night. Stefon was an easy person to talk to. He always had a story or two to tell. He had a way of making who ever he was talking to feel like they really mattered. Stefon loved to just watch people in a crowd he had a way of seeing something wonderful in everyone.

The conversation involved details from both of our lives, as we knew very little about each other. I told Stefon that I had been in town for about a year before taking the job at the restaurant. He had lived here for more than ten years and owned property on the out skirts of town. Stefon was not married but he had been in a ten-year relationship, which had ended about two years before we met. Informing Stefon that I had also been in a relationship, which had ended about two years ago. Being completely honest with myself and with him, telling Stefon that I liked my life and that I knew I was not willing to give up any part of it for a new relationship. We spent the remainder of the conversation in discussions about life and how it was to be enjoyed. We seemed to have concluded that personal relationships were meant to add too and not take away from a person's life.

We spent a lot of time together over the next six to eight months. Stefon was self employed and often worked away. When he was in town, we would see each other as often as we could. I had been to Stefon's property several times. What a magnificent place. Twelve acres straight up a forested mountain. No hydro, drinking water from a creek, black bears, rabbits and the motor home were he lived. He spent much of the last ten years with his partner travelling in his motor home, the last few years it had been permanently parked on his property.

There was a narrow winding dirt road, which wound up to the top of his property. He built a machine shop at the top. The property was terraced with four levels; the motor home was on the second terraced level. Stefon would run up and down this mountain several times a day from the motor home to his shop. The first time I walked up the road to the top of his mountain I was huffing and puffing and had to sit at the top for a rest. He was older than I was and could run up this mountain with the energy of a twelve-year-old boy.

Stefon loved this place; he ran his machine shop off a generator and made his own system for electricity for the motor home using the water from the creek that ran down the mountain. Stefon had a genuine love and respect for nature. He co-existed on this mountain with black bears, deer the occasional cougar, several rabbits and on one occasion a bobcat. He loved his rabbits. He would be working in his machine shop and there would be a half a dozen or more rabbits wandering around under his feet.

As we walked up and down this mountain together, Stefon would give me tips on how to watch out for wildlife. He pointed out the path which he did not disturb as this was a bear trail that was used daily for the trip to the river for the bears to drink. On one occasion, I watched as Stefon was placing 2x4 lumber in a large puddle on the first terrace level driveway. There did not seem to be any particular logic to the placement. Inquiring as to what he was building, He replied, "nothing; I am making a bridge for the ants." Looking down into the puddle there was a trail of ants marching across his impromptu bridge. He showed me the base of a large tree on the other side of the puddle. There was a massive ant-hill. Stefon was concerned that the ants could not return to their home as the puddle covered a large area of driveway.

As we were inspecting the ant colony, he commented that if the nest got too large he would wait until it was dormant in the winter and move it to a more private place for the ants on the mountain.

Stefon was well known and well liked in this small town. As it was becoming apparent to those who knew him that, we were a couple I would have a steady stream of customers relaying what they knew about Stefon to me. Unlike the friendly information that I had received about Bill; the picture that the community had of Stefon would turn out to be accurate.

The community knew Stefon as the guy you went to anytime you needed a hand with anything. He was known as Mercedes for his cars he was also called a genius for his ability to make, repair or create just about anything. Farmers and the mechanics all raved about his skills. If you need a tractor fixed, a hole dug with his backhoe or some obscure part for an outdated machine that was no longer in stock; Stefon was the one who could study the machine and make you a part, stop in the middle of the day to help his neighbour get his tractor going or assist just about anyone who asked in any way he could. The gas station, hotel and even the grocery store had all called on Stefon for assistance at different time.

It was about a twenty-minute drive from the restaurant to Stefon's acreage. Much of the drive was down a winding mountain road. When you entered the town limits, it was only a short drive to the main street in town. Anyone living on this road near the town limits would have about a twenty-minute walk to the grocery store. Driving towards Stefon's acreage, we were just about at the town limits heading to his place. There was a local woman walking on the side of the road heading in the opposite direction towards town. Stefon waved as we drove by. He said to me, "I bet she is walking into town, I should ask her if she needs a ride." He turned the car around drove to where she was walking and asked if she was heading to town. She answered, "Yes she was heading to the store." Stefon offered her a ride, waited for her to do her shopping and drove her home. What a wonderful thing to do, some how no matter how busy he was he always made time for the important things in life.

He managed to fit so much into his life and do it all with joy. Stefon genuinely loved helping people. He often told me that he had to earn his living out of town because he had a hard time charging his neighbours. He could have made a reasonable living locally with his skills. Most of the time, he fixed a tractor or made a custom part he would charge for the materials if he had to pay out of pocket to purchase them and a small fee. Many times he simply would say, "don't worry about it, I might need something from you some day."

Stefon seemed to enjoy what ever he was doing and did everything exceptionally well. He had a natural love for people. If he knew a neighbour or the waitress in the restaurant or any of his, many friends liked a particular thing it gave him great joy in finding something special and presenting it to who ever it may be. There was a waitress in the restaurant that collected Mickey Mouse items; he had a friend who was into antique tractors. If Stefon spotted something in a store or at an auction he would often say, "oh I know so and so is looking for one of those" and he would gladly purchase what ever it was and give it to the appropriate recipient.

I had never known any one who seemed so content and so appreciative of everything in his life. Stefon was an excellent cook, he could use a sewing machine, he could choose the appropriate plants and herbs to make whatever ointments or medications he required for himself or to doctor a sick animal and he loved to garden.

His previous partner of more than ten years, although they were no longer together was driving one of Stefon's Mercedes as she hit a deer with her car. Stefon still looked after her car maintenance and when he was not able to fix the vehicle that she had damaged he gave her the money to purchase another car. He promised to fix her car and he was not able to do it so he loaned her his car until he could afford to buy her something else. He said that he still cared for her, she was not happy in their relationship and he wanted her to be happy; so they simply agreed to move on with there lives separately.

I would look at Stefon and tell myself what a wonder man he was. I thanked God for bringing such a wonderful gift into my life. As I am writing this in 2007, this fall Stefon and I will have been together for ten years. He was then and is still today truly a wonderful gift to me from God. Thank you Stefon and Thank you God.

28

THE BEAR NECESSITIES

Eight months or so into this new relationship we were discussing moving my business to Stefon's acreage. This would lower my expenses, allow the business room to grow and allow my partners business room to grow, as we would no longer be sharing a facility. This would also allow Stefon to be away for work without having to pay someone to care for his rabbits.

We would share living space in his motor home. Loving this idea and loving Stefon, there was no place I would rather be and no one I would rather be with. Laura had taken a job in the City and was living in her own suite at this time. The two of us would share this magnificent mountain and his motor home for the next six years.

Stefon used to joke and say that we had to get along because the motor home was so small there was no room to fight. A friend and neighbour was moving to the coast and asked Stefon if he would keep his Big Bouvier cross dog. A City townhouse was not the place for a huge dog. Stefon agreed, in the winter when we let Cindy sleep in the motor home with us we would joke that when Cindy was in the house we had wall-to-wall carpet.

As we completed the fencing and the building required to house my business, which was a small dog breeding kennel Stefon would give me tips on living on the mountain. Cindy was an excellent bear dog; she would alert you to the presence of a bear without intimidating the bear or being afraid and running to you with a bear behind her as many dogs do. During the times that Stefon was working away and I would be alone on the mountain, Cindy was a great companion as we walked to the top of the mountain to care for the rabbits.

There was an incident I would like to share with you, which happened before Cindy lived with us. Stefon often gave me tips, as we would walk up the mountain. He always said that if you see a bear do not be afraid, a bear can tell if you are afraid. He would tell me, "if you see a bear do what I do; just talk to him. Tell the bear to go back into the bush. Talk to him in a calm even voice and don't be afraid." He would add if this doesn't work than just throw a rock at him, hit him in the butt and he will run away.

Telling myself, that this seemed liked good advice, having not yet seen my first bear. Would it be possible not to be absolutely terrified if I actually came across a bear while walking up or down this mountain?

As Stefon would be away at times two or three weeks at a time I would travel to the top of the mountain daily to care for his rabbits; making this trip countless times and not yet encountering a bear.

One day arriving at the shop as usual opening the door and shutting the screen door behind me, I proceeded to feed and water the bunnies. My work was complete; I was about to open the screen door and there in front of me only a few feet away from the screen was a black bear. Stefon's advice was rushing through my head. Don't be afraid. Remembering a bear tip from my time living in Bella Bella. If you see, a bear just make a loud noise bang a pot or a pipe or something and this will scare the bear away.

Deciding to opt for the loud noise idea first, I picked up a piece of metal pipe and banged it against the steel doorframe. It made a loud bang. The bear that had been wondering in front of the building exploring was not afraid of the loud bang. All the noise did was alert the bear to my presence. This bear that up to this point had been minding his own business was now interested in me and was staring at me through the screen.

Time for plan "B;" Stefon's bear advice would be put to the test. I started talking to the bear saying, "Nice bear; go back into the bush. Go back into the bush nice bear. Please don't eat me, go back into the bush." The more I talked the less interested the bear seemed to be in me. He was again wondering in front of the building exploring the assortment of parts etc. that were on the ground.

Thinking to myself; Stefon is out of town; no one knows that I am up here. This could take forever if this bear does not heed my advice and go back into the bush. I kept on talking, repeating the same phrases. It seemed like the conversation through this screen door was eternal. The bear who clearly was not listening to me and who in fact seemed to be completely ignoring my presence stopped snooping and sat down.

He actually sat down a few feet away from the screen and was staring at me, Tilting his head from side to side as though he was trying to figure out who or what I was and why I had been talking to him non-stop. I was not afraid; this bear did not look scary. He looked curious. I just kept talking to him asking him ever so nicely to go back into the bush so it would be possible for me to leave this shop. Finally, out of boredom I believe the bear stood up and turned around. He now had is rear end towards me. Turning his head to look back over his shoulder at me, he walked back into the bush.

Over the next six years, I would encounter many bears. Some at the top of the property others who would stroll down to checkout the motor home on occasions. There was one magnificent mother bear and her cubs. This mother bear lived on the top of this mountain for about three years. She had cubs with her. If Stefon or I would arrive at his shop, this momma would come to the same spot in a clearing of trees a few feet away. She always had her cubs behind her. It was as if she was coming out to say hello and let you know she was there. I would feed the rabbits and leave talking to her the entire time as I had talked to the first bear I met. Starting with saying hello and saying thank you for not eating me, I am just going to feed the bunnies and then I will leave you alone.

Sadly, this magnificent momma was shot and killed on Stefon's property by poachers; they took her paws and her hide and left her body for Stefon to clean up. Stefon had taken a close up picture of her that we planned to have blown up and framed. He gave the picture to the game warden that asked for it to be able to identify the hide if it should ever turn up. She had two cubs the year she was killed, one cub we saw again the following spring, I do not know if the second cub survived the winter.

Stefon loved animals he talked to the bears he talked to the bunnies, the deer the squirrels and to my dogs. He had a wonderful way of calling whatever creature he was holding a conversation with "little buddy." He would greet them all with, "how are you doing little buddy?" It was such a delightful name that I borrowed it for my kennel business, Little Buddies Breeding Kennels.

As my business was now able to expand we travelled together to Alberta to purchase a new breeding male for my kennel a pure bred Bichon Frise male. It was important to register this male with a name that would reflect his new life as a handsome stud. His registered name would be Willie Nelson. I now had two handsome new males in my life. It just doesn't get any better than that!

My business was slowly growing and expenses were now much less, than they had been. It was time to contemplate how much longer to keep the hotel job. As my life was improving, I had given some thought to adding a second World Vision child to my family. Being a sponsor for many years my first African child was now an independent adult who no longer required my assistance. I was currently sponsoring a second child. As life seemed so wonderful, it was time to consider whether my budget could afford a second sponsored child. Concluding that it would wait a little longer to be sure that my business income could completely support me at some point. I would not sponsor a second child and then have to withdraw my support should this extra expense not be affordable.

I received a phone call from World Vision; the lady on the phone was thanking me for my support and asking about the possibility of sponsoring a second child. Explaining that the idea of a second child was not something planned for right now, however it would be in the near future.

Hanging up the phone it was time to count out my change; Loonies and Toonies (one and two dollar coins) these coins were my tip money from the hotel. The cook shared in the tips. In a small town, there were not a lot of tips to share. Counting my change and contemplating the purchase of a pack of cigarettes on my way home from work the following day, thinking about the $5.50 that a pack of cigarettes would cost I had one of those "ah ha moments."

Thinking, "wait a minute! I just lied to that lady on the phone." Spending $5.50, a day on cigarettes was not a necessity but a choice. There was enough money for a second child. There was in fact enough money to sponsor four more children if I counted a whole month of $5.50's. All that was required was for me to choose to wait and smoke again, when it was affordable rather than to choose to sponsor a child again when it was affordable. I picked up the phone and asked to sponsor a second child and have not had a cigarette since that day.

Things were progressing; able to pay off some debts including a small car loan it was time to leave my second job. Living only on my business income would mean no regular paycheque coming in. I gave the hotel a month notice and was now two weeks away from my final day of working two jobs.

Daniel called. Living and working in the BC lower mainland he had been diagnosed with arthritis several months prior to this phone call. His condition had deteriorated to the point were he was no longer able to do physical labour. The past several months he had been living on Unemployment Insurance and was jumping through the required hoops to have Unemployment sponsor him for retraining before his claim would run out.

This phone call was to tell me he was finally approved and accepted for the course after waiting for several months. His Unemployment claim would run out in about three weeks. Daniel had been waiting, filing out forms, obtaining the correct medical documentation etc. for more than eight months. He was finally accepted and Unemployment was willing to extend his claim and fund this course. Daniel received the acceptance news the day that he was calling.

It was wonderful that he was accepted. The day that the Unemployment office called to tell him that they had accepted his application, they also informed him that they would only pay for half of the course. This course had a price tag of $10,000.00.

Had he known they would only fund half; he could have spent the past eight months applying for a student loan or looking for financing. If financing was not available, he could have pursued other career options. There was now only three week left before he would have no income. Daniel was commenting on how ludicrous it was for the Unemployment office to tell a person who has not worked for close to a year that they have three weeks to finance $5,000.00.

They were aware the day that Daniel put in his first application form that if he were accepted they would only fund half; yet none of the several people he had contact with over the past eight months felt the need to share this detail.

As Daniel was not employed, a loan would not be possible for the $5,000.00 required. I called my bank and explained the situation to see if there was anything we could do. The person on the phone stated that in order for anyone to qualify for a student loan a co-signer would be required as a full time student is not usually employed. I would be willing to co-sign if qualified.

Stating to the person on the telephone that I was self-employed the Bank considered a person who was self-employed to be a high-risk client. The application required my income. I quoted my gross and net incomes from my business for the previous year and my income for the first three months of the current year, as we were having this conversation in March.

The voice on the other end of the telephone stated that the bank would only be able to consider the income that was already earned for the current year. I asked why? It was obvious to me that if a business made this amount in the first three months and there were clearly nine full months left in the year that it was likely that the income for the year would be higher than only the first three months. Bank policy was that they could only consider what a business actual made up to this point for the year as being self-employed meant a regular paycheque was not guaranteed.

As we were talking the representative from the bank had been viewing my current bank file, it was noted that I had recently paid off a car loan with this bank, it was also noted that I was employed at the hotel. The voice on the other end of the phone asked, "Are you still employed at the hotel?" That little voice inside of my head was saying yes but I have already given my notice and have only two weeks left to work. My lips were saying, "Yes I am still employed at the hotel."

The bank could only consider the amount of money that was earned for this year up to today. I was being asked today if I was still working at the hotel. My answer was yes. The question was not how much longer did I intend to work for the hotel. The loan was approved.

Daniel graduated with a degree in Broadcasting and was hired out of the school for a job in radio, which did not require any physical labour.

Once the loan was approved, Daniel and I met in the City to sign the appropriate papers at the bank. It was early afternoon as we walked down the sidewalk toward the bank. There was man in his late twenties or early thirties sitting on the sidewalk playing a guitar. He had his guitar case open for donations. Daniel stopped in front of this man and listened to the song he had been singing. When the song was finished Daniel shook the man's hand and said enthusiastically, "Hey man, I really like your music" the man replied with a thank you.

Daniel did everything in life with enthusiasm. He continued his conversation with, "hey man I would really like to help you out; but I'm kind of taped out myself right now, but I enjoyed listening to you." Both Daniel and this entertainer parted with smiles on their faces.

As we continued toward the bank Daniel was telling me that he usually gives money if he has it. He continued with, "or sometimes if I don't feel comfortable giving someone money and they are asking for food I will go to McDonalds and buy a bag of cheap hamburgers and a coffee and bring it back to them. It always surprises them and it makes me feel good." As Daniel was relaying this information with his usual bubbling enthusiasm, I was telling myself how proud I was of the man that he had become.

This day in the City with Daniel reminded me of a similar personal encounter on a previous trip to this City. It was early morning I had parked my car in the back parking lot and was walking to the bank. The bank was not yet opened my intention was to make a deposit in the bank machine. There was a young man in his early twenties sitting on the back step of the neighbouring building. As I walked by he said, "good morning, nice day isn't it." I replied, "yes it is, it is going to be a beautiful day." His next comment took me by surprise. He looked up at me and said, "thank you." I replied, "thank you for what?" to which he added, "thank you for talking to me." He had been sitting quietly and now appeared to have some excitement in his voice. He continued with, "thank you, thank you that a beautiful lady like you would talk to me." I said, "You're welcome" and thanked him for the complement adding, "You have a wonderful day."

The forty-five minute drive home had me thinking of this young man. It appeared that he said good morning to everyone who passed by his step in the morning. What a sad statement that in a City full of people this young man felt so alone that a simple good morning acknowledgement was so rare he was bursting with excitement wanting to say thank you to a stranger who had simply said hello.

Remembering this young man and thinking of Daniel; I felt proud that Daniel was a man who would not only have said good morning but would have taken the time to talk to a stranger just because he knew it made them feel good.

29

A HEART OF GOLD

Running the kennel was not providing a large income; it was providing me with reasonable living expenses and the freedom that comes with being self-employed. The time that had been previously spent at my hotel job was now spent on the things I loved.

The Food Bank was open to clients only twice a week. It would take another two days to complete the required shopping, stocking shelves, picking up donations, organizing, planning and volunteering for various fund raising events. The two years volunteering as Treasurer also meant finding times to do the books and the banking.

Having attended church on only a few occasions with Laura and my mother I was now able and willing to attend services on a regular basis as Sunday was no longer a day to work at the hotel. The one thing each town, village or City that I have lived in had in common was wonderful people. This little town was no different it was full of the most remarkable individuals.

The first day Laura and I accompanied my mother to church it was wonderful to see so many familiar faces. Most of the people in this little church were friends or acquaintances. Not one of them had ever mentioned they attended church. The most remarkable person in the room was a woman who would become an amazing friend and guardian angel to me. She has given me permission to use her real name in this book and has volunteered to be one of my editors.

Valerie is the picture of grace and elegance. This magnificent woman glows with enthusiasm and absolute, genuine, affection for; and acceptance of each and every person she meets. When we met, Valerie was only a few years away from retiring as the Reverend of this little church.

My religious background was almost non-existent. Laura had not grown up in a home with any type of religion or spiritual background. Yet here we were, feeling absolutely comfortable and welcome in this little church. Laura at seventeen-years-old was attending church with her grandmother out of choice during the time that I was working Sundays at the hotel.

Valerie was close to retirement age, yet she was fit as a fiddle and was jogging down the street with my seventeen-year-old daughter and another friend in preparation for an upcoming run to raise money for breast cancer. We became friends and co-workers, volunteering for the Food Bank and other local events.

We often shared lunch and stories from our lives. It was wonderful watching Valerie with children. Her bubbling, nurturing, loving instincts just poured out. Valerie had been a single mother; she had run a day care as a means to support herself and her children.

One of her sons she adopted as a special needs infant. It was interesting swapping child rearing philosophies. There were also many discussions involving strategies for which every project we were tackling at the moment. As we were sharing lunch one day Valerie commented on how much she enjoyed talking to me because I was so honest. Whatever the subject I simply stated how I saw things in the world. She also commented that it was difficult to have friends when you are the Reverend. People think of you as a Reverend or a councillor not just as a friend.

Several months after this lunchtime comment, I was stocking Food Bank shelves with a fellow volunteer and church member. This volunteer asked me a question, which reminded me of Valerie's comment on friendship. This question took me by surprise. The question was, "if you want to go out to lunch with Valerie what do you do?" The woman asking the question was a few years older than I was and possibly a few years older than Valerie, she knew that we often had lunch together.

It was a simple question, which I simply answered, "When I want to go out for lunch I pick up the phone and say hello Valerie its Rose do you want to go out for lunch today." In my ignorance of religious protocol and lack of church upbringing, I had missed the actual question being asked.

This woman was asking the proper protocol to invite the Reverend out for lunch. This was obviously an important issue to this friend and co-worker, which I had just brushed off as an almost ridiculous question.

It had never occurred to me that there was a proper way to invite some one out to lunch. During the many lunches we shared, I had not considered Valerie's occupation at all. We were two friends sharing lunch, what either one of us did for a living never entered my mind.

This was one more time in my life when I was glad that I was ignorant. Although, sorry for not understanding the importance of this question to the person who was asking it. Accepting Valerie for the woman that she was and not only her job description was the way I accepted everyone in my life. This was something I never wanted to change.

One of the projects we worked on together was Valerie's creation. As co-workers for the Food Bank, we were blessed with the opportunity to share many personal stories with friends and neighbours that in different circumstances may never have been told. There are those in every community, which at times require an economic or spiritual boost. Rose's world and Valerie's world were no different. Difficult times are not reserved only for an unfortunate few.

Valerie often commented on how wonderful it felt to join a friend for lunch. Somehow, a simple lunch, great conversation in a nice place with good service, real tablecloths and flowers on the table just brightened your whole day. This comment was often followed with how nice it would be if everyone could enjoy such an event. There were seniors in town that may be able to afford going out for lunch, however many of them would be sitting alone. There were working moms, new comers to town who would love the opportunity to socialize and meet people, and many families who simply could not afford such a simple pleasure. This repeat conversation was the springboard for a free lunch program, which Valerie created and coordinated out of the Sunday school room in her church.

There are many churches with free lunch and hot meal programs for the needy. This one was very different. Valerie has this unique, magical way of painting everyone in her world with the same brush. Bright vibrant colours for all, it is not possible to feel less than in Valerie's company. She simply does not see anyone as being less than.

This unique program would be a once an month free lunch for all. Complete with real tablecloths, flowers and no line-ups, meals to be served to the guests and every one sitting together sharing conversation. Those who volunteered to cook and serve would enjoy lunch and conversations as soon as the serving was complete. Volunteers would share seats at different tables making sure everyone felt included, thus joining, being one of all the towns' people. There would be a donation basket at the front door for anyone who would like to donate.

The entire community was encouraged to come for lunch. We asked the business owners and local workers to share their lunch breaks. Valerie wanted this to be a community free lunch. This was a place for all. It was a special once a month social gathering. No religion, no stigma attached as being only for the poor this was a place for all to enjoy.

There was no shortage of volunteers to donate desserts or make a pot of soup. My specialty was corn chowder. Valerie's free community lunch was so successful it would be shared with the other churches in town. Those large enough to hold the event would rotate locations. Those churches without facilities would rotate with offers of hosting the event at Valerie's church. There was one church, which decked the dinning room out with pink tablecloths, candles and maroon napkins it was simply magnificent. Summer time often included a free community lunch barbecue. The donation basket meant there was never a shortage of grocery dollars. The day of the barbecue a loaded logging truck parked out front. The driver not only ate, but also ended up flipping burgers.

One Monday a month the Sunday school room in this, little church would come alive with fine diners and stimulating conversation. Old and young, employed, unemployed, rich and poor, served by gracious hosts who were encouraged to sit with their customers. What a wonderful way to brighten your day. Leftovers were given to moms and dads with kids so they could eat homemade soup and cake another day.

This same little Sunday school room would double as a distribution centre once a year for the Food Bank Christmas Hamper program. It is truly amazing what can be produced in small spaces.

As with most charities the needs seem to steadily increase. With the increasing need for assistance the challenge of fundraising to keep the Food Bank doors open never ends.

Fundraising in a small town has its own limitations. Many of the systems, which work in a City environment are greatly reduced or do not exists at all in a small town.

This small Food Bank had a small completely dedicated group of volunteers most of whom had experiences at some time in their lives, which required and hand up from a stranger or a community. Some had memories of hard times where there was no help there was no place to go for temporary assistance. Each volunteer had their own story, their own personal reason for giving back to this community. Each one had a passion for the friends and neighbours we assisted and a determination to keep the doors open.

Most of the volunteers who were available to show up on a weekday were retired seniors. Laura and I took on the responsibility of shopping for and picking up donations, as we were more physically able to load and unload cases of canned goods.

Being a small town with limited resources the Food Bank also coordinated and completed the Christmas hamper program each year. The City had a Santa's anonymous program which covered City residents and a certain distance out side of the City. The boundary for our small Food Bank clients was all those living outside the City boundary to the town limits. All those living in the town limits and all those living in the other direction up to the boundary, which was set for the next neighbouring town. This meant that although the town limits had a population of about 1500 people the Food Bank boundaries included a population of about 4000. One hundred plus Christmas hampers would be provided to families each year with the exception of my last year with the program where more than 300 hampers were provided. My first experience with the Christmas hamper program was as a volunteer when I was still employed at the hotel. There were toys and mittens etc. donated by the community. The reality of being in the room trying to find an appropriate gift to place in a food hamper box for an eight-year-old girl on my list, when the few gift to choose from were a fire engine, Tonka trucks and toys suitable for a three or four year old was breaking my heart. The thought of this girl (8) on my list opening her only present Christmas morning and it is a Tonka truck meant for a four-year-old boy was in bedded in my mind.

Laura and I spent every year since this first Christmas hamper volunteer day shopping for and donating gift for the hamper program. Shopping was something I avoided if possible for myself yet somehow shopping for the Food Bank was different. This was enjoyable. March turned out to be the best month to buy children's toys. This is the time of the year when the stores are clearing out last year's stock and making room for beach toys and new bicycles.

All year long every year both Laura and I would look for suitable items, which may be on sale. We walked into Canadian Tire one day to by windshield wipers for the car. There was a display in the entranceway of tabletop pool games clearing out for about eight dollars each. We purchased twenty.

We could give this gift to a boy or a girl. If I were short a gift for a five-year-old boy, a twelve-year-old boy or a ten-year-old girl it would fit. There were ten dollar watches in individual display cases, hand held video games on clearance. Any time we spotted trucks, dolls or art supplies on sale we would purchases a dozen or so and store them in my mother's basement. Little Buddies Breeding Kennels bought a hundred or more gifts each year. Spreading the shopping over the year meant spending only a hundred dollars or so at a time. These gifts were added to the other donations each year with out anyone knowing who donated them.

There were years when I was the coordinator for the hamper program where there would be a shortage of gifts for a particular age group. Laura simply went shopping for the needed gifts and added them to the pile. Each and every child on every hamper list received at least one reasonable gift appropriate to their gender and their age.

As a child I do not recall even one Christmas that was a happy occasion. The gifts whatever they may have been were never a disappointment I had learned as an infant to have no expectations. Christmas meant drinking, fighting, my father may leave or my mother may end up in the hospital again.

As an adult and mother Christmas was a time that was completely devoted to making my children feel wonderful. For me Christmas was a time that I would go through all the motions all the magic of Christmas for my children yet inside feeling somehow detached from it all.

The Christmas Hamper program for six years allowed me to feel absolute joy all year round. There are no words to describe the feeling inside as I watch one hundred plus mothers and fathers smiling as they pick up the hamper with ingredients to assist in creating a Christmas of wonder for their children.

There were several years Little Buddies anonymously ordered and paid for Christmas cookies or candies to add to the food hampers.

Christmas is one time in the year when the ability to fund raise for any charity increases. People think of others at Christmas. As coordinator for the hamper program Christmas was on my mind year round.

Laura and I were in the City it was July or August. We had stopped at Costco. As we were entering the store, a wall full of paper teddy bears caught my eye. Each bear was individually signed, while paying for our purchases; the cashier asked if I would like to buy a teddy bear. The proceeds were to go to the children's hospital. I purchased a bear, put my signature on it at it was placed on the wall.

On our way, home this day we drove through a McDonalds drive through window. The window was covered with paper baseball mitts. The girl in the window asked if we would like to purchase a baseball mitt for charity.

As we ate our lunch on the drive home the picture of this huge wall full of paper teddy bears and a window covered with baseball mitts was playing in my head. How teddy bears and baseball mitts had me thinking about Christmas and the Food Bank I do not know.

The picture in my head was of paper turkeys. The remainder of the conversation involved the possibility of me borrowing the teddy bear and mitt idea to raise funds at Christmas time to purchase turkeys for the hamper program. We can call them turkey bucks. Three different coloured turkeys one dollar, two dollar and five dollar turkey bucks. A customer would sign the appropriate colour to match his or her donation. Imagine an entire wall at the local grocery store or the gas stations, the hotel restaurant covered in turkey bucks.

The turkey bucks campaign was launched December 1st of that year and was an amazing success. Several local businesses competed for who could fill the wall or window with the most turkey bucks. Turkey bucks would return each December 1st.

Another fundraising idea that was borrowed was an annual breakfast with Santa. The department store where I worked before giving birth to Daniel had an annual breakfast with Santa held in the public restaurant.

Fundraising in a small town can be difficult. People are generous, however asking the same small group of people to give over and over again to a variety of causes can become overwhelming for both the fundraisers and those who donate.

Coming up with creative ways to ask for money was not an easy task. What was needed was a way to raise money while providing a product or a service that people would choose to purchase and the money would be donated to the Food Bank. The Food Bank once a year would sell barbecued hotdogs in front of the local grocery store. The store donated the wieners, buns and pop with the Food Bank providing the barbecue and the volunteers. Shoppers would purchase a hot dog and a drink for two dollars, which would go to the food bank. The customer receives lunch for a two-dollar donation. This is much more appealing to most people than simply asking them to donate two dollars for a cause.

Breakfast with Santa had a similar theme. The customer receives breakfast and entertainment for their children and the proceeds would go to the Food Bank. My idea was to find businesses that would be willing to donate the product, such as pancake mix, a case of sausages, butter, syrup etc. If all of the ingredients were donated and if it were possible to find a donated facility one hundred percent of the money raised would go to the Food Bank. Each restaurant in town offered to donate something, the grocery store donated several items. The Legion donated the kitchen and dinning facilities. Local music and singing students donated the entertainment and we had a magnificent volunteer Santa.

My restaurant experience came in handy with the cooking. There was no shortage of wonderful volunteers for serving and cleaning. We even had a volunteer to take pictures with Santa for an additional two-dollar donation. Little Buddies donated the film for the camera. Tickets were pre sold so we knew how many we were cooking for. We sold out each year. The families who were Food Bank clients received complementary tickets and were not charged for a picture with Santa. As tickets were pre sold no one knew who had paid or who may have received complementary tickets.

The introduction of turkey bucks and breakfast with Santa were opportunities for the community to be directly involved with the Food Bank. With turkey, bucks hanging in various locations around town people were thinking about Christmas and about giving. It is amazing what can happen when caring people share their ideas of how they would like to help.

Several larger communities and Cities run various programs at Christmas where a family or a group can adopt a family and provide Christmas dinner and gifts on a personal basis. This idea had been brought up before my time volunteering with the Food Bank. The Food Bank members had agreed no to allow individual sponsors for families.

The reasoning was that the families requesting Christmas hampers wanted to remain anonymous. Especially in a small community, privacy is essential. There was also a concern that a sponsored family may receive much more in a hamper than the Food Bank was able to provide for its clients.

My second year as hamper coordinator the subject of private sponsorship was brought up at a meeting in early fall. One of the long time members stated that this subject had been debated in the past and stated the reasons why it was dismissed. As Treasurer at the time I pointed out that with the current financial situation and the constant need for fundraising the Food Bank was realistically not in a financial position to turn down offers of any kind.

I suggested that it was possible to create a system by which a family could be sponsored without the identity of the family being compromised. It was possible that a potential sponsor could be given the particulars of the family, mother, father, boy eight, girl three and even ask the parents for gift suggestions for their children without the family being identified.

The family would apply for a hamper through the Food Bank the Food Bank would pass on the particulars to a willing sponsor. The sponsor would deliver the completed hamper to the Food Bank for pick up or delivery. This system would allow those who were willing to sponsor a family to feel personally involved in the giving. For every privately sponsored hamper there would be one, family the Food Bank would not have to find resources for.

This in turn would allow more funds for the hampers, which are not privately sponsored. If a sponsored family was fortunate, enough to receive a huge Christmas hamper with extra groceries and gifts what a wonderful Christmas it would be. For those who are not sponsored the Food Bank hampers would possible contain a few extra items, as there would be fewer hampers to fill.

My suggestion was that as a Food Bank we not only accept the offer to sponsor a family we actually have a campaign to encourage individuals and groups to sponsor a family. Those who choose to sponsor a family and personally shop for the children are likely to remember this family and the Food Bank throughout the year. Awareness is the best thing that could happen for this Food Bank.

We kicked off the sponsor a family campaign, which grew each year. There were businesses, church groups, baseball teams, elementary and high school classes and individuals all wanting to sponsor a family. If an individual or a group could not afford to sponsor and entire hamper including the groceries and gifts partial sponsorship was welcomed. If a sponsor was to supply only the gifts, or only the groceries, some chose to sponsor only the turkey. The Food Bank welcomed each and every offer as the gift that it was intended to be. Any item supplied by a sponsor was an item the Food Bank or Little Buddies would not have to supply. What a wonderful combination.

There were people who sponsored a family at Christmas who would approach me in August or September of the following year asking if they could have the same family again, or if I could let them know as soon as possible, so they could start shopping early. This was a community full of people who could not wait to give. One of the larger employers in town started collecting money each payday in about October from the workers to go towards the dozen or so hampers that they jointly sponsored. This magnificent tiny town was displaying its heart of gold.

Life truly is amazing. Life truly is what you make it. Make yours magnificent!

30

LOOK AT YOUR WORLD WITH BOTH EYES OPEN

Being known in town as the Food Bank lady meant often people would stop on the street or in the grocery store to give me a donation, ask questions or offer suggestions and advice. There were those who would offer editorial comments on their personal opinion of people who use a Food Bank. One comment or question, which was repeated often, was; why did I waste my time on people who just drink their welfare cheque because they know they don't have to budget for groceries, they can just go to the Food Bank. There were people who felt compelled to inform me that they knew for a fact that Food Bank clients just sell their free groceries so they can buy booze or drugs. Valerie had a man stop her one-day and accuse her of stealing from the Food Bank. This man informed Valerie that he watched her fill her jeep with groceries from the Food Bank and that he knew she did not need the food. What this man had witnessed was Valerie filling her jeep with Food Bank groceries to deliver to clients who were either too senior, too ill or had no means of transportation to pick their groceries up. Valerie did her best to explain the situation. This man was not interested in her explanation. He was sure he witnessed her stealing from the Food Bank.

Not being Food Bank clients these well-meaning individuals who were sharing their advice had no way of knowing that clients were provided with groceries only once a month. The mandate for this small Food Bank when I began volunteering was that we would try to provide one weeks worth of groceries. With the increased demand and diminishing resources, the actual groceries provided once a month would provide meals for about three days.

Three days supply of no name brand macaroni and cheese, brown beans, dry Oriental noodle soup and perhaps a can of fish if it were available would hardly be sufficient to feed any one for a full month if they chose to drink their welfare cheque and not budget for groceries. Clients were able to pick up bread items weekly as we shared bread with one of the City Mission.

For a family these items would be multiplied to match the number of family members. There were occasions when cookies or granola bars would be donated and would be given to families with children for school lunches. When resources permitted, the Food Bank would purchase milk and eggs to provide to families.

For a family of four no name brand canned meals for three days one jug of milk and a dozen eggs would hardly bring sufficient funds if a client were to sell his or her groceries to fund an alcohol or drug problem. If one of my clients had the talent to turn a profit on selling such items, I would certainly like to have this person utilize this talent and sell all of my no name brand macaroni. Perhaps we would be in the position to purchase Kraft dinner.

I cannot imagine the person who would be willing to purchase such items. If a person required food, he or she could simply go to the Food Bank and receive his or her own groceries free. If the need was not for food, what could possible motivate anyone to pay two or three dollars for a fifty-cent box of no name brand macaroni and cheese? The well-meaning citizens who believe that these situations are actually taking place are sadly mistaken.

There are Food Bank clients who may have alcohol or drug problems and there are a few individuals in the world that will take advantage of any charitable situation. I prefer to devote my time and energy to the many who truly appreciate the assistance and not the few who may abuse it.

As for parents who have substance abuse problems, which limit their employment abilities and who literally do drink their welfare cheques. I know the box of macaroni and cheese in their food hamper is going to feed their children.

I was one of those children! My father drank many a welfare check in a time when Food Banks did not exists. His children still needed to eat.

As a child I overheard many an adult comment, "she's got parents, what's the matter with them? They should be made to look after her." Well there was plenty wrong with my parents. They were responsible for looking after my siblings and me. They were also incapable for whatever reason to live up to their responsibility most of the time. I choose to look after all children whatever the reason may be that they are in need. A box of macaroni may not be much; it is better than no dinner at all.

I would like to share the circumstances of a few special individuals and families I had the privilege of sharing. I will never forget these truly remarkable people.

In six years of being at the Food Bank counter the dynamics of the clients, being served changed. The largest increase was assistance to seniors. The pain, shame and hurt in the eyes of new Food Bank clients multiplied when the client was a senior. A new application would be accompanied by several apologies and promises that they would not return unless it was absolutely necessary.

With the increase in home heating costs and many seniors requiring over the counter medication or prescriptions, which are not covered by a medical plan, those on a fixed incomes are left with the choice of heating their homes, purchasing medication or groceries. Many seniors wait until they are absolutely desperate before asking for help.

Several seniors assisted by our Food Bank were too ashamed to ask for help. A neighbour or the medical clinic often would inform us that there was a senior who was in need. As many of our volunteers were also senior's they would simply stop by the persons home for a visit.

One elderly woman living alone in a mobile home park was a cancer patient. Our Volunteer stopped in for a visit after receiving a call from the medical clinic. The only food items in the house were a small bag of rice and tea bags. This frail woman was insisting that she was just fine. The volunteer simply asked, "If I show up for a visit with a bag of groceries will you accept them?" The woman was in tears as she said yes.

There were several clients who where too ill, too ashamed or not physically able to pick groceries up. Our volunteers simply delivered to their homes. There were handicapped clients we delivered to in the winter. On two occasions, our volunteers found people living in homes in minus twenty-degree weather with no heat. Many homes had fuel tanks. A minimum delivery was $250.00 this simply was not doable for some people. One handicapped client who used a walker had no heat or hot water for the winter months. She had a fireplace in her mobile home. We did our best to find donated wood. This woman was physically not capable of picking up, loading and unloading firewood.

Valerie begged wood from the mill scrap and could often be seen with her jeep full of logs and odd chunks of trees.

One single mother with three elementary school children worked three part time jobs. She would ask for assistance only a few times a year. Christmas, back to school and on a few occasions when her children were ill and required medicine. The cost of children's Tylenol and cough syrup left very little in her already minimal grocery budget.

A family man in his mid thirties was on a disability pension. His wife passed away leaving him with three elementary school age children. His wife had always worked and his pension was added to her income. Physically unable to work he was grateful for the groceries he received.

Two single clients we assisted every week rather than once a month. Both were single men. One in his mid forties was mentally handicapped and was incapable of remembering which Monday or Wednesday he was permitted to come to the Food Bank. He usually asked for one or two items and a loaf of bread each week. The second man was in his sixties. This man had a life long drinking problem. There were times when he had been homeless. This man was in ill health and suffered from memory loss; he would receive one or two items each week. Although he struggled both mentally and physically, he was at the door first thing every Monday morning. The Food Bank had a pot of coffee on for our clients. My car trunk on Monday morning usually contained food items to be unloaded into the Food Bank. I had a regular assistant to carry items in from my car as he waited for the coffee to brew.

One large blended family with six children both parents were employed. The mother had Crones disease. This is a very debilitating illness. There were many times when she physically was incapable of going to work. There were several times when she would be hospitalized. The cost of housing, feeding and clothing six children even on two wages can be a struggle. It is almost impossible on one wage. The times when this mother was incapable of working, she was also in need of medication.

We often put aside a box of cereal, cookies, or crackers, which had been donated to add to this families groceries once a month. Providing school lunches on a regular basis for six children was a constant struggle for this family.

We assisted several families on a monthly basis as the primary wage earner had been diagnosed with cancer. One family a single working mother of three was recovering from the removal of both breasts. Two families; where the husband's in their late fifties were now cancer patients. These families had lived on one wage. The wives were now in a position to try to find employment in there late fifties. These women had not worked outside of the home. If work were available, it would be for minimum wage and often only part time.

One client's story I have saved for last. This magnificent woman and wonderful family I will always remember.

A small thin women walks down the roadside through town. She is walking slowly with her head down to protect herself from the cold October wind. Her steps are uneven giving the appearance that walking is difficult. She approaches the door and enters the Food Bank.

She is an aboriginal woman very soft spoken. It is difficult to determine her age, somewhere in her late thirties maybe early forties perhaps younger. She wears what looks like years of struggle on her face. Her difficulty in walking gives the appearance that she is staggering.

Without knowing her circumstances on first impression alcoholic, junkie, hooker all would fit the picture of the woman standing at the Food Bank counter. She is applying for assistance for herself and two elementary school age children.

Laura escorted this new client through the Food Bank explaining procedures and choosing appropriate food items for her family, they arrive at the bread freezer. Laura had already explained that the Food Bank was available to her family only once a month and although resources were limited that the Food Bank was privileged to share bread with several other charities which allows our clients to receive extra bread on their regular visits and allowed her to come to the Food Bank once a week to receive bread items.

The tension on her face and in her movements lessened. Gratitude and relief now show in her hollow eyes. In a shy meek voice she said, "thank you" to Laura. She now feels relieved and safe enough to share that her children had had no breakfast and nothing to take in their lunches this week. This was late afternoon on a Wednesday. One can only guess what dinner for the past week may have been.

As her story unfolded this meek little lady with the appearance of bad lifestyle choices was a new arrival in this town as she had relatives near by. She had moved her children to be closer to family she wanted them to get to know. It was important that her children meet their relatives as their mother (this woman) was on the top of the transplant list as she was dying from kidney failure.

This frail woman had walked across town in the October cold to obtain a few dinted cans of food and some stale bread and was now intending to walk what would be an hour at her pace to carry her groceries home.

We would deliver groceries for this family. Delivering groceries to this home it was obvious that this family had moved with little or no belongings. Food Bank volunteers managed to obtain donated furniture items. Christmas of this year volunteers donated a tree and ornaments for the family.

I received a phone call in early December from this mother. She was calling from the City hospital. She had been hospitalized and realized that the complementary tickets the Food Bank had given her family for breakfast with Santa were in her purse at the hospital.

Her daughter who was about six-years-old was so excited about breakfast with Santa she did not want her to miss it. She told me over the phone that she had made arrangements for someone to take her children and was asking if we would allow them to attend even though the tickets were in her purse.

Her children attended the breakfast and received a complementary picture with Santa. A hand written note arrived at the Food Bank a few weeks later. The note was a thank you for allowing her children to attend without the tickets. The note stated that her daughter was thrilled with seeing Santa. There was a paragraph saying how grateful she was and how wonderful it was that we had allowed her children to have their picture taken even though they did not have the two dollars. The last paragraph was an apology for forgetting the tickets in her purse as she was being rushed to the hospital in an emergency.

The next two years I would watch this magnificent mother with her son and daughter. This little girl was a super nurse to her mother. Both children would make there mother tea or help her in every way they could. I would see these young children walking in the snow to the grocery store to pick up a few items and struggle with their mother's bankcard to pay the bill.

I would often deliver milk or fresh fruit and vegetables to this family in between Food Bank deliveries.

Sadly, this loving, caring, wonderful mother would pass away with her name on the top of the transplant list. I will never understand how it is possible in a Country as rich as Canada that citizens who are too ill to care for themselves and their families are not given enough resources to simply feed themselves.

This loving caring mother struggled through her last two years of life with her physical illness. She struggled with the emotions of leaving two young children she adored behind. How is it possible that she was also left to struggle with feeding her children during this time?

These are only a few stories from one small town Food Bank. These stories and many more are repeated over and over and over again in every City and town in this great Country.

It is not always possible to know the story by simply looking at the cover. This amazing woman who I will never forget showed up in my world looking very much like a drunk, an addict or a hooker. I ask you all to dare to look at your world and each and every one in it with both eyes open.

31

I LOVE YOU DAVID

During the time that my mother was living in a house in this small town, David arrived in town. I had not seen or spoken to him in more than twenty years. My mother had relayed stories over the years of when he was in or out of jail. I arrived at my mother's house and there was David. My mother had not bothered to tell me that he was in town.

Stories of David's life, his drug habits, his criminal behaviour, details of times he stole from my mother were all I knew of my own brother. My mother had relayed stories of times in the last few years when David was ill. "I wonder if he has AIDS." Went through my mind on more than one occasion when the details of his illness were being relayed.

Seeing David sitting in my mother's kitchen was a shock. I said the usual high how are you? David answered with one or two words and then sat silently in front of the television. Knowing the total source of my information on David's life had come from my mother over the years and being fully aware that my mother despised David since his birth yet somehow I was also seeing David as being exactly who my mother said he was.

Thoughts of, what is he doing here? What does he want? Was he planning to steal from our mother? As I drove home this day pictures of David were playing in my head. David looked thin and ill his body was covered with tattoos, there were open sores on his hands and his face. This was a man who looked like the worst case junky slumped in a skid row door way. One again I was asking myself if David had AIDS?

A few week went by David was still in town. Other than, a hello David would usually sit in silence as I visited with mom. More than a month had gone by I asked mom how long David was planning to stay. She answered that he was sick and she did not know how long he was staying. Looking at David, my thoughts were that he was dying. I was telling myself that it was mid summer David would likely be dead by Christmas.

213

The words just came out of my mouth. I asked, "What is wrong with him? Does he have AIDS?" My mother answered, "He doesn't have AIDS he only has HIV". Clearly, by looking at David, he had full blown AIDS. My mother has a limited understanding of most issues including this one. In a conversation months later the topic was AIDS. My mother commented to me that you could only get AIDS if you already have HIV and then you sleep with someone who has AIDS. This was her attempt to explain to me that David did not have AIDS.

Two or three months passed. I was talking to mom on the telephone. It had been a week or so since I had been to her house. At some point in the conversation, she commented about David being in the hospital. I asked, "When did David go into the hospital?" She answered, "Oh he's been there for about a week, I don't know if he will be coming back here." My assumption was that David was hospitalized due to his AIDS and that he was dying.

Conversations with my mother can often be disjointed and difficult to follow. Somewhere in this conversation, my mother mentioned the police taking David to the hospital. I asked, "why did the police take him to the hospital?" My mother proceeded to tell the story of David being driven to the hospital by the police after he had attempted suicide. David was in the psyche ward not the hospital ward. Her story continued with, "the people from the AIDS Society are trying to find him a place to stay in the City." AIDS Hospice was the thought in my head. Several weeks had passed with David in the City. My mother was not sure if he was still in the hospital or if he was with the AIDS people as she called them. I stopped in to visit my mother and there was David sitting at the kitchen table.

He did not look well although he looked much better than before he left. On this visit, David actually said hello and sat at the table for a while. He told me that he had a councillor that he had been seeing with the AIDS Society and that he was feeling much better. This five-minute conversation was the most we had spoken to each other in twenty plus years.

David met with his councillor once or twice a week in the City over the next month or so. Arriving at moms house one afternoon, David was there alone. Mom had gone to the City with our younger sister for a medical appointment. I was about to leave when David said he wanted to talk to me. David had been feeling and looking much better for some time now. On this day, I was not sure if he was nervous, agitated or worried, something was different with his demeanour and his body language.

I was not prepared for what came next. David was pacing back and forth near the kitchen table, looking at the floor, he finally said, "I just need to know why you hate me." I had never felt hate for David not sure what to say I answered his question with a question, "what makes you think I hate you?" The answer was so predictable it should have been obvious to me. David answered, "Mom told me you hate me."

The voice in my head said, "of course she did; hate was a word she used on a daily basis. My heart sunk, my stomach was hard as a rock; the emotions from my childhood, hiding listening to David scream while he was being hit with a belt or what ever else was handy were flooding my very soul. David was standing in front of me in a grown mans body yet he was still that trembling little boy; for the first time in his life he was able to ask why? Why did I and everyone in his life hate him?

Again, I answered his question with a question. "How could I hate you? I don't even know you." We had not had more than a five-minute conversation in more than twenty years; we knew nothing about each other's lives. David was telling me that his councillor was the one who had encouraged him to ask me why I hated him. He continued to tell me that it had taken him more than a week of not sleeping and thinking about it to gather up the courage to talk to me.

As we talked, David admitted that he did have AIDS. When he first arrived in town looking like he was dying, it was because he was dying. His blood count was at a point that the doctors told him he might only live a few more months. For reasons only known to David, he had a need to spend his last few months with the mother who had neglected and abused him since birth.

I asked David what had changed. He obviously still had AIDS, yet he seemed to be much stronger both physically and emotionally. David explained that he had arrived in town dying from AIDS and using drugs. He had been a junkie since he was twelve-years-old. The AIDS cocktail he was taking was not working as his body was contaminated with other drugs.

It took being close to death for David to stop using heroine. With out the heroine in his system the other medications appeared to be working. The explanation of his blood count I did not fully understand. What was clear was that currently he was in some sort of remission.

David admitted his life of drug use had resulted in most of his teenage and adult life being spent in and out of jail. When mom was undergoing surgery in intensive care in Vancouver, David stole her chequebook, forged cheques and cleaned out her bank account. As he relayed these stories to me, he wanted me to know that he was sorry and that he would never intentionally do anything to hurt mom when he was not stoned.

David was assuring me that he could never do drugs again or he would die. As we parted on this day, I hugged David and told him that I loved him.

David continued his visits with this counsellor. We now shared regular conversations on my visits to moms house. David had mentioned on several occasions that he was available if I needed a hand with the kennel or at the Food Bank. It would give him something to do.

As our relationship grew David would spend time on the mountain mending fences or doing light chores. He tired easily but what a difference it made in his life. The phone rang one morning; there was a pick up truckload of donated groceries unexpectedly being dropped off for the Food Bank. Several phone calls later it was looking as though I would be unloading the truck without any help.

I called David and asked if his offer to help at the Food Bank was still good. We met at the Food Bank, unloaded the truck and stocked the shelves together. David was exhausted as he left he was actually smiling saying call me anytime you need a hand.

This was the beginning of David's volunteer career. Mending the odd fence and assisting at the Food Bank gave David a sense of purpose and the opportunity to prove to himself that he was not worthless.

I was in awe of the absolute genuine compassion David showed to each client. There was David opening doors for seniors, carrying groceries for clients who had no idea that David was as or possibly more disabled than some of them. There were days when David would have to leave early out of shear exhaustion.

David was still living with mom. He received a disability cheque each month, which he used to pay her for room and board. The first Christmas after David began volunteering for the Food Bank, he was donating toys for hampers. David asked what he should buy for Laura's son who was two or three at the time. He commented that he wanted to buy him something special. "It's only money, I have no need for money these days," was the comment he made as we discussed appropriate gifts.

It was absolutely amazing to see so much love, caring and compassion pouring from this man who had literally lived the childhood from hell and an adult life with circumstances that could have left him angry, cold, heartless or unable to feel anything at all.

Watching this transformation, remembering that little blond hair boy with the perpetually sad eyes I found myself asking how was it possible for anyone to look at the boy or the man and hate what they see. Yet this magnificent person, my little brother had lived forty plus years in his world where he believed he was not only worthless but hated.

David was still terminally ill. He had AIDS and nothing was going to change that. Having David back in my life even for a short time was a wonderful gift. It is not possible for me to erase the memories of David's tortured childhood from my mind. It is possible for me to replay the tapes in my head of David smiling as he opened doors and carried groceries for others. I will always remember David as the loving, caring and compassionate man that he is. There is no circumstance in this world, which cannot be overcome with a little love. I love you David.

32

B.C. is BURNING

It was spring of 2003 I had lived on this mountain with Stefon for five years and was in my fourth year as President of the Food Bank. This was an unusually dry spring. Our water supply was from a creek, which ran down the mountain. This creek flowed year round with a good supply of water. The previous year we had a month or so in late summer when we had no water. This year the creek was dry in early May. Stefon had been hauling water from the river twice a week for the animals and to fill the tank in the motor home.

Due to the water situation and the need to pump water from the river on a regular basis Stefon stayed home for the better part of the spring. He was concerned that it would be too difficult for me to haul water if he were away for a week or two at a time.

It was late July Laura and her son; my daughter in-law, my youngest grandson and Richard had been visiting for a week or so. Daniel was working in the City and was not able to join us. The kids and the grandkids were camping at the lake, which was about a twenty-minute drive from our mountain home.

I received a phone call from the hotel. It had been a few years since I had been employed with them. I did help occasionally if they were short a cook. This call was from the restaurant owner. The neighbouring town had been battling a forest fire for a few days. The fire crew wanted to set up camp in the hotel. This call was to ask if I would be willing to come in the morning and cook for the fire crew, as the hotel was not prepared for such a large volume of customers.

The phone rang it was early morning. I answered expected it to be the hotel. A neighbour who was part of the local search and rescue was informing me that the town was on a one-hour evacuation alert. The fire had spread and was heading our way.

Stefon and I drove to the lake, woke up the kids, packed up the camping gear and headed back home. I called the information number I had been given for an update as soon as we arrived home and was told the alert was over and we were to

218

evacuate immediately. The kids and grandkids packed into Richard's car and headed for the coast. Stefon was loading the animals into the back of the pickup, which had a canopy. Richard had agreed to drive the pickup, I would drive the car with dogs loaded in the back seat and Stefon would follow with Cindy and the other yard dogs who were to big to ride with the smaller dogs.

The kids had taken the pick up to the lake with the camping gear. The gas gauge was almost on empty when they returned. Stefon and I both needed to fill our cars if we were to leave town. I headed into town with my car intending to fill it with gas and bring back jerry cans full of fuel for the other vehicles.

This allowed Richard and Stefon to load the animals into the truck while I went to town for fuel. Arriving in town, I could not believe my eyes. The main street in town was lined up with vehicles from the small gas station on one end of town to the grocery store at the other end.

Being on the mountain were we did not have hydro there was no way of knowing that the power had been out in town. The power poles on the highway had been burnt and no longer existed. This town had three gas stations; the two larger stations were closed. The little independent station at the end of town was operating with the help of a generator. The owner of this station had purchased the generator for emergencies from Stefon a year or so before the fire.

Waiting in this long line in 100+ degree heat the young man who worked at the gas station was making his way down the row of cars speaking to each driver. He arrived at my window to say, "we are almost out of gas; each vehicle can have twenty dollars worth until we are out." Twenty dollars worth of fuel would be a drop in the pick up and I required fuel for two other vehicles.

Arriving at the pump I receiving twenty dollars worth in my tank, with nothing in the jerry cans. I entered the station to pay and realized that I had no cash. My Interact card would not work without power. The station owner's wife who knew me well was attempting to process interact transaction with the system hooked to the generator. It was a hit and miss situation. Some cards processed others did not. Mine was one that would not work. The owner simply wrote my name on a piece of paper with a hundred or so other names and said pay me later.

Driving back to the mountain, my head was racing with thoughts of where I would go and a million other things. Talking to myself asking, "who would have thought that in an emergency, when you are trying to run from a forest fire the most important item you need would be gasoline?"

Each vehicle in the long line in front and behind me absolutely required gasoline. Had any of them had half a tank they would not be sitting in line waiting for twenty dollars worth of fuel when their families were at risk.

I am not sure what any of us would have done had one independent gas station owner not had the foresight to purchase a back up generator and the will to stay behind and fill his neighbours tanks with gas on credit when he had a family which needed to evacuate.

I am grateful that he chose to stay. The station owner and his wife were honoured as citizens of the year when the crises had passed.

Arriving home with gas in my tank and no fuel for the truck or Stefon's vehicle we had no choice but to hit the road and hope to make it to the next town for fuel. The biggest question was where were we going with a truck and a car full of dogs.

Remembering a neighbour down the road from me had a friend she often spoke about who raised dogs in another small town. Calling this neighbour, fortunately although she was in the middle of evacuating horses she answered her phone. Asking her for her friend's name and phone number stating I was hoping to call her and see if she had temporary space for my kennel.

I called the number, explained to the lady on the phone that I was her friend's neighbour, and was looking for an emergency place for my dogs to stay. She said she would make space. Asking her where she lived, she answered in Chase BC. I had no idea where Chase BC was. She said for me to head towards Kamloops and follow the signs.

The truck was loaded I would follow Richard. Stefon was to load his car and leave shortly after we were gone. Giving Stefon the phone number of where we were heading, I said we would be in Chase.

With the fire burning across the highway, there was only one way out of town. The RCMP had the roads blocked and was directing traffic to head north. Kamloops was directly south. Richard and I joined the slow moving procession of vehicles heading north. The next town was about twenty minutes away; the plan was that we would head to the first gas station. I hoped that the fuel in the truck would be sufficient. At about the ¾ mark to the next town there was an RCMP vehicle stopping traffic.

Vehicles were turning left as directed. The officer stated that the next town had no power and no gas stations open. His instructions were that I follow this back road and the signs will eventually lead to Kamloops. Ten minutes down this road the traffic stopped, there was a line up miles long and in 100+ degree heat many people were standing outside of their vehicles waiting. Asking the people waiting in front of me what was going on. There was a small tourist store down the road with a gas pump. This line up was for gas. Ten minutes of waiting in line with no shade in site, if this line did not move quickly I would have a truck-load and a back seat full of animals that would die from heat exhaustion.

Waiting outside of the vehicle, I stopped a motorcycle that was travelling in the opposite direction to ask if the gas station at the end of this line had any fuel left. The man answered that they were still pumping gas. He also said that if any-one had enough fuel to make it another mile or so there was another gas station on the main road.

Richard was driving on fumes; we decided that we would try to make it to the next station as if we stayed here much longer our animals may not survive. Before turning around we passed on the message to the vehicles beside us that there was another station down the road.

The vehicle directly behind me was an Aero Star van; the windows were rolled up tight as they did have air conditioning. The driver rolled down the window so I could pass on the message. There were five or six people crammed into this vehicle with at least two full size lamas in the back. The driver stated that he did not have enough fuel to go any further. Richard and I made it to the next station and were able to fill both vehicles.

Six or seven hours had now passed since we loaded the animals and headed north. Finally, we arrived in Kamloops. Neither Richard nor I had cell phones at this time. We pulled over at the first phone booth with a shaded area to park the vehicles. After several attempts to call the number in Chase, I was getting voice mail. It was likely the woman I was calling was in her kennel making room for my arrival.

We would be able to find someone to direct me to Chase, however I did not have an address to this kennel. My phone book was in my purse. As we were waiting to make another call hoping for someone to pick up the phone I remem-bered that in my phone book was a number to the Treasurer of a dog-breeding group that I had met with on a few occasions.

If the Chase kennel was a member of this group, the Treasurer should have an address. Calling the number a woman answered the phone. Not sure if she would remember me I explained that we had met at a couple of meetings. I asked if she had an address for the Chase kennel or if she knew the kennel name so I could look it up in the phone book. She answered that the kennel owners had only ever attended one meeting and that the only information she had was a phone num-ber.

Explaining the short version of the situation, I asked her if she was able to give me directions from Kamloops to Chase. We would drive to Chase and wait for someone to answer the phone. The woman on the phone said, "if you don't know were you are going why don't you come here?" "Where is here?" I asked. Kelowna was the answer.

I knew where Kelowna was and had driven there several times. We pulled into the agreed meeting place in Kelowna and followed this kennel owner to her home. It was now 11 p.m. Richard and I left the mountain before noon. The kennel owner Debbie and her husband Ron helped us to unload the animals, feed and water everyone in the dark.

As we were unloading Debbie was telling us that after receiving the phone call from me she received a phone call from another kennel in a small town which was also being evacuated due to a forest fire. The second kennel owner was on her way and would likely arrive after midnight.

In 2003 in BC forest fires affected several small towns and Cities. The entire Province at one point was under a state of emergency.

This wonderful couple who took my animals and me in on a moments notice would take in more than 250 dogs from several different evacuated kennels over the next two weeks that I stayed with them. We found a company in Kelowna who rented temporary portable fencing.

This company erected as many new spaces as were required as the numbers grew. As the number of towns on the evacuation list grew and this Kelowna kennel grew; people were absolutely amazing. The second or third day after my arrival as we were feeding, watering and pooper scooping for constant new arrivals plus this kennels own animals the TV news cameras arrived. The six o'clock news that night there I was being interviewed by a reporter wearing borrowed clothes, dog poop on my T-shirt, no make up, bags under my eyes, looking like I had just been through a disaster. Which is exactly what had just happened.

Once the story aired about this wonderful couple and the number of animals they had taken in there was a steady stream of vehicles in the driveway with people volunteering their time to clean pens or walk dogs. There was also a steady stream of vehicles dropping off donated dog food and milk bones. Several people called to ask what brand of dog food the animals were eating, as they knew the animals were under stress and they wanted them to have the food they were used to eating. What an amazing wonderful caring world we live in!

In the ten days that had gone by since my arrival, some kennels were able to return home with their animals others were still arriving. My time was spent caring for animals, watching the news every night and calling the forestry numbers constantly to update the situation in my hometown to know when the evacuation order may be lifted.

The fire update stories both by telephone and on the news were full of contradictions. Watching the late news only a few days after my arrival Debbie, Ron and I watched in horror as the reporter stated that the entire town of Barriere BC had been levelled. The reporter was showing satellite images and stating that there was nothing left of my town.

Three or four days had now gone by with me having no contact with Stefon since leaving town. I had left messages with the Chase kennel as to where I could be located if Stefon called. Laura and Daniel were in constant contact by telephone. Stefon had their numbers and Jason's number where he could leave a message. No one had heard from him since the day we left. Before we left the town, each citizen had stopped to register with the Red Cross emergency centre giving details as to where they were heading and recording that they had in fact left town. The Red Cross had no record of Stefon registering that he had left town.

It felt as though my heart had stopped as I watched the TV news reports that my town had been completely devoured by fire. My thoughts were of Stefon there was the possibility that Stefon had not left town.

Three more agonizing days would go by before I received a call from Stefon. He had not left town. The reason he had not contacted anyone was there was no phone service anywhere in town. He knew if he left town he would not be allowed to return as the roads were blocked, Stefon had stayed on his mountain, which thankfully was not touched by the fire. There was one neighbour who had no transportation for himself or his animals who also stayed and two old timers as everyone called them who refused to leave. Stefon and the two old timers were sure that if the worst happened they knew the back logging roads well enough to exit the area safely.

Several families on this mountain road evacuated on a moments notice having no choice but to leave farm animals and some large pets behind. Given the choice of leaving with your children and your neighbour in the car or your Sainte Bernard, a handful of chickens or pigs there was no other option for some but to leave animals behind.

Stefon and the two old timers checked each property. Anyone who had livestock or animals of any kind left behind these three men would stop in every day to feed and water each and every one. It would be ten days or more before the SPCA and a crew of volunteers would arrive to take over this job.

With no phone service the entire town evacuated, the only source of information on fire damage and casualties was the nightly news or the forestry emergency number. In the two weeks before my return, the information would be contradicted several times. During one phone call, before connected with Stefon the person on the forestry emergency line confirmed to me that the mountain road we lived on, which was the only way off our mountain was in fact burning. The person on the other end of the phone told me that the fire fighters were working on this road just as you enter the town.

Finally, contact with Stefon would confirm that our mountain had not burned. My sister who had evacuated to a hotel in the City with my mother and David was told and had it confirmed on two occasions that her acreage property had been completely destroyed and that there was nothing left. After talking to Stefon, he was able to make his way to her property and called me to report that the property had burnt to the back fence line. The house and the barn were still standing.

The news story, which I understand was broadcast throughout North America stating that the entire town had been destroyed, was also an error. The satellite image did make it appear as though two fires had merged directly over the town. The reality was more than seventy homes; several businesses, the industrial park and the sawmill were all gone.

About a week had gone by; Debbie and I were watching the late night news cast. Bill Good was reporting on disaster relief efforts. They were showing a picture of a highway truck being loaded with clothes, toys, etc. destined for the Barrier Food Bank. As the President of the Food Bank, I knew that our small facility was not able to take a fully loaded Semi full of anything no matter how much it may be needed.

Our little food bank was housed in what used to be a small two-room rural dentist office. Calling the television station to explain the situation, arrangements were made for any donated items to be delivered to Kamloops. The Co-ordinator for the Kamloops Food Bank was able to secure the use of a donated empty store space for temporary storage for items destined for Barriere. The TV news and several radio stations broadcast a message to the Barriere Food Bank volunteers to contact me at the Keolwna number. Contact with the regular volunteers was essential to begin planning to assist the town once the evacuation order was lifted. There was no way of knowing where each volunteer may be. The media was wonderful in helping us to connect.

I was now dealing with the daily feeding and caring of the evacuated animals while attempting to coordinate Food Bank volunteers and the arrival of donations by telephone from Kelowna. Connecting with the Kamloops Food Bank provided a temporary solution for donated items. Once people were permitted to return to town, there was a need for a place to distribute these items and for transportation of the goods from Kamloops to Barriere without cost to the Food Bank.

The picture of this semi trailer being loaded with item destined for our Food Bank was playing in my head. What would be required to temporarily store and distribute these items? The answer came to me. How about a semi trailer for temporary storage? I picked up the phone going through the yellow pages for transport companies. Going down the list one at a time I simply called and asked if anyone had an available trailer they would be willing to donate for temporary use by the Barrier Food Bank. There was sufficient room in the Food Bank parking lot for a trailer to be dropped off.

It did not take long to find a Company that said yes. Arrangements were made for a trailer to be dropped off in the parking lot as soon as the evacuation order was lifted. This Company would actually loan the Food Bank the use of two trailers one with refrigeration, which we used for storage and distribution for the remainder of the summer and into the fall. These temporary storage facilities in the Food Bank parking lot would be transformed into a distribution centre for the remainder of the summer.

Finally, ten days or more after being evacuated the order was lifted and residents of Barriere were allowed to return. The town would remain on a one-hour evacuation alert. There was a need to return to town to coordinate Food Bank relief efforts there was also a need for me to remain in Kelowna to assist in the care of my animals. With the town, being on one hour alert it was advised not to return animals or livestock unless you were sure you would be able to evacuate again on a moments notice.

The stress of the first evacuation and being housed with several other animals in a strange facility was already taking a toll on my dogs. Transporting them home and repeating this ordeal would be too much stress for the animals and me. Leaving Debbie to cope with my dogs without my help on top of the others she was caring for was not reasonable. The decision was made that I would remain until the weekend. Perhaps by then the one hour alert would be over.

I would return home without my dogs on Friday to check out the situation and would return with Stefon on Saturday to transport the animal's home. This would allow me to be in Barriere for the Monday to assist with Food Bank issues.

The few days remaining in Kelowna I was in constant contact by telephone with the Food Bank volunteers who were now in Barriere. More than ten days, no electricity, 100+ degree temperatures meant residents returning home were instructed by the health department to seal their refrigerators and deep freezers with duct tape or whatever they had and take the entire fridge or freezer out to the curb for pick up. Every household would have their refrigerators and freezers carted off to the dump.

For the Food bank this meant the loss of six deep freezers many full of bread items. There were no stores or businesses operating. It would take a week or so for the only grocery store to be cleaned out restocked and approved by the health department to reopen.

The Salvation Army had set up in town and was providing meals for citizens. Electricity was provided to the town by temporary generator systems. People were being asked to limit the use of electricity including not using electric stoves.

During the last, few days spent in Kelowna the Food Bank Treasurer and other regular volunteers were busily cleaning and restoring the Food Bank to a reasonable state. The Red Cross had arrived in town. The Red Cross and the Food Bank Treasurer had co-ordinated a food distribution program to take place on the following Monday. The Red Cross provided the Food Bank with groceries and boxes to package and distribute to each family returning to town. The groceries were meant to replace some of the items each household lost with their refrigerators and freezers.

My plan was to bring my dog's home Saturday and be there to distribute groceries with the Red Cross on the Monday.

Driving home on Friday afternoon I passed through several areas of BC, which showed signs of being charred by fire. Including part of Kamloops, expecting to see scorched trees, black mountains and missing power poles along the highway-entering town the image in my mind of what was to be expected would pale in comparison to the actual sites as I arrived.

The trees were black or completely gone. A friend's farm, which bordered the highway, was no longer there. The entire trailer park where I purchased a mobile home for Laura was gone, the antique store and a small restaurant were gone. The Mill, which was a massive presence on the highway, was now a small pile of twisted metal. The industrial park contained a few burnt out shells and several individual homes many belonging to friends of mine were completely gone. It felt as though I was driving through the TV news scene of a devastated war zone.

The fair grounds at then end of town were now the fire coordination centres. Stopping in at the office to inquire as to when the one-hour alert may be lifted. The answer was that the town was expected to be on alert for some time. There was no way of predicting the situation until the fire was out or at least considered under control.

My heart knew that people were counting on me. The Food Bank had to be my number one priority. Knowing the work involved in carrying for so many animals, asking Debbie to care for mine without my help was not an option. The only option was that I bring my animals home and hope for the best. I hope that the evacuation alert would be lifted soon.

Stefon had been hauling water from the River and preparing for the animals return. The plan was that we would drive to Kelowna later this evening and return early in the morning with the animals. This would leave all day Sunday for me to coordinate with the Food Bank volunteers and do what I could to fit into the distribution program, which was to begin Monday morning.

Stefon and I were in the truck about a half an hour away from the Kelowna kennel. As we were driving, a news bulletin came on the radio. The announcer was saying that Barriere was once again being evacuated. Stefon was concerned that if we did not return immediately we may not be allowed in to collect Cindy and the other yard dogs.

We were almost in Kelowna we arrived at the kennel to explain to Debbie and Ron that we were once again being evacuated. Debbie suggested that we head back right away to see if we would be allowed to collect Cindy and the other animals. Debbie offered to keep my dogs. I knew this was an enormous hardship adding to the he mounting workload. We agreed that Debbie would care for my dogs until the following weekend. This would allow us to return for the other animals if permitted and perhaps by next weekend, the people would be back and the one-hour alert would finally be over.

We would be evacuated three times and the one-hour alert would not be lifted until late September. Stefon and I returned to Barriere. The entire town had not had to evacuate, only some of the areas directly threatened by the fire.

Monday morning arrived and the town was able to collect their food boxes provided by the Red Cross with the help of the Food Bank. As the distribution was winding down about 3p.m., we were again notified that we were to evacuate. This time the town centre was okay to stay it was our mountain that was being evacuated. Rushing home to load Cindy and the other yard dogs into my vehicle I was able to stay in the town with a friend who had a large fenced yard for the animals.

It would be a week or more before we were permitted to return to the mountain. Before the weekend arrived, I received a phone call from Debbie she was calling to tell me that her kennel had been evacuated on a moments notice with the flames in site. Kelowna was now on fire! Fire fighters helped her to evacuate the huge amount of animals she was caring for plus her own and had set sprinklers on the kennel roof in hopes of buying some time and saving the building.

Debbie and Ron were now in the position I had been in two weeks earlier trying to find a place to go with not only their animals but also hundreds of animals belonging to other people.

Decisions had to be made with no time for planning or organization. Every kennel in the province which, was not under evacuation, was now taking in someone's animals. Volunteers simply loaded animals in their cars and headed to wherever there was an available space to deliver their cargo. These strangers made these trips at their own expense on a moments notice with no idea who it was they were helping. I thank each and every one for their kindness and their help.

Debbie had to instantaneously make decisions on which animals to send where, some how she managed to keep track of every single animal. Several of the dogs had litters of pups with them when they were evacuated from their home kennels. Finding instant places for dogs, which could be housed in groups under these circumstances was difficult enough. Mothers with a litter of pups had to be housed separately. The decision was made to take any pups, which looked old enough to be weaned off of the mother, record the owner and send the pups to a broker on the coast who would be able to sell the pups and return the money to the correct owner.

The pups who looked too young would be placed with who ever they could find who was willing to temporarily care for a mother and a litter of pups. My dogs were cared for from Langley to Quesnel BC by various kennel owners. There were several moms with pups when I evacuated to Kelowna. My kennel was small. Moms are only bred once a year. This was August; the time of year when I had the most litters to sell. Some of my moms normally had pups in the fall. The money from the summer puppy sales was meant to carry me through until the fall sales and the fall money would have to last again until late spring or summer.

It was not a large income it was enough and my kennel provided me with the freedom to work for the Food Bank which I loved, however the Food Bank job was 100% volunteer with an salary of $0.

All of my pups were thought to be old enough to leave their mothers. It is difficult to tell if a puppy is three week old of five weeks old when you are not familiar with the mother or the breed. All of my pups were sent to the broker on the coast. All of my pups would eventually die, as they were too young and likely too stressed to survive.

I had now lost my entire income for half the year. There was nothing I could do, except to say thank you to Debbie and Ron and everyone else who did their best to make instant decisions for my animals, trying to help me while there were going through their own crises.

My dogs would finally return home by mid September. Most were skinny and stressed. These animals were used to being cared for by Stefon or me. They had been loaded into a hot vehicle not once but twice in a two-week period. Crammed into housing with animals they were not familiar with in more than one location. Although the kennels, which took them in cared for them as well as could be expected in over crowded conditions, many small dogs when the are stressed either don't eat or if they are shy they may be intimidated by having to share a pen and food with animals that are more aggressive. My dogs had not seen me for weeks, which also added to their stress.

The mothers who would have been bred for the fall were evacuated over the time period that they would have been bred. I had no idea whose animals or even what breed of dog my females had been housed with. Some mothers may not have cycled due to stress. Anyone who was bred I would have no idea who or what the father may be. Looking at the condition of most of my mothers I knew anyone who was not bred would not be able to be bred before spring.

I had one Bichon mom who had two pups in late November. They looked like Bichon pups; there was no way to determine what other breed may be involved. I sold them as Bichon cross pups. My entire income for the year was $400.00.

I had contemplated having to sell my animals and close my kennel before win ter would arrive. Stefon was the optimist; he would tell me not to give up. This was my lively hood we would find a way to recoup. Doing the math things just did not add up. Sefon had not gone to work since early spring due to the water and then the fire situation. Until the one-hour alert was lifted leaving me alone to haul water and possibly deal with having to evacuate on my own with no help was not something Stefon was prepared to do.

The dog food bill and heating bills alone would add up to $2000.00 per month from October to March or April depending on the weather. Expenses of $2000,00 per month which, did not include heat, food or gasoline for the vehicles for Stefon and myself and an income of $0 meant if we survived the winter financially my kennel would be thousands of dollars in debt by spring.

If it were possible for all of my mothers to have a litter in the spring, which realistically would not happen there would not be enough income to pay off the winter debt. Even if the debt were paid there would be no income left to support the kennel or myself trough the next year. Being able to recoup my losses and support, myself on my kennel income was not realistic. Any real recovery would take years.

With many businesses burnt and the mill gone the prospects of finding employment at the hotel or anywhere in town was slim to none. The few remaining businesses were trying to survive in a town with the major employer gone, many families were unemployed or in the process of moving away for work. Others were recouping from a minimum of two weeks lost wages and evacuation expenses on top of loosing their fridges, groceries and freezers, which many families had expected to eat out of for the coming winter. Many families had returned to dried up or burned out gardens, which would have stocked their freezers for the winters. This was not a wealthy town before the fire. In the short term, many families including my own were facing desperate financial situations.

In between three evacuations, my animals being cared for across the province and personal concern over financial survival was the need to focus on the immediate situation. The Salvation Army had been feeding the town for a week or so. With no power, no grocery store and many families with literally no money the focus had to be taking care of each other.

I met with the Salvation Army representatives to discuss a plan for immediately after their meal program would end. They would remain in town and provide meals until there was sufficient power to allow residents to use their stoves and until the grocery store was able to reopen.

The concern was for the many residents who would literally not have the funds in the short term to buy groceries. Many families would not have a paycheque for some time. Families eligible for unemployment benefits would have six weeks or more after applying before receiving any funds. Those who were self employed including myself would not be entitled to unemployment or Social Assistance. Many small family businesses, which were totally destroyed, were left with no income. Some were insured many were not. Several families who lost their homes were also not insured.

The Salvation Army representative proposed that when they pulled their meal program out of town the Food Bank would provide basic groceries for families in need. Pasta, canned items etc. It was anticipated that the power would be restored and the grocery store able to open in about a week.

This was a very logical plan, however the Food Bank existing stock was nowhere near enough to supply the amount of food we anticipated would be required. The Kamloops Food Bank had been storing donated items for a week or so.

The Barrier Food Bank would be able to deal with the volume of food required with the assistance of the two donated storage trailers using the parking lot for distribution. I contacted the Co-ordinator for the Kamloops Food Bank to discuss arrangements to transport the donated items.

Most of the donated items were clothing and household goods. There were some food items, however not enough for distribution to begin in a week's time. The Salvation Army agreed to set up a temporary location in Barriere to deal with clothing and household items. This would free up the Kamloops storage space for food items only.

The Kamloops Co-ordinator suggested that I make an immediate appeal on television and radio for the food items required macaroni and cheese, pastas, rice, beans, canned meat and fish etc., food items which, can provide several meals and could be easily stored. My appeal was on every television newscast, several local radio stations and nation wide on "CBC TV" and radio. Kamloops called to say that a truckload of donated groceries had arrived.

On Thursday, morning two Food Bank volunteers and I met with the Kamloops Food Bank Co-ordinator at the storage facility. The donations had arrived with the help of several other Food Banks and a central Food Bank distribution centre on the coast. The Barriere Food Bank received a truckload containing Cadbury peanut butter Easter eggs, several pallets of granola bars and a few pallets of mixed canned goods. The Co-ordinator explained that this was all that had arrived. We were grateful for whatever was available, however it was now almost noon on Thursday. There were families expected to be able to pick up groceries on Monday morning and all that was available were peanut butter Easter eggs!

The Food Bank Treasurer was one of the volunteers with me in Kamloops. She had been the one who coordinated the distribution of the Red Cross groceries while I was in Kelowna. The Red Cross had not yet set up an office in Barriere as they were looking for a temporary space they did however have an office in Kamloops. We decided as we were already in Kamloops we would stop in and share our dilemma.

We arrived in the middle of a Red Cross meeting. The emergency co-ordinators were meeting to discuss the need for assistance through out the Province including Barriere. Although we were not expected, we were welcomed to join the meeting.

There are no words to describe the workings of this magnificent organization that we were privileged to share a small part in. Most of the Red Cross workers we would work with over the next few months were volunteers as we were.

Many were from other towns and Cities, some from out of Province or from the US travelling at their own expense volunteering their time to help complete strangers. As we joined the meeting, it was explained that they had been discussing the relief program for Barriere.

The Red Cross had put out television and radio appeals for donations for all BC fire victims including Barriere. It was explained to us that the donated funds raised for Barriere would be used for the programs being discussed.

The Red Cross Co-ordinator explained that their primary concern was to set up an office in Barriere before the end of the month. It was expected that many families would be unable to pay their rent or mortgage payments for September 1st.

I was given the opportunity to explain the Food Bank situation and that the Salvation Army kitchen would be closing as of Monday. Families would need to pick up groceries, that the Food Bank did not have.

Although we arrived at the Red Cross office unexpectedly on a Thursday afternoon the Food Bank had the groceries required delivered early enough to be packaged and distributed by volunteers Monday morning.

We left this meeting with a program in place where the Red Cross agreed that the Barriere Food Bank would order the required grocery items through the local grocery store paid for by the Red Cross. The Food Bank would package and distribute the dry grocery items. The Red Cross would set up an office in Barriere and would take applications to assist families with their up coming rent and mortgage payments. Those families who qualified for Red Cross assistance would be sent to the Food Bank for groceries with the Red Cross providing grocery vouchers for vegetables, milk, meat, etc. which the Food Bank was not able to supply.

This arrangement allowed families sufficient groceries to survive the short term, and allowed the only grocery store in town to survive the temporary economic situation. Over the next six months, the Red Cross would purchase and our little Food Bank would distribute over half a million dollars worth of groceries. This allowed the Food Bank to utilize the many wonderful cash donations from carrying citizens across the country to cover future expenses once the Red Cross assistance was complete.

The Red Cross was also able to provide each small business owner with $500.00 worth of what ever was most necessary. Little Buddies received Red Cross vouchers for dog food and heating fuel. I thank each and every one who donated to the Red Cross through this fire season. I want you all to know what an amazing gift dog food and fuel can be at just the right time.

For all those who donate their time and resources to the Red Cross I thank you. The Red Cross was there for all who needed assistance. No red tape, no hoops to jump through, they simply saw an immediate need and filled it; where it was needed, when it was needed for as long as it was needed. What an absolutely wonderful, amazing world we live in!!

The Food Bank had become a full time job. Food was distributed three days a week with the other days used to unload groceries and pack food hampers. The pay was still zero. There was no shortage of volunteers. We had a steady stream of volunteers many who had lost their jobs at the mill or other businesses in town. Unloading groceries, packing food hampers and distributing food was not only full time work for many it was also mental therapy.

One unexpected, uncontrollable event had transformed hundreds of lives overnight. One close friend and neighbour who had lost her husband to cancer only a few months before the fire had now lost her job at the mill. She had been employed at the mill for twenty plus years. With only two or three years left before being eligible for a full pension. For her this fire meant the loss of twenty plus years of life, as she knew it. She would eventually have to declare bankruptcy and move to Alberta for work.

Several families had fathers who would leave town to look for work leaving wives and children behind. Mortgages had to be paid. Many of the Food Bank new volunteers simply required a place to be everyday so they did not have to think about tomorrow, bills and slim job prospects. Volunteering for some helped to alleviate some of the guilt when it was their turn to take groceries home.

I was hearing the same comment from so many shattered people. The comment was that they could not believe that they were standing at a Food Bank counter waiting to take much needed and appreciated groceries home. What was most surprising to many was the realization of the poor opinion they had of people on that side of the counter until today.

The comment was always the same, "I can't believe I am standing in a Food Bank" followed by, "if it can happen to me it can happen to anyone." Many of these people had worked all their lives, paid their bills, did what they believed to be everything right, yet here they were. Can't pay their mortgage, can't feed their kids, can't pay their car loan or their hydro bills. Can't pack up and leave with no money and there was not a line up of people waiting to rent their homes if they were to go elsewhere. How could they afford to move away for work, if they could find it and pay the mortgage payments on their empty homes? There would be some who would loose their homes to the mortgage company and not the fire.

Amongst the daily happenings with people trying to rebuild their homes and their lives were the TV cameras, radio and newspaper reporters. Over the next few months, a variety of media would turn up at various locations throughout the town.

The Food Bank was a regular stop for most media at some point when they were in town. Some reporters simply wanted to film the activities, others would ask one or two questions and others would ask for an interview.

A reporter from one of the Vancouver newspapers stopped in at the Food Bank. He was asking questions about donations and what if any government assistance the Food Bank had received.

I answered that we received that same government assistance that we received before the fire, "Zero". His next comments were regarding the various politicians, local, Provincial and Federal who had either flown over or dropped in for a visit during Barriere's State of Emergency. He asked if I was aware that the Governor-General Adrienne Clarkson was on the list of visitors to come next week.

Politicians who wanted to drop in for a photo op made no difference to me. I had been too busy coordinating food distribution to pay much attention. I had heard that Adrienne was planning a visit and the thought had gone through my mind that we would be better off if she stayed home and sent the Food Bank a cheque for the money she would have spent on the trip. I did not share this thought with the reporter. He asked if I felt her trip would make any difference to Barriere or the Food Bank.

In answering his question I said, "ask her to bring a case of macaroni and cheese with her if she wants to help." The reporter left and I continued with my work. A few days later, there was a message on my home phone. It was Adrienne Clarkson's Press Secretary asking me to return her call.

I returned her call. She said that Adrienne had read my comment in the newspaper and wanted to invite me to meet with her when she arrived in Barriere. I agreed to attend the event. There were several people invited to one of the local restaurants for this meeting. There were representatives from various charities, churches, government groups and some of the residents who had lost their homes, businesses or both. Laura was with me for this meeting as she was a regular Food Bank volunteer.

Adrienne made her way around the room spending time with each table of guest. I had no great expectations of Adrienne or any other politician showing up and actually making a difference to our situation. At this time although several visitors including Paul Martin had made the Barriere tour the only real financial help reaching the people, was provided by the Red Cross.

Although I had every reason to be sceptical about the purpose and value of this visit as I watched and listened to the various conversations, Adrienne said something that stood out to me. She was speaking to a man who had lost his home to the fire and his job at the mill. After listening to this mans story Adrienne said to him in a very sincere, caring manor. "Things will get better, you will find another job, but you are going to have to leave."

The voice inside of my head was saying, "WOW finally a political figure who actually tells it how it is." She was not here to promise to make things better, she was not here to patronize this man and tell him what she thinks he wanted to hear. She was not here to make him feel special because he got to meet the Governor-General of Canada.

She was simply here to tell this man that someone cares and that life will go on. In the short term, realistically, for a man who has a mortgage and a family, life will not go on in Barriere. No amount of wishful thinking or political promises could change that.

Adrienne arrived at my table; once the introductions and hello's were out of the way, she sat beside me. Her first comment was that she did not bring me a case of macaroni and cheese. She said that she wanted to meet me because she thought that my comment showed that I cared. She asked if once the meeting was over if I would be willing to give her a tour of the Food Bank.

Adrienne, her bodyguard and two of her invited guests spent half an hour or more with Laura and myself in the Barriere Food Bank. Most of the time was spent sharing stories of some of the circumstances of the families we were assisting and some of the evacuation stories, including the circumstances of families returning to literally throw out refrigerators and freezers and eat from the Salvation Army kitchen. Concern for the long-term survival was also discussed. There were some families, which simply would not be able to stay.

A visit from the Governor-General did not change the circumstances for the families in Barriere in 2003; for some including myself it felt good to know that so many really do care. As they were leaving, Adrienne's bodyguard handed me a twenty-dollar bill and said, "here buy something nice for your grandson." The invited guests with us were from Kamloops. There was an article in the Kamloops paper about their visit with the Governor-General. The article stated that one of the most memorable and touching parts of their visit was the time that they spent talking with Adrienne and the representative from the Barriere Food Bank.

There were several volunteer groups from various organizations, which had arrived in town. There were church groups with volunteers rebuilding houses for families who had no insurance, there were groups cooking meals, volunteers dis-

tributing clothing, there were out of town businesses that donated freezers. May-
tag donated several new freezers to the Food Bank. Volunteers from each group
would meet to coordinate current and future needs.

With September, approaching the concern was if and when the schools would
open. Many families would not have the funds for school supplies etc. The concern for the Food Bank was with winter approaching and no sign that the economic situation would change in the near future it was looking as though families
would require assistance with groceries through the winter.

It would not be possible to distribute groceries from the parking lot once the
weather got cold. The trailers, which we were using for storage, might not be
available for the next six months. Although it was September, my mind was constantly reflecting on Christmas. This was the time of year that the Christmas
Hamper program details should be looked after; September was the month for
the motorcycle toy run.

My kennel would not be in a position to purchase toys for those hampers,
which may be short. The number of families affected by the fires that were now
unemployed and receiving groceries from the food bank was not going to be
reduced in the short term. Many of these families would need assistance this
Christmas for the first time.

With the immediate issues for many families of rent, mortgage payments, groceries and how to pay bills Christmas seemed like a subject that should somehow
be unimportant at the moment. I could not imagine children who had lost so
much, many who would return to school without new clothes or books, living in
families that are stressed by financial survival being told that there would be no
turkey dinner or gifts for Christmas.

The mill employees had been one of the larger contributors to the Christmas
Hamper program. The mill was gone and many other businesses, which were
now gone had sponsored families or sold turkey bucks. I knew many of the families who had given so much in the past would be in a position to receive this year.

My immediate concern was a place to house the Food Bank for the winter.
There were not many large buildings in town. The Salvation Army or the Red
Cross was temporarily using all available space. Most of the churches were tem-
porarily housing out of town volunteers.

There was the old IGA store in town, which had been closed and boarded up
for a few years. If I could track down the owners perhaps, they would permit the
Food Bank to use this building for the winter.

The North Thompson Relief Fund, which collected donations for fire victims
offered to pay the Food Banks electricity and heat bills for the winter. The own-

ers of the building were in Richmond BC and were more than happy to donate the facility for as long as it was necessary. We now had a new winter home and a space sufficient to store and produce as many Christmas hampers as would be required.

The fire situation throughout BC had dominated both TV and radio news for some time. The media was instrumental in letting the Country know the situation. Donation, cards and letters were arriving from across the Country. The cash donations would be used to stock the Food Bank shelves once the Red Cross donations ended.

These funds could not be used to provide Christmas hampers for families at the expense of having no groceries on the shelves in January or February. If the opportunity presented itself in any of the TV, radio or news papers interviews I was a part of I would make a comment about this being the time of year that the Food Bank would normally be focused on Christmas hampers.

I received a call from Kathryn Gretsinger of "CBC Radio 1." I had been a guest on her radio show a few times and had managed to work Christmas into the conversation. This call was Kathryn telling me that she had personally taken up the Barriere Christmas cause.

"CBC Radio" had agreed to spear head the Christmas for Barriere Campaign. Listeners were encouraged to purchase toys and gift for Barriere. Kathryn played interview tapes from our previous shows each time she encouraged her audience to donate. People would stop in at the Food Bank to drop off a cheque and say that they had just heard me on the radio; they were passing through Barriere and thought they would like to donate what they could. On many of these occasions, I had not been on the radio for weeks. It was Kathryn replaying bits of previous interviews to keep Barriere in the spotlight.

The little Barriere Food Bank received cards, letters, donations and phone calls from across the Country. There were schools, dance classes, boy scouts, and individuals, calling with offers to collect and donate gifts. There was a small Indian band on Vancouver Island that sent boxes of hand knitted hats, mitts and scarves along with a letter, which stated they were not able to donated financially so the villagers made personal gifts for the children. Tilley Endurables in Ontario insisted on the amount of their donation remaining anonymous. This Company offered to pay for each and every turkey required with extra funds to help fill each grocery hamper. A branch of the same company in Vancouver called to say they could not send such a large donation but they were also sending a cheque and asked that the amount remain anonymous.

One toy manufacturer sent boxes of Disney Monopoly Games. Toys R US chose the Barriere Food Bank as the Charity this year that would receive the toys from their annual toy show. We received top of the line must have toys from this years show. Quilters groups from across the Country communicated with each other and each group hand made quilts of every size. Each one labelled from the town and group who made it, there were enough quilts for every family who lost a home to receive one quilt for each family member. There were enough quilts for each child receiving a Christmas hamper to receive a quilt. There was also a special batch of quilts sent as a Christmas gift for each regular Food Bank volunteer.

We received pallets of chocolate Christmas candies; there were pallets of cookies and juice. Several of the smaller groups donating gifts called "CBC Radio" with concerns of the transportation costs.

For some groups the transportation costs were more than the donated items and were just not doable. Kathryn called Greyhound. Greyhound agreed to ship gifts to Barriere for CBC at no cost. This was truly a Christmas Miracle. The Barriere Food Bank was able to provide Christmas dinner with all the trimmings; gifts for every child and several adults. There were gifts, chocolates, cookies and juice, which we were able to send to neighbouring Food Banks and Christmas Hamper programs.

Kathryn sent me a personal Christmas Gift. It was a magnificent cookbook. Inside the front cover she wrote: "For Brenda; the wonder woman who made sure that kids in Barriere got what they needed for Christmas; with thanks Kathryn "@CBC Radio 1". (Rose) is the name on my birth certificate I use my middle name Brenda.

Thank you Kathryn for asking your audience to take part in the Christmas for Barriere Campaign. It would not have been possible without your help and without the love, caring and sharing of so many amazing people. Thank you to each and everyone for Barriere BC's 2003 Christmas Miracle.

33

YOU ARE GOING TO HAVE TO LEAVE

Groceries and gifts arrived daily leading up to Christmas 2003. Volunteers packed food boxes and selected appropriate gifts for each child. The old IGA store was transformed into a food distribution centre and Santa's workshop.

David had volunteered for the Food Bank regularly before the fire. After the fire, he never missed a day. Those perpetually sad eyes were full of compassion, caring and unconditional love for each person who walked through the Food Bank door. I am not sure if any one else could see what I saw in David.

I knew he felt the grief and the pain in the souls of those who arrived for groceries as deeply as I did. There were many occasions immediately after the fire and again at Christmas when those receiving groceries needed someone to talk to and a hug as much or more than the food. David, myself and several other volunteers shared a lot of stories, tears and hugs while we distributed groceries.

Grocery boxes and selected gifts were carefully labelled and customized to fit the particulars of the recipient. There was half a grocery store full of sealed black garbage bags filled with unwrapped gifts and boxes of groceries stuffed with Christmas goodies.

Distribution for those who were able to pick up their items would take place over three days the last weekend before Christmas. A steady stream of volunteers offered to deliver Christmas for those who had no transportation or were unable to pick up their packages in person.

August 1, 2003 the day we evacuated to December 20, 2003; just less than five months filled with chaos, stress, uncertainty, hard work and no pay. These same days and months were also full of incredible people, events, opportunities, miracles and love.

This was five months I never want to repeat. This was also five months I wouldn't have missed for the world. Saturday December 20, 2003 with the

Christmas Hamper distribution complete, I officially resigned as the Barriere and District Food Bank President. As Adrienne Clarkson had so eloquently stated to the man she spoke to on her visit. Things will get better, life will go on but you are going to have to leave.

My heart was with the Food Bank clients. The reality of my own financial situation had taken a back seat to the busyness of the past five months. Dealing with Food Bank, issues and Christmas hampers had been my mental therapy. It was a way of avoiding personal reality.

The Food Bank would not reopen for grocery distribution until after the New Year. Systems were in place to care for the clients. The hand full of original dedicated volunteers before the fire were still there. There were more than enough new regular volunteers to help with the lifting and stocking of shelves. The Food Bank was well equipped to survive without me.

It was time for me to retreat from the hectic seven day a week non stop, go, go, go, life I had been in the middle of for the past five months. The time had come to contemplate the reality of Adrienne's words for myself, "But you're going to have to leave!"

Driving home after distributing my last Christmas hamper, I felt both full and empty at the same time. I was full of the joy and satisfaction of being a small part of a Christmas morning that would be special for so many. At the same time, I was feeling totally drained, empty and numb at the thought of leaving.

Eight years in this magnificent place, our mountain, the business Stefon and I built together and the charity that I loved. Realistically it was over. It was time to focus on how and when to move on.

As predicted in early September to feed and heat my animals through the winter would leave me thousands of dollars in debt. With the holiday season behind us, Stefon left to work in Alberta in early January. He returned for only one or two weekends over the next three months.

My world had come to a dead stop. Before the fire I had worked two jobs in order to build my business to the point were it was self supporting. Replacing my second job with volunteering at the Food Bank meant living a busy, full, rewarding lifestyle. It may not have been fancy living; it was a life I loved. I was happy and content with my life and my lifestyle.

With the shift from five months of chaos and stress to dead calm, came the realization of what it would take to recoup and recover financially in my personal life. I had done the math months ago, Stefon wanted to hang on and believe we could turn things around. A part of me was hoping he was right. The busyness of the past months had allowed my personal life to run on automatic pilot. It was no longer possible to ignore the situation. Alone on our mountain in January the only subject left to deal with was me.

Stefon and I had contemplated moving to Alberta a year or so before the fire. This would put him closer to his work. We had looked at a few properties at that time. The plan was if we could find a property we could afford that we would move the kennel business.

My thoughts were now of moving to Alberta to be closer to Stefon's work and to be in a place were there would be more job opportunities for myself. Remaining in Barriere and attempting to recoup my business would mean years of debt and bare financial survival.

Properties were not selling in Barriere. A move to Alberta would mean having to sell the dogs and close the kennel. We were not in a position to buy a property and set up the kennel again anywhere. In order to find employment for myself that paid above minimum wage I would need to be in or near a City. Renting a place in any City would not allow me to keep the dogs. Staying in BC was not an option. The job prospects in Kamloops were slim and minimum wage. To move to a BC City made no sense, as Stefon would have steady work in Alberta if he lived closer to the job sites. The idea of living in any City was not appealing to either of us. It seemed like the only logical option. I hope that it would be a short-term option.

Option number one; moving to Alberta without my kennel was now playing full time in my head; there did not seem to be an option number two.

Alone with my thoughts, taking care of the animals required only a small part of my day. Greeting each one while cleaning their kennels, I was asking myself; where would they go? Who would take care of them? Would their new owners know which one liked this and which one didn't like that? I was beginning to dread the part of the day that required me to be in the kennel. Many of my dogs had been with me since birth. They had been traumatized by the evacuation how could I be contemplating sending them away knowing they would never come home?

The emotional toll of the past months was no longer hidden under mountains of daily details. My mind and my body had nowhere to go to escape the feelings attached to this new reality. So many had lost so much, somehow, my loss seemed as though it should be trivial when compared to those whose homes and businesses had burned to the ground.

At this moment the thought of starting over, financially broke, nothing to show for fifty years of struggle and hard work; the old voices from my childhood were screaming in my head, "Failure! No good for nothing! Useless! Looser!" I was left searching for answers in my mind, which was now clouded by thoughts of failure, and mind numbing depression.

It was not logical to define my entire life by the financial position I found myself in at this moment. Logic was not a part of my current thinking. Some how the voices from my past, the voices that said from birth that Rose was less than were the only voices I was able to hear.

In the fog of depression, there was no room for remembering the many successes of my fifty years. Starting over at the bottom, my self worth being directly tied to my current financial position, all I was able to see was absolute failure. With the negative voices drowning out any logic and reason, the picture being painted in my mind of my future, as I sat alone on this mountain was; a job I did not want; in order to pay for a bare minimum life style; in a place I had no desire to be.

My children were grown. I was telling myself I was no longer needed. Life at this point was a matter of choice. Choosing to start my life over again, feeling as though the past fifty years amounted to absolute failure. Illogically imagining any future to be full of more sacrifice, more struggle with the same of perhaps worse results.

How had I managed to work so hard, struggle through so much of life, picking up the pieces over and over again, only to end up an absolute failure. Had I struggled through almost fifty years of life, trying to convince myself and the world that I was not worthless, only to discover that what I had to show for fifty years of living added up to less than zero. My life's work totalled a net worth of minus thousands of dollars.

The energy, adrenalin, and shear determination, which had driven me for the past five months to care for others, was completely drained. The only thoughts running through my mind were of impossible tomorrows. Much of what I had survived in the past was credited to shear determination. There did not seem to be a drop of determination left in my soul. At this time in this place, I felt completely emotionally and physically drained. The only one left to rescue was me; yet, there did not seem to be an ounce of determination or the will to go on left.

I had conceded defeat. This had been one loss too many. There was no desire to return for another season. Nothing inside of me was willing to give it another try, the formula of try harder, work harder do more, do what ever it takes had expired. In this moment in time, depression had consumed what was left of me.

My mind was now calculating possible future circumstances and events. Analysing the affect of my not being here for my children and grandchildren. My children were grown. They were competent adults. They would do just fine without me. My grandchildren were young enough that they would not be affected by my departure. My children would tell them about me as they grew. Stefon who I dearly loved had survived alone before we met. He would survive again. There appeared to be no logical reason why I should choose to continue through years of hardship and unhappiness. My mind consumed with thoughts of failure and loss concluding to end my life seemed a reasonable choice.

My animals would have to be sold no matter what my choice for the future may be. Waiting until a few days before Stefon was to return would ensure that the animals would be cared for. Until Stefon returned no one would know that the animals were alone. Somehow, it all seemed so logical.

I overfilled the dog dishes and left plenty of water for a few days. Laying out half a bottle of painkillers and tranquilizers left from a previous back injury and every headache pill, antihistamine and cold capsule in the place. Every pill I could find was lying on the counter top. It seemed so simple. Just swallow and go to sleep. Eternal peace.

Starring at the pills on the counter, pouring a glass of water my mind was asking what if questions. The; what if I were no longer here questioned had been asked and answered. The question now cutting through this thick depression was, "what if there are not enough pills?" What if there are only enough pills to do permanent damage? What if I were to wake up? What if the rest of my life was spent as the equivalent of a recovering stroke victim? It would be the ultimate failure if I could not even do this right.

There was no way to determine if the pills in front of me were enough to complete the job or only enough to leave me in a possible state where my family or Stefon would have to care for me forever. I would not do this to my children or Stefon was now running trough my mind.

With only negative images of myself playing over and over in my head the message coming through was; I failed at everything else in life what made me believe I would not fail at this too. It was more likely that my efforts would again result in failure. To fail at this had far greater consequences than to go on with my miserable life and fail.

Somehow, in this moment I made the decision that to go on with life, as a failure would be more acceptable than failing this attempt and possibly ending up as a vegetable.

During this time of depression, reverting to patterns from my past allowed me to temporarily convince myself that somehow the circumstances of my current life were caused by something I should have or shouldn't have done. It is not possible to have a positive outcome when feeding your mind only on negative thoughts.

Given the choice of soaring with both eyes open; seeing my life as it had been, full to overflowing with both struggles and accomplishments, or closing my eyes and seeing only today. With my eyes closed, I allowed myself to be defined by one moment in time. A moment in time, which was not caused by, constructed or designed by me.

Once again, the only thing that had changed was my mind. Yes, my circumstances had changed. It was not possible for a current change in circumstances, caused by an act of nature to negate a lifetime of achievements. It was not possible for my current circumstances to define my future abilities or the outcome of my life unless I chose to allow it.

I believed that I had long since let go of the negative influences of my childhood. Yet, when presented with circumstances, which seemed to prove the old voices of worthless, useless, no good for nothing and statements from people like Kathryn Gretsinger who signed her gift to me, to the Wonder Woman; the negative voices were a more natural fit. Choosing to listen to the old negative voices allowed no room for Kathryn's positive words.

34

A TIME TO SEE

I had concluded that to choose life as a failure over life as a possible vegetable seemed for now my only option. My still foggy mind had switched to thoughts of how and when to move on. Formulating some sort of a moving on plan was now required. Alone on this mountain day after day, test scenarios were playing in my head. We could do this or what if we did that. The how, what, where and when questions were repeating over and over again; somewhere in the middle of all the questions I remembered similar questions running through my mind before selling the acreage and moving to Barriere.

As I have mentioned in previous chapters, there were times from 1978 when Daniel was born through 1996 when I first moved to Barriere that I started to consider and question if there was a God. Like most people, I started praying to God out of desperation for answers to various problems in my life. Although I distinctly remember thanking God when Daniel and Laura were born and saying thank you on other occasions.

At the time contemplating leaving the acreage I had simply concluded that if I were meant to move to Barriere it was logical that there was someone, somewhere who was meant to move on to this acreage. I distinctly remember thanking God for everything in my life and saying to him; if I am right; and there is someone out there who is meant to be here; could you please find him or her and bring them to me so that I can move on with my life. I ended my request with another thank you to God for everything in my life.

Not only did a family show up to move onto the acreage. This was a family who would love and appreciate the bats, the birds, and the coyotes, even the dandelions as much or more than I did. The timing was perfect; they were ready to move in as the school year-ended, which was when I would be ready to move on.

I asked God for a very specific gift and he provided all that I had asked for and more. I had attended church for a time when Valerie was the Reverend. I had not been to church now more than once or twice since Valerie had moved out of town well before the fire. I had on several occasion over the six years living on this mountain walked to my special spot halfway up the mountain, sat quietly and talked to God.

The view from this silent spot was breathtaking. It was always so calm, so warm, so totally relaxing and uplifting at the same time. On this day, I climbed to my special spot with Cindy my bear dog at my side to sit quietly and ask God what I should do with what was left of my miserable failed life. It was time to reconnect with God whom I must admit I had forgotten through all the drama.

Sitting silently alone allowing my body to simply relax and my mind to empty. No questions, no ideas, no thoughts of any kind. With my eyes closed, I am able to see the darkness. First, I see black and then the most calming shade of blue followed by yellow. Almost as though watching a gentle flickering flame inside of my eyelids. This is a peaceful place I had found inside myself many times while living on this mountain.

Somehow, with the events of the past months this had been a place completely forgotten. The non-stop, go, go, go, chaos and stress had consumed all of me. In the middle of the past events going full out, dealing with the avalanche of every daily detail without taking the time to breathe seemed normal. Only when the tidal wave of events was over was the personal, physical and emotional toll even acknowledged.

Today sitting in this familiar, calm, warm spot with my mind purposely emptied as I stared into the inner coloured spaces of my soul; pictures drifted through the empty space floating in front of my closed eyelids.

The pictures floating by, some in colour others not, my mind completely calm, I had seen these pictures before. This was a repeat performance of a vision I shared with God a year or more before the fire while sitting in this same magnificent spot.

This was a vision I had shared with Stefon, as it was absolutely vivid. Like watching, a full screen movie playing in front of my eyes, large as life and detailed. Neither Stefon nor I had any idea what the movie I had watched in my head, while sitting on this mountain in the middle of the day, with my eyes closed, yet fully awake could possibly mean.

As I have said, this vision took place a year or so before the fire and was now repeating itself with no changes. The movie playing before my closed eyes was of my kennel building. I was inside the kennel, Jesus Christ, dressed, as one would expect, including sandals was standing just inside of the kennel door. On his right was a ¾ size pen, which looked similar to the other dog pens. This pen was normally used to store bags of dog food. In this vision, Jesus was filling this pen with cloth bags full of money. The exact picture was of the moneybags one sees in cartoons with the $ on the outside, tied around the top with a rope or a string.

I watched as he continued to toss moneybags into this corner pen. No words spoken just watching. This corner pen was being filled with bags with $ on the outside. Some time passed with Jesus continually tossing in bags. Jesus then spoke to me; he simply said, "It is not for you." Jesus was filling my kennel with bags of money; yet as he spoke the words, I knew it was absolute. He was telling me he would provide bags of money and none of it was intended for me.

Sharing this original vision with Stefon, it made no sense. Stefon referred to it as a dream. This was a dream a vision what ever you want to call it; it happened during a time when my eyes may have been closed however, I was absolutely awake.

It had occurred to me at the time that it may have some connection with the Food Bank. Perhaps this meant that I would receive a large donation for the Food Bank, which of course would have meant that it was not for me.

Repeating this scene, duplicated exactly as it had been showed in the past as I again watch Jesus tossing the identical moneybags in the same corner of my kennel. This time the words are not spoken. I simply knew that the money was not intended for me. Without spoken words, without any words at all I now knew what Jesus had told me long before the fires.

Jesus was telling me that he would provide. In both visions, he never stopped tossing in moneybags. There was no end. There are no words to describe how I was now able to understand the message. The communication was absolutely clear without actual words. The repeat performance was Jesus telling me; that he had showed me there would be more than enough. It was not for me; but **through me**; he would provide all that was required.

In this spot on this day, the repeat performance was to show me that all that had been required of me was to have simply remembered the message. All that was required for me to know the outcome of my efforts for the town, the Food Bank and the Christmas hampers was for me to have simply remembered to ask Jesus first.

In this relaxed state, in the silence it was so clear. The message filling my body and soul in this moment in time was; had I simply chose to stop for a moment in the midst of the chaos to remember. Had I simply stopped for a moment to ask Jesus first; I would have known the outcome was absolute.

I would have still gone through the daily details, the meetings, the stocking shelves, the distributing food and the appeals for Christmas. What I would have not gone through was the stress, the uncertainty, the worry and there would have been no devastating depression to overcome.

The vision was of endless dollars that were not for me. The reality was a forest fire, a town in need and a half a million dollars provided by the Red Cross to our little Food Bank, plus donations of cash, clothing, food and Christmas gifts from across the Country. With more than enough to be shared with neighbouring Christmas Hamper Programs.

Had I remembered the vision, these past months could have been filled to overflowing with feeling of accomplishment, ability and an absolute knowing that we would all be cared for.

The message on this day with this repeat performance was a message meant personally for me. With the movie replay over, the message remaining was Jesus had done exactly what he said he would do. He told me he would provide. He was here today repeating the message. He has provided in the past. All that was required of me in the past and in my future was to simply remember and to simply ask. He was and would always be there.

As I opened my eyes on this day my thoughts were now of realizing that the events of the past months were anticipated well in advance. If I was watching myself receive moneybags a year or more before the fire, the circumstances were predicted long before they happened. The details were not shown to me, they were not required. The message to me was that Jesus would provide what ever the circumstance may be.

If the past events were known before they would occur, perhaps this was the reason for my choosing to move to Barriere. Was it possible that my work in this small town Food Bank was somehow predestined? It seemed like both a logical question and a totally ludicrous question at the same time.

Again, I was thinking of the events, which occurred when I left the acreage to move to Barriere. There was someone out there who was meant to take my place on that acreage at that time. If they were meant to be there and I was meant to move on, perhaps pre determined destiny was more than Guru talk for a chosen few.

Was it possible that these events and perhaps other events in my life or maybe even all the events in my life were somehow mapped out in advance? Was it possible that there had been a blue print for Rose's life long before Rose began drawing her own blueprints?

The depression I carried up this mountain was completely replaced with endless what if questions. What to do with what was left of my miserable failed life was the intended question on this day. The question was never asked. The, "what to do question" had been replaced with a rolling review of what had happened up to now.

Days of mental reviews of my life would follow. The same repeat scenarios and endless what if questions. The silence of this magnificent mountain wrapped around me like a warm blanket. My thoughts seemed to end at the same place with the same repeat inquiry. If life was wholly or partially predestined and clearly a part of mine had been; to what end? What was my purpose? What comes next?

How many messages had I missed? How many messages had I miss interpreted. Clearly there were messages directed at me at my life. The past few months could have been so different had the interpretation of my early vision been understood.

My mind and body were filling with the desire and determination to see more, to understand more about both my past and my future. I sat endlessly talking to myself and to God at the same time. Rambling on in my head with various questions and scenarios of current and past event. It was becoming so clear that the recent past events were meant to be; and were both known and unknown to me before they took place. The vision was mine; it was graphically clear. The interpretation only became clear after the event was over. My attempts at interpreting this vision resulted in questions rather than conclusions.

Sitting at the kitchen table in the motor home I found myself writing out question after question, which somehow ended with a list of questions at the top of the page followed by a list of statements. The statements were of absolutes. As Oprah would say, "what I know for sure is" the questions were of what to do with what I absolutely know?

I knew for sure that my vision of bags of money, which were absolutely not for me were shown to me both before and after the fire. The money had arrived and it was not for me. I knew for sure that I had asked God to find me the person who was meant to take my place on the acreage and he found the person who exceeded the expectations set out in my request. I absolutely knew for sure; that God and Jesus were present in my life.

Religion had not been and was not now a part of my life. Personally talking to God on several occasions and seeing Jesus with my own eyes, both showing me and telling me things that I have now witnessed take place; I absolutely knew and know; that God is and Jesus is. This was not a matter of faith this was a matter of fact. For me in my life God and Jesus are an absolute.

In a few short weeks with the only changes in my life again being in my mind, thoughts of how to end my life were replaced with thoughts of finding and fulfilling what ever my life's purpose may be.

Armed with the knowledge that it had been possible for me to communicate with God and Jesus and actually see an event before it happened gave me the determination to want to know the how and why of what had occurred. More importantly was it possible for such an event to happen again.

It had happened therefore it was possible. Was it possible to preview a future event on purpose? Perhaps preview my life's purpose or a least a small glimpse of what was to come next.

The need to move on was very clear. During the time spent contemplating what may come next, it was becoming obvious my time here on this mountain and in this town was over. Moving on was beginning to feel like a natural fit rather than something that I had been dreading. My focus had shifted to the future rather than what I may be losing or leaving behind.

If any part of what comes next had been predestined, or pre told to me, now was the time to determine what if anything I was meant to know or remember. Now was the time to decipher any missing messages, guidelines or clues to my past, present or future life, which may have passed me by unnoticed.

Climbing to this peaceful spot on countless occasions over the next few weeks, my mind filled with unanswered questions. Closing my eyes sitting in the silence saying thank you and asking question after question. Asking God to please teach me how to see. Teach me how to see more of the path I have been on and of the path to come. Teach me how to soar with both eyes open. Teach me to see all that you want me to see. Help me to remember any messages that may have been forgotten or not understood.

Most of all tell me what you want me to do now, today and tomorrow. I do not want to spend any of my time worrying, struggling and creating a new beginning only to be shown at some point in the future that had I only done it your way it would have been so much easier. Teach me your way now, before I leave this place. If this is no longer the place for me, please show me which place is waiting for me and for what purpose.

The same endless questions asked in as many different ways as possible with no response. Perhaps the past vision had been a one-time communication with a single purpose.

I absolutely knew that it was time to move on. Somehow knowing that Alberta was the place to move on to, remembering the same feelings inside of me before leaving the acreage and moving to Barriere. Everything inside of me was

saying that there was a purpose for what ever would come next. I was not prepared to leave without some knowledge of where to go and why.

Again climbing to this placid mountain spot, saying thank you for everything
in my life and asking question after question. On this day somewhere in the middle of rephrasing the same questions thinking perhaps that different words for the
same questions would somehow be heard; in the middle of my barrage of questions I was not sure if I was thinking or hearing the words; "you have to stop asking questions long enough to hear the answers." With my eyes still closed the
realization that although I was sitting in this same spot my body was not relaxed,
my mind had not been emptied, my eyes were not watching soft colour displays.
My body was tense my mind was filled to overflowing with questions, thoughts,
ideas. I was trying to communicate while all of me was in hyper drive.

Taking deep breaths, consciously relaxing by body one section at a time, slow-
ing down my thoughts. It was a real effort to empty each thought and each question. Watching the inside of my eyelids as left over thoughts and questions
drifted by. I could hear myself say let it go. Finally, the blue and then the yellow
were floating in front of my eyes. Relaxed, simply sitting embracing the dancing
colour patterns.

The colour patterns were changing the blue and the yellow, a glimpse of red
were drifting peacefully by. The colours were forming a pattern. I was now looking down at a floor. The colours had formed a carpet. This was a carpet I had
seen before. No words, no messages, just a multi coloured familiar carpet.

Opening my eyes on this day the picture of the carpet playing in my head.
This carpet was very unusual and very familiar. This was the carpet on the floor
in Valerie's church. Something inside of me was saying, "You have to go to
church." This was not a desire to go to a church service. This was a desire to be in
the church building alone.

That same day I found myself at the church talking to the new Reverend. We
knew each other only through the Food Bank. I had not attended even one service with the new Reverend. Simply stating that I would like to reserve a time to
sit in the church for a while alone and asked if this would be possible.

One o'clock the next afternoon was arranged. One o'clock arrived the reverend unlocked the door to the room where Sunday services were normally held.
She showed me how to lock the door so I would not be disturbed and said, "Take
as much time as you need."

Entering the room sitting in a middle pew. So much time had passed since I
had last been in this room I had no idea that the multi coloured carpet had been
replaced. Most of the room was unchanged, with the exception of a table at the

end of the aisle, with a large opened book, which I assumed to be a bible displayed on it.

Closing my eyes, relaxing my body and emptying my mind, knowing this was not the time to ask questions but was simply a time to see. Silently watching the same colour patterns pass in front of my eyelids, nothing more, no thoughts and no messages just floating silent colours. How much time had passed I did not know, for a brief moment there was the feeling that nothing is happening; yet at the same time there was the feeling that I did not want to open my eyes or leave.

There is a picture hanging in the front of this room. It is a large picture of Jesus Christ. He is holding a reed in his hand. There is something unusual about this picture. You know the man is supposed to be Jesus somehow the image is not quite right. Valerie has commented on this picture saying it's really not very good.

Sitting quietly although my eyes are closed this is the picture floating in front of my eyelids. Jesus is talking to me. He is handing me the reed he is holding; only when he hands it to me it is a microphone. I am looking at the picture seeing him hand me the microphone and hesitating to take it. He tells me, "Its okay, I know the picture is not right but it is me."

As he hands me the reed, which is now a microphone he says the word, "speak." Jesus is handing me a microphone and telling me to speak! The only other words spoken to me were, "save the children." My body was feeling so light, so at ease, almost as if it were floating. The message was clear, "speak and save the children" in this relaxed, completely connected state as I found myself saying yes to both requests, I knew I had no idea what "save the children" meant. Jesus was asking me to save the children and to speak and all of me was saying yes.

Opening my eyes, I found myself sitting and staring at this unusual picture hanging on the wall. The words "save the children" were repeating themselves in my head along with my reply "I will save the children, whatever that means." Standing up ready to leave something drew me to the end of the aisle, which had the open book displayed. I did not have my glasses with me, yet somehow I was able to read the small print. The book was open to a verse, which read: "I will put the words in thou mouth and you will speak them and together we will save the children!"

Driving home feeling light as a feather, completely content thinking my life is some how about saving the children. I had absolutely no idea what this meant, what children were to be saved? What were they to be saved from? In this moment, it did not seem to matter. God and Jesus had asked me to save the children and I had said yes. If this was truly, what comes next in my life surely God or Jesus or both will tell me what it is they are asking me to do.

In the days that followed, there were again more questions. Replaying the events in the church brought back a memory of a previous forgotten message. I have mentioned in a previous chapter that a year or so before the fire Stefon and I had contemplated moving the kennel business to Alberta. We had taken a trip to Alberta to check out real estate prices.

During this time period part of me had been feeling disconnected. My life was completely content yet some how there was the feeling that either something was going to change, perhaps moving to Alberta, there was a subtle nudging that perhaps there was something missing or something more I should be doing.

The events in the church brought back a memory of a previous conversation in my spot half way up this mountain. During the time period in the above paragraph, I had been sitting quietly communicating with God. At that time, I was also asking if there was something missing in my life. I was asking God if there were more for me to do. The answer was simply, "feed the children." My conclusion was that Barriere was where I belonged feeding the children through the Food Bank. This conversation had been forgotten until today.

Today remembering this past message to feed the children; again my interpretation was this message was connected to staying in Barriere with the Food Bank. The new message in the church was to save the children. I still had no idea what this meant. Somehow, I absolutely knew that it meant moving on. My connection to Barriere and the Food Bank was over.

It was late March, moving to Alberta was now a certainty. No more doubts, or questions the when and where details needed to be sorted out. The time had come for action. It was not possible to travel to Alberta to look for work or a place to stay with animals in Barriere needing to be looked after. Step number one would be to sell the dogs.

I picked up the phone and called every kennel owner I knew. My entire kennel was for sale. There would be some dogs, which would go to retirement homes and others who would go to reputable breeders. A few months before the fire I had purchased my first Chihuahua dogs, a breed, which was fast becoming my favourite. My plan was to sell the Chihuahuas last. Perhaps if we had to live in a City we would be able to keep one or two little ones.

Two week later, they were all sold with the exception of the yard dogs and a few Chihuahuas. Arrangements had been made for someone to take Cindy if we could not keep her. The Chihuahuas would not be difficult to sell. We would keep them until we knew where we would be living.

One of the men who had lost his job at the mill and had contracted out his truck to help with the burnt wood cleanup, offered to stay on our place and care for the remaining animals. This would allow me to head to Alberta to look for work and a place to live. He agreed to stay until September if need be. This would give him free rent and help us out at the same time. He offered to permanently keep one of the other yard dogs. Things were starting to fall into place.

My older sister Bernice lived in Calgary. Over the past twenty years, we had spoken maybe a handful of times. In the past year or so we had actually been communicating and trying to get to know each other again. On the trip, Stefon and I made to Alberta before the fire to look for property to move the kennel we visited Bernice. In March of 2003 Bernice received a Woman of Vision award for her accomplishments in business. As we had started communicating before the award, Bernice had called and asked if I would like to attend, which I did.

During the fire, evacuation Bernice sent me a cell phone while I was in Kelowna so I would have a way to keep in touch. It was now late March of 2004; I called to tell her that we would be moving to Alberta. When and where we did not know. She offered to let me stay with her in Calgary for as long as it may take to find a place to stay and a job. It would be so much easier to look for both from Calgary. I would head to Calgary the last week of April 2004.

The plan was for me to leave for Calgary the last week of April. The remaining animals would be cared for by our new tenant, which allowed me until September to find a place where we may be able to keep them.

The remaining three weeks or so would mean countless trips to my favourite spot. Sometimes asking questions and sometimes watching pictures and waiting for answers. There are a few visions I would like to share with you.

The first one was a picture of Bernice and me. We were about five-and-six-years-old. Bernice was wearing a yellow dress and I am wearing a red and white checked jumper. I have seen pictures of us as children in these outfits. We were both standing on this mountain. Jesus was sitting on a large bolder on the grass just off the lower driveway talking to both little girls. Jesus stands up, takes Bernice by the hand and begins to walk away. He turns to look back at me and says in a gentle voice. "Don't worry I will be back for you."

The next scene was of me as an adult, standing on this mountain in the area between the motor home and Laura's mobile home. I am standing in front of a large group of children. There are too many to count. The children are hungry and I am handing out food. As each child approaches, I hand him or her a food item.

It now appears that I am standing next to a large fruit tree. Perhaps a cherry or apple tree, as each child approaches I pick a piece of fruit. Handing out piece after piece. There is now no more fruit and endless children in front of me. Looking at the next child in front of me, I cut a branch from the tree and hand it to the child. The next child receives a branch. There are now no more branches. Looking at the child's face in front of me I cut into the tree trunk; handing each child a piece of tree trunk until there are no pieces left. The tree is no more and there are still endless hungry children in front of me. My thoughts were to give a child a branch or a piece of tree was better than having nothing to give.

I do not see Jesus or God although they are speaking to me. Jesus is showing me that had I handed out the fruit and not cut the tree, the tree would have been full again with fruit to feed the children in a few months. Jesus is now filling what appears to be a glass of wine. No words spoken and no picture of Jesus yet the message was clear.

Jesus was saying, "You did not have to be afraid of not having enough. I would have filled your cup and the children's cups while you waited for the tree to produce more fruit." "What you did not see was you had abundance, you had the tree. Yet, you chose to cut the tree. If you cut the tree, there is no more fruit. If you cut the tree all will starve."

The message was repeated in a soft gentle voice. "Do not fear lack of. There is enough. Do not cut the tree. You cannot give what you do not have. You have all you need. You simply need to ask."

The final picture was of Daniel my daughter in law and grandson, Laura and her son and Stefon. We are in a hotel room. Daniel and his son are wearing suits. We are all dressed as if we were celebrating something. We are holding glasses of champagne and toasting something. I am now holding a large oversized cheque and having my picture taken for the newspaper. I have posed for several such pictures accepting donations for the food bank.

This one was different. It is clearly a Lottery Foundation cheque made out for $2.5 million dollars, no explanation and no idea where the hotel room might be, no details although it did feel as though this money was for me. This vision would repeat itself several times in the near future.

About a week after talking to Bernice and accepting her offer to stay with her while looking for a new home, she called. The month of May would be holiday time for some of her employees in the office. She was calling to ask if I would be interested in filling in for holiday relief.

My office skills were ancient. I could still type however the last time I worked on a computer they still used key punch cards. She said I would be fine. She offered to mail me some information on the job and the company to familiarize myself with how they operated over the next couple of weeks.

Not only was there a temporary place for me to stay, there was also a temporary job, which would allow me to earn money while renewing my office skills. Things were moving along so smoothly it seemed obvious that Alberta was were I was meant to be.

Stefon and I were determined to find a place to live that was outside of a City, perhaps acreage outside of Calgary or Edmonton. Somewhere where we could both commute for work.

The last couple of weeks passed with more trips to my favourite spot; there were still many questions and no answers. Every day several times a day while talking inside of my head I had asked, "what did save the children mean?" "Save what children? Save them from what with what?" There was no answer.

Some how there was the knowing that this was my destiny what ever it meant. There was the uncertainty of where we would live, where I would work, how we would pay the many bills we were leaving behind. Yet, there was also an unexplainable contentment. I was leaving this magnificent mountain for places unknown feeling the same contentment that I felt living here before the fire.

A contentment in knowing what ever and where ever comes next it would be the right place for me. The final day had arrived. It was time to leave. Stefon was still in Alberta I would take a Grey Hound bus to Calgary to begin our new life. As Grey Hound bus rides are not, overly exciting there I was watching the telephone poles pass by one by one contemplating my future. Again silently talking to God and myself at the same time.

This time my eyes are, open my mind deep in thought, remembering Jesus taking Bernice by the hand and telling me that he would come back for me. Remembering the hotel room and the Lottery Cheque, remembering the microphone Jesus handed me as he asked me to speak. Most of all remembering saying yes to Gods request that, "I save the children."

What does any of it mean? If there were ever, a time to have the answers this was it. This bus would arrive in Calgary Alberta and I had a one-way ticket.

Sitting in the window seat seeing only the questions and images in my mind the internal conversation was getting serious. There was an absolute need to know. If the answers were not available to all of my questions, surely it was not too much to ask for answers to some of the more important ones!

I actually said; "Okay God, I need talking to God for dummies; no puzzles, no riddles, no pictures I may misunderstand. You know me better than I know me. You know exactly what I will understand. Please tell me; the hotel room with the

Lottery cheque, does this mean I will win the lottery? Does this mean I will find a really good job in Alberta? If it means that I will somehow have money, don't you think now would be a good time for it to arrive, as I am on the bus heading to Alberta looking for a place to live with almost no financial resources?"

God's answer was absolutely clear. He said, "What difference does the delivery system make? I told you, it will be!" What an amazing answer. There I was smiling to myself and saying your right; thank you, picturing the bags of money for the Food Bank. Jesus told me it would be and it was. My next question was, "please tell me what did you mean when you asked me to save the children? What children do you want me to save?" The answer again was clear. God answered, "All of them."

I found myself saying yes again. Yes, I will save all of them. At the same time thinking it sounds impossible, but if God wants me to save them all I will find a way to save them all. God finished his answer with, "For which one would you not save?" My heart stopped with that answer. Of course, you would save them all; for which one would you not save? I was seeing the endless sea of children's faces as I was handing out food in the tree vision. Thinking to myself how would you choose which ones to save?

My questions continued with, "Save them from what?" God answered "Duh! From whatever they need to be saved from." I actually laughed out loud. God had a sense of humour. The duh! Inflection in his voice was saying, "isn't it obvious, save them from what ever they need to be saved from." It was so very obvious and seemed so simple.

This was such a marvellous conversation. With the big questions answered sitting in this bus seat feeling absolutely content. The sure knowledge that what ever comes next God was leading me. God was taking care of me. God has answered me, "What difference does the delivery system make? I told you it will be!" Every part of my being knew that it will be!

Again came the picture of the fruit tree, which is now a cherry tree, this was the tree from which I handed the children fruit and then chopped down. I am standing under this tree with a little boy who is about five years old. The little boy is holding a fishing rod. God is saying to me, "Teach them how to fish".

The scene changed. I am now inside of a luxurious building with a large reception counter. Behind the counter is a fancy wood panelled wall. The gold lettering on the wall says, "B. Lavis Empowerment Centre." The lettering on the reception counter says, "Teaching the world to fish; we grow angels." I have seen these words before in a previous forgotten vision. God told me, "to talk to Oprah; she has already grown angels." The first time I saw this, my understanding was it had something to do with Oprah's Angel Network. Perhaps this Empowerment Centre would be a similar charity.

The vision continued; somehow, there was a knowing that this centre was in Red Deer Alberta. The door opened to one room in this centre. Bernice was in this large room in front of a group of people. She was teaching something; the subject was not shown to me. Opening another door, there was Daniel in front of a crowd of people also teaching an undisclosed subject. Some how there was a connection to his radio career although it was not clear.

Another door opens and I am wearing a business suit and speaking to a large group of people. Telling them to choose God first, yet there is a distinct message that this is not religious. I am talking about the Food Bank, the fire, people's attitudes etc. I am teaching them to nurture the tree. Do not cut the tree, there is enough, we are all one, is part of the message.

As the pictures, fade there is a clear unmistakeable message. My purpose in life is to save the children; all of the children; from what ever they need to be saved from; to teach the children how to fish. An absolute knowing that what ever comes next is filled with all that I need. What ever comes next is filled with every resource including money. The message is unmistakable. "What difference does the delivery system make? I told you it will be!" Where we would live etc. did not seem to matter. We would live where we were meant to be. All that was required of me was to simply ask and be still enough to hear the answers.

What a magical place this world is. It may have been a Grey Hound bus, but man, what a ride!!!

35

OUR PLACE WAS IN THE COUNTRY

Arriving in Calgary suitcase in hand ready for what ever comes next. So much uncertainty, yet I was walking on air. Totally content, no worries, no fear. Although completely illogical, my soul was full of excitement; determination and awareness of the fact that whatever tomorrow holds would be wonderful.

My plan was to stay with Bernice, work in her office and spend weekends and evenings looking for somewhere to live and a permanent job. Stefon would stay with me while he worked for Companies in Calgary. We would have to time house hunting with his work between Calgary and Edmonton.

The money from selling the dogs was partially spent on bills. As much as was possible to save was what we had for start up cash plus Stefon's wages. The remainder of the kennel debt would have to be paid off slowly over then next year or so.

I had a temporary summer fill in job, Stefon was self employed; we had barely enough funds for a damage deposit, no savings for a down payment and no way to qualify for a mortgage between us. Yet from my first day arriving in Alberta my mind was set on finding us a place to own, away from City life.

Remaining in this City or moving to any other City would have been more realistic and practical, and yet all of me was focused on finding a place in the country we would own. The place in the country I knew was waiting for us. How we would pay for it when it showed up did not seem to matter. There was just a knowing that it would be.

Monday to Friday was spent working in the office. Every evening was spent with every newspaper and real estate flyer available. Reading ad after ad, had we wanted to remain in Calgary the paper was full of ads for assumable mortgages, no qualifying, low down payments. $500.00 down etc. The rental situation was equally attractive. Columns of rental accommodations, many with incentives

259

such as first month free and the majority of well paying jobs were in the City. None of this mattered.

My place was in the country. Driving 45 minutes or so for work would be far more meaningful for us both than having to live in any City. Real Estate papers and City newspapers had very few ads for out of town properties. Stefon and I would spend every weekend and some evenings driving between Calgary and Edmonton looking for "our place." We stopped in every small town and village we could find, collecting local newspapers, advertising flyers and real estate listings that were available. We read every sign tacked to a telephone pole or farm fence, stopped in grocery stores and gas stations to read local bulletin boards with "For Sale by owner listings" and talked to locals.

Sunday evening we would arrive at Bernice's place with a stack of papers to scan during the coming week. Searching for anything, which might be suitable. Making phone call after phone call asking if the listing had an assumable mortgage and after being told it did not asking the same question, "does it come with any creative financing?" This question was always greeted with a no.

Two weeks or more had gone by with the same results. There were many properties for sale, not a lot of properties with assumable mortgages or alternative financing. The Realtor's we spoke to repeated the same information over and over again. "What we were looking for did not exist. In Alberta, acreage will run you about $350,000.00. There are not many acreages available." We would leave whatever Real Estate Office we may have been in and have the same conversation in the car. Stefon would comment, "We will find something private. There are lots of farmers who may want to sell a part of their land or perhaps we will find a farmer who is willing to lease us part of his land."

Finally, I found an ad for acreage property with an assumable mortgage. The person on the other end of the phone was saying yes this one is assumable, so much cash to mortgage. The location was somewhere north of Edmonton which was too remote and too far to commute for work. Hanging up the phone, it did not matter that the one acreage with an assumable mortgage was too far away. Circling the ad in red, I told Stefon that the owner said it has an assumable mortgage. We both agreed it was too far and too remote for us. My statement to Stefon was, "we have been here less than three weeks and I have already found one acreage we could own if we chose to. If there is one, there are others. We will find the one for us.

The comment on the phone by the owner of $30,000.00 cash to mortgage was replaying in my mind. Any assumable mortgage would have some cash requirement. Stefon may be able to borrow a down payment privately from a friend. How could we come up with cash required?

My mind was now thinking dollars and cents, when I find the property that is for me how will we come up with the funds required. Remembering a previous business proposal from a few years ago gave me an idea. There was a friend who a few years back had planned to invest as a silent partner in a restaurant I was considering purchasing. This friend wanted an investment for her money, which would give her future returns for retirement. She had no plans on working the business, just investing as a silent partner. At the time, her reason for wanting to invest with me was she said she knew I had integrity. Another party beat us to the purchase.

I picked up the phone and called my friend asking if she was interested in another business deal, which would show a return on her investment better than the interest currently offered at the bank. I asked if she would be interested in providing a private mortgage. She asked how much money was required. Approximately $40,000.00 was my answer.

The reply was that there was only $50,000.00, which could be invested; she was not willing to part with $40,000.00 but would be willing to offer half. Twenty five thousand dollars would be wonderful. We signed the deal. The funds were to be paid back over 5 years.

In between house hunting and working, there was some time to reconnect with Bernice. It was now late May, Stefon had spent the last few days working in Edmonton and was expected back Friday for the weekend. Bernice was scheduled to attend a three-day weekend seminar booked months in advance. At the time that she booked this seminar, she was attending an event in the US. There was a bonus offer with this seminar that she could invite someone to attend. The name of the person had to be provided at that time. She was aware that we were considering moving to Alberta at some future date, when asked for the name of her invitee she signed me up. The event was far enough away she thought that perhaps I would be available.

She was telling me that the weekend she signed me up for was this coming weekend. It sounded interesting. This would be my first seminar. This was also a weekend that Stefon would be in Calgary and available to house hunt. The seminar was called the Millionaire Mind Intensive. This was a three-day intensive seminar involving managing money. Part of me wanted to go and part of me wanted to house hunt with Stefon. I compromised with attending the seminar for at least the first day. If it was not for me, the next two days could be for house hunting.

What an amazing event. The seminar, which Bernice signed me up for without my knowledge months before was absolutely where I was meant to be. Three days of T. Harv Eker's methods of looking at money. Learning my money blue print. The how and why of the way I see money or the lack of money in my life.

At the time in my life were God has shown me money and told me that, "it will be!" At a time when money would be one of the prime ingredients in what ever formula was meant to save all the children; I find myself sitting in a room with hundreds of people adjusting my mind to accept the concept that thinking about choosing money was not only OK it was part of my destiny.

Reaching back to my earliest childhood where asking or even thinking of wanting something for me, anything including necessities was considered ungrateful and greedy. Today after a lifetime of successes and failures the words of my mother referring to my rich aunt, "she doesn't want you she's got money, she doesn't care" resonate in my mind. Hearing her scream at me for being greedy and an ungrateful brat for taking an extra cookie.

These memories were helping me to see that a large part of my soul is attached to the belief that if I were to have money, if my life were full of abundance rather than lack of or just scraping by there was something wrong with me. To have more would be greedy, to be rich or well off would mean I did not care. A very large part of me believed that to struggle and to have less was to be at least acceptable. Anything more was pure selfish greed.

T. Harv Eker helped to open my eyes to a very different theory. God and Jesus had both shown me money. There was money, which was not for me and there was future money that was meant for me. Jesus told me after the tree was chopped with nothing more to give, "you can't give what you do not have" my eyes, my heart and my soul were opening to the realization that to have more is simply to be able to give more. To live my life in lack of is to be less capable of fulfilling my life purpose.

Sitting in this room surrounded by hundreds of people sharing "ah ha" moments the following events would prove to be both amazing and a complete confirmation that there are no coincidences in life. Sitting in this room on these three days sharing this experience with Bernice who just happened to put my name on the invitation months before my arrival in Alberta with out my knowledge. The picture of Jesus taking the hand of that little girl in the yellow dress, looking back and telling me that he would come back for me was replaying in my mind. This was also no coincidence after twenty years apart Bernice and I were sitting side by side today.

The seminar shifted to explanations and a large drawing easel on the stage. The man who is talking is giving an explanation of foundations and roots. As he speaks this man who I have never seen before today draws on the easel a large tree. This is the exact large fruit tree, which is a cherry tree that I chopped down in my vision. The explanation and story, which goes with his drawing emphasizes the roots and the trunk as the foundation. I am sitting in this room watching a presentation with the same tree and the words do not cut the tree. Strengthen the roots. "Don't cut the tree" the words Jesus spoke to me under this same tree. Some how at this moment in time, this was the room meant for me. Months before today to reserve this spectacular space for me was God's intention.

As we left this seminar, every part of me was seeing a present and a future full of all I would need. Knowing that the future would not only include all that was required, the future would hold abundance. Clearly God and Jesus intended that my life include more money, they had both shown me mega money, some for me and some not for me. Whatever, "save the children" may entail the future wealth coming my way is intended to be shared between all the children and myself. This time some is for me; abundance includes me! If God does not see this as greed, if God chooses wealth for me then surely choosing wealth for myself is not only okay it is part of my destiny.

This wonderful weekend was over it was now time to resume house hunting. During the early stages of my work in the hotel in Barriere, there was a woman that worked with me who since moved to Alberta. Calling and hoping she would remember me, I discovered she was living in a small town in central Alberta. Her parents lived in Barriere so she was well aware of the fire situation. Explaining that we were looking to relocate I asked if she would mind watching the local papers for land for sale and asked if she knew anyone who may have a private acreage for sale. She was happy to help and would call me with whatever was available.

She did call to say that she had not found any new ads, however she was having a barbecue on the weekend and invited us to attend. We agreed, this would give us a chance to be reacquainted and we could collect newspapers etc. on the drive.

We followed the directions to her acreage and enjoyed the barbecue and the company. As we were leaving this day Stefon turned right out of her driveway instead of returning on the same roads in order to explore more of the country-side.

Five minutes down the road, although it was daylight we spotted a large owl sitting on a fence post beside the road. The owl turned his head to watch the car as we drove by. Continuing down this gravel country road Stefon was winding his way to a main paved road. About twenty minutes into the drive, we passed a telephone pole with a hand written sign on it.

I asked Stefon to back up, as this may be a, "For Sale" sign. It was a, "For Sale" sign which, simply read, "acreage For Sale by owner" and a phone number. We sat in front of the sign wrote down the number and used the cell phone to call.

A young girl answered the phone that had no details, so we kept the number and headed back to Calgary. That evening I called the number. The man on the other end of the phone said it was a six-acre parcel with a ten-year old mobile home. Now for the important question, does it have an assumable mortgage? The answer was yes. Thirty five thousand dollars cash to mortgage. My mind was thinking we have $25,000.00, my mouth was asking when can we look at it.

We made a return trip the next day. This was a partially treed, fenced acreage with a meticulously kept mobile home. No neighbours across the road, no neighbours on one side. It was the last parcel on a dead end gravel road. The closest neighbours were a half a mile across two hay fields behind and half a mile back down this road.

Stefon and I had wanted a piece of land with trees and privacy. The living accommodations did not matter. We had considered if we found bare land, we would simply move the motor home. On my many conversations with God, I would ask for help in finding the place we were meant to be. Details did not matter, I had on a couple of occasions added to my internal conversation; a bathtub would be kind of nice. Living in the motor home for six years with only a shower there were occasions when taking a long hot bubble bath was something that I missed.

We toured the acreage and were sure this was for us. The quality of the mobile made no difference. This was six acres with an assumable mortgage. The outside tour ended and we were shown into the mobile. It was meticulously kept. Only ten years old. With blue carpet on the floor and rose coloured blinds on the windows. It was more than we had ever-expected three bedrooms, two bathrooms, and not one but two bathtubs. The wallpaper on the bathroom walls was bunny rabbits and butterflies.

The little voice inside of me was saying this is the one God chose for us. Bunny rabbits for Stefon and two bathtubs; once again, God was exceeding my expectations and provided more than I had asked for.

The terms were $35,000.00 cash to mortgage. This was the last week of May 2004. We signed the offer to purchase with the possession date being July 1, 2004. This left us one month the come up with the remaining $10,000.00 plus legal fees etc. to complete the purchase. Between the money in the bank from selling the dogs, both of our wages and having to borrow a few thousand dollars we made the deadline.

We took possession of our new home the last day of June 2004, as July 1 was a holiday. We stopped at the acreage to pick up a key and headed to Barriere to collect the Chihuahuas, Cindy and whatever belongings would fit in the pick up truck. Monday July 5, 2004 we slept on the floor in our new home. We had clothing, dogs and a few of Stefon's rabbits. The remainder of the furnishings we would acquire over time mostly from garage sales.

Leaving Barriere to head to Alberta the last week of April with a few saved dollars and a large debt, yet we moved into our new place, which we now owned July 5th. Thank you God for this amazing achievement. Thank you to my friend for inviting me to your barbecue. Our new home is 45 minutes from Red Deer Alberta, an hour and a half from Calgary and about two hours from Edmonton. This was the perfect central location for Stefon to commute for work.

At a time in my life when God and T. Harv Eker are showing me abundance is mine if I choose it. God had found me a secluded spot in the middle of one of the richest Provinces in one of the richest Countries in the world.

My new home is twenty minutes away from the one friend I have currently living in Alberta. My life and my eyes are open to learn how to create the wealth and the formula required to, "save the children, all of them, from whatever they need to be saved from!"

Thank you to all who have helped me on this magnificent journey, which has just begun.

36

THANK YOU JESUS FOR DRIVING MY BOAT

During my first month of working in the office and house hunting, Bernice had offered me a full time job in the Calgary office if we could find a place close enough to commute to work. This was a fantastic offer and I needed a permanent job. Calgary is so large and so spread out that there was literally no affordable country living close enough to commute for work.

After several house hunting trips covering most of the province both Stefon and I preferred the Red Deer, Rocky Mountain House area. The first few weeks of no assumable mortgages and continued road trips we made the decision that we would concentrate our search on the area where we both preferred to live.

Explaining to Bernice that although the job would be perfect we both decided that we would concentrate on finding a place closer to Red Deer Alberta. If we found a place in this area taking the full time job would be impossible.

It seemed so ridiculous to be turning down a spectacular full time job opportunity an office job for the uncertainty of whatever future employment opportunities may await me. A month or two of current office and computer experience would hardly be significant on my resume.

I moved to Alberta to find a place to live and a good full time job. Here I was turning down countless ads for rental or purchase deals in Calgary and turning down a full time office job, which may not be offered by anyone else as my office skills were no where near up to today's standards.

Logically this made no sense, spiritually the knowing that this was not where I belonged, it did not feel as though these were opportunities lost. My whole being was searching for what was absolutely meant to be.

There was an absolute knowing that at this time in my life there would be no compromising. This was my time, illogical or not this time was meant for me to follow my heart and my soul. The need to be practical or sacrifice just to get by etc. was no more. My children were grown. Following my instincts and not my intellect seemed such a magical fit. My instincts or spirit whatever you want to call it lead me to this quiet, majestic place between Rocky Mountain House and Red Deer Alberta, which is now our home.

Bernice's reaction to my turning down the full time job offer was even more astounding. After explaining that Stefon and I would prefer to live in the Red Deer area she said, "wow, our clients have been begging me to open up an office in Red Deer."

"If you can find a place near Red Deer, you could run the Red Deer office." What a gift! Bernice was not loosing a full time employee she was gaining a new branch office. In staying true to myself it was as God had so elegantly spoken, "what difference does the delivery system make? I told you it will be!"

And so it was. We moved into our new home July 5, 2004. The Red Deer branch of Bernice's company was in business July 6, 2004. The month between when we put the offer in on our acreage and when the actual move would take place was spent going over details of the new Red Deer office. During our discussions and negotiations, there was the realization that perhaps the work carried out in the new Red Deer office could be carried out through a home office.

I had two full bedrooms, which were not being used. This would save the company the expense of renting and operating a second location and save me the commute time. With some innovative thinking and the help of a good courier company, this would be very doable.

What a journey; from the last week of April to the first week of July so much had happened. The feelings that I carried off of that Grey Hound bus that what ever came next would be absolutely wonderful was the same feeling I was now carrying into my new home and new job.

The events of the past few months had shown me once again that God was absolutely guiding my life. The remainder of July was spent adjusting to our new home and visiting potential businesses and clients in Red Deer and Edmonton dropping off printed information and letting them know that the Calgary Company was prepared to service clients from Red Deer and Edmonton.

The work started to trickle in. With the events of the past few months moving so quickly there was an expectation that my job and any future events involving saving the children would also happen quickly. My expectation was of full time work and some sign of what my work with the children might be would appear immediately.

August, September, October went by with business being a slow trickle. No new visions, no revelations of saving children and no bags of money turning up on my door step. Our new property contained several large boulders set in various locations under the trees. Two of these boulders were now my special thinking spots, my connecting with God spots.

With work being slow, there was plenty of time for sitting quietly on top of these boulders again asking questions and clearing my mind to receive the answers. There did not seem to be any answers available.

Stefon's pay would have to cover the mortgage and any other expenses until the business built up to full time. Three of four months had now gone by without what I considered any real progress. My conversations on the boulders consisted of asking God for direction. Asking God to show me what comes next, thanking God for everything in my life and asking God for more.

To write these words it sounds greedy to have been given so much and yet there I am asking for more. Asking God for more, yet there was this absolute feeling that this was exactly what should be done. There was no greed involved. Sitting on this giant boulder day after day saying thank you followed by request for knowledge and tangible assets.

No answers, just questions and requests. My internal talk was turning to old patterns. Although so much has happened, so much has been shown to me, so much has been given to me. All that God said would be had been; my thoughts were returning to the old thinking of everything has stopped, perhaps this is it, perhaps what ever comes next is up to me to create. This may be the time to listen to my intellect to listen to logic rather than waiting for some spiritual future event.

Over the winter months the trickle continued. There were some months where my total take home pay was $400.00. Stefon was paying all the bills and living expenses. Telling myself over and over again perhaps it is time to give up and just get a job. Any job would pay more than $400.00 a month gross.

My get a job speech to myself was always followed by the same comment to myself. "No! I don't want a job I want an income!" This sounds ridiculous, not wanting a job yet wanting an income. This was exactly what I wanted. Having a job any job comes with restricted hours. Working for someone else means being on his or her timetable not mine. Being self employed for so long the freedom of choosing my work hours, making decisions for myself was something I loved.

Telling myself that as much as I felt guilty expecting Stefon to carry the full financial load, to take a job would mean to concede that the business expansion had failed. It would not be possible to take an outside job and continue with the business even at a trickle, as the documents I worked with had legal dead lines, which had to be met. Should a project come into the office it would have to be out on time to meet what is normally a very short deadline. It would not be possible to meet this deadline while working elsewhere.

Telling myself over and over again to give the business more time to take off. Trying not to feel guilty about not contributing financially at this time. Telling myself to be grateful, that at the time when I need assistance to pay the bills Stefon was here and willing to contribute for as long at it takes to establish the company in new area.

The waiting and the boredom were making it difficult to hold on to the idea of whatever comes next will be wonderful and my future will be full of abundance. My conversations and request with God were completely one sided. I was doing all the talking and all the asking with no connection and no answers now for months.

Being still and emptying my mind in order to hear the answers I had repeated over and over again with no results. My questions were shifting from asking for more resources in order to save all of the children and asking for guidance as to how any of this was to be accomplished to questions containing self-doubt.

That positive bubbling expectation that somehow my future would unfold in front of me instantaneously was being replaced with questions to God of how was I to teach the children to fish. How was I to teach any one to fish when it appeared I could not fish for myself?

After been given so much so quickly my newfound purpose of moving to Alberta to somehow save all of the children had ground to a halt. God had provided all that he said he would. After receiving so many magnificent gifts, when left to produce something from those gifts I did not seem to have the required ability.

I had been here for months and had not completed one step towards saving any child and it seemed that Stefon was required to save me financially. What was I doing wrong? Were there missed messages, was there a path meant for me, which I did not see?

My new request to God was to repeatedly ask him to please show me how to fish, so that I may teach the world to fish. My second question was, "what did Bernice's company have to do with any of this?" Something was telling me to hold on to this opportunity, did God want me to hold on or move on? Still no answers no connection with God.

Stretched out in a hot bubble bath with my eyes closed again I am talking to God. This is yet another one-sided conversation. "What does Bernice's company have to do with it? Is this were I belong or is this a stepping-stone to something else? Please teach me how to fish. How can I teach anyone to fish if I am not able to fish for myself?"

This time there is a picture floating in front of my eyelids. It is a picture of Bernice's book. This was a book she was in the process of publishing dealing with her business. The book cover was shown to me and nothing else. No explanation, nothing else. My interpretation of this picture was that is was some kind of a message not to give up on the company yet.

It was now early December 2004 other than the bathtub vision above there had been no changes, no revelations or visions pointing me in the direction of my future work. Once again sitting in silence asking God to teach me how to fish. This time there was a connection. This time there was a full coloured movie playing in front of my eyelids staring Jesus and me.

I am standing on a beach in the sand. The water is not in the picture I am holding a fishing rod and fishing in a bucket, a small tin bucket, which contained a single fish. Saying the words, "God please teach me how to fish." Jesus is now standing beside me. He gently takes the rod from my hand and we turn to see the ocean. Although it was only a few feet away, at this point I had been totally unaware that the ocean was there. We walk together toward the water. When we arrive at the water, my expectation was that we would fish with my rod. Jesus tosses the rod away and showed me a boat, a fishing boat, which was right beside us. Thinking are you sure this is okay? As we boarded the boat, Jesus said to me, "cast your net out over the water and know it will be filled." I saw my net come back filled with fish. Jesus then said, "cast your nets out over the water and know they will be filled." I saw three nets come in filled with fish.

God then said to me words he had spoken to me before, "It will be! It cannot not be!" Only this time he added, "AS LONG AS JESUS IS DRIVING YOUR BOAT!"

There was now a complete understanding that my entire life had been spent fishing in a bucket. No matter how hard I try, how long the wait, how dedicated and determined I am it is only ever possible to catch one fish the one fish, which was always just enough, never anything left!

Although we are standing beside the ocean, I had not seen the water or the boat. Even when Jesus shows me the ocean and the boat I am willing to dip my rod in the ocean which would net me once again, one fish, just enough. It never occurs to me that it is possible the boat and the ocean were meant for me.

Being taught since birth that I was less than. There was always just enough or I physically would not have survived. As an adult, the only picture I knew was survival the hard way. Fish every day all day and the result is just enough I may have been willing to change the bucket once in a while but never considered anything bigger anything more. Even with Jesus drawing me a picture the idea that the ocean and the boat were available to me and that it was okay to choose a net, it was okay to want more, even expect more was difficult for me.

After all God has shown me, after all that I know to be true, a part of me was holding on to and reverting back to old beliefs. A part of me believed there was nothing for me to teach. To be qualified to teach the world to fish I must first be a successful fisherman. Clearly as my days were spent constantly asking God and Jesus to teach me how to fish, I did not picture myself a success. God wanted me to see myself as he saw me, as completely whole and competent.

Jesus was now showing me the way that God intended for me to fish. God intended for me to share in all his creation. God saw that I was not only capable of fishing from a boat with multiple nets he showed me that this was my boat this boat and this ocean were intended for me, a gift from God.

(Borrowed from unknown author) **Your net worth will improve as your self worth improves.**

I now see a vision of a fisherman (unknown man) with a net full of fish. He is sorting through the net throwing back all manner of things. He is mumbling under his breath as if he is annoyed. When he is finished, he has a few fish, which he has selected to keep. Although annoyed with the excess items in his net he seems quite pleased with the fish he has kept. I understand that these were the fish he had intended to catch. He viewed any other items in his net as unwanted and discarded them.

Although not in spoken word I am communicating with Jesus he is showing me all the wonders which are in my nets, each shell, each fish, even the sea weed, it all has a purpose it all has value the message is; that if I recognize and utilize all that is in my nets even that which appears to have no value. I not only have enough I have abundance beyond belief. And I have only made one trip on this vast ocean. It all has a purpose it all has value. It is only when we have predetermined what we are fishing for, and where we are worthy to fish from, that we have placed are own limited values on our catch. We are throwing away the pearls in our nets in order to hang on to shells. Whether you see the shells or the whole picture depends on whose eyes, you are using to see. I now choose to see the world through Gods eyes. Both the pearl and the shell have value one is not possible without the other.

I now see the life of abundance that God intended for me. Abundance has always been there, God and Jesus have always been there; the ocean and the boat have been a few feet away since my birth. It took Jesus to turn my head and open my eyes; the courage to ask for assistance was always mine.

Today God is offering me the tools to make fishing the joy it was meant to be. To simply turn my head and acknowledge the ocean, to completely accept that Rose is worthy of a net that Rose is worthy of a full net. God is asking me to tell the world that each and every one; each and every child is equally worthy of a full net. To teach the world to fish is to simply teach the world to soar with both eyes open and to open each mind to accept that all that appears in your nets is truly a gift.

God has shown me to, "save the children; all of them;" is to simply empower each and every child to save themselves. To see themselves as God sees them.

The absolute ability to fish for ones self from an ocean of abundance results in a lifetime of joy. God is now showing me a book cover. It is a white cover with gold embossed lettering. The words read: "Teaching the World to Fish. From Food Bank to Big Bank."

The picture on the cover is of the same five-year-old boy holding a fishing rod. I am standing behind the boy helping him to cast. We are both standing under the same large cherry tree from my pervious vision. This time the tree is made of gold.

God and Jesus were showing me that my life, my world lacks nothing. I have been fishing all my life in a bucket saving each child who crossed my path by sharing crumbs. God has shown me abundance to replace the crumbs and asked me to teach the world to fish thereby saving them all by empowering each and every one to save themselves.

I have chosen to share this vision with you, as God wants you to know that he intends for you all to fish this way. The ocean is available to each of you, you are all worthy of your own boat. Each and every item in your past, present and future life's nets, regardless of how they appear was, is or will truly be a gift, if you are able to see them through God's eyes. With Jesus driving your boat it is not possible to overlook the gifts in your nets, it is not possible to over fish the oceans.

I THANK GOD FOR CHOOSING ME FOR THIS MISSION!
I THANK JESUS FOR DRIVING MY BOAT!

37

SEVEN

The winter months slowly turned to spring. Spring did bring the expectation that business would pick up due to natural business cycles. The trickle turned into a slow running stream, which was still not enough to draw full time wages. The Calgary office was booming. Now fully trained to complete the work required my office is running at a third or perhaps at times half speed while the Calgary office is in need of relief.

My skills could be utilized if it were not for the distance between us. Couriering work from Calgary to me would not be possible. The Calgary office was well established, clients were not used to factoring courier time into deadlines. This was possible with new clients in Red Deer and Edmonton, as deadlines had not been previously established for these areas.

What a ridiculous situation, I needed work; they needed help there had to be some way to make the distance between us disappear. The high tech solution was not an option as my location left me with a telephone dial up service for the Internet, which was not sufficient to transfer the volume of documents required.

After talking to several technical companies, Bernice was able to set up a web site through which documents could be transferred at a more suitable rate even with my computer relying of telephone dial up. I am now able to do work for the Calgary office. This was worth waiting for.

Full time wages, working from a home office, no travel time, it would take a year and a half before Stefon and I were finally able to pay the last debt remaining from Barriere.

Business cycles would be up and down. We had some super months followed by some slow months. Always contemplating new and better ways to improve business at the same time never forgetting that my purpose for being here was to save the children. All of them, yet somehow the timing of when my mission was to begin was still unknown.

Sitting at my computer one morning completing work for the office the television was on in the other room. Listening to the daily "World Vision" program, which, happened to be a rerun. This was a familiar situation. I would often listen to the morning news while working. "World Vision" followed the news daily.

For some reason on this day while working, my mind was thinking of my original mission of saving the children. So much had been accomplished, some of it in a short time span, others like full time work took longer to achieve. All that had been shown to me had now materialized. All but saving the children.

Somehow saving the children seemed to me the most important part of my moving to Alberta I believed it was the new purpose for my life. Yet although everything which had been accomplished was magnificent not one step had been taken towards saving even one child.

On this day in this moment for some reason, although this was a rerun television program the words being spoken seemed to stand out. My mind was now thinking of saving the children mixed with the dialogue from the television.

This was another, "ah ha" moment. The realization that although my life had been blessed with so much, my world had gone from debt to abundance as Jesus told me it would. The more that was requested had arrived. I had more yet I had not given more. The picture I was waiting for was mega dollars. To save them all would require all of the resources available. The vision of my Centre was clearly something funded by big dollars. There had been no further visions or pictures not even a clue as to what this Centre was meant to accomplish. The one vision of rooms full of people being taught subjects unknown and my speaking was all the information acquired.

Something on this day was telling me there was no reason to wait. The universe had provided more for me; it was time for me to provide more for the children. Mega dollars had not arrived. The ability to open a Centre and somehow save them or empower them all to save themselves was not available to me. Yet questioning when to start, telling myself that my mission to save the children was not able to begin on this day did not seem logical.

The man on the television in the other room had repeated over and over, "you don't have to do everything. I am asking you to save just one child." It was so simple; my mission does not have to start and the end with saving them all. It could simply start at the beginning with saving one more.

As stated in an early chapter I supported two World Vision children. My first World Vision child had grown and no longer required assistance. Although my income was in the negative numbers after the fire, World Vision never misses a payment. What ever we were temporarily lacking was nothing compared to the hardships my sponsored children faced every day.

My financial situation had vastly improved since the fire; my contribution toward saving children had remained the same. I picked up the phone and asked to sponsor another child. The man on the other end of the phone asked if I would be interested in spending just a small amount more to sponsor and AIDS orphan. Of course, I said yes. Whichever child was at the top of the list in need of sponsorship most will be my new sponsored child. An eight-year-old boy from Africa named Godfrey was on the top of the list.

That evening while enjoying another bubble bath with my eyes closed I was thanking God for everything in my life. There was a special thank you for helping me to see all that was in my nets. There was no need to wait for larger, fuller nets to come in. Abundance had arrived I was still sorting the items in my net not always seeing the value of my catch. On this day, Godfrey would share my wealth.

While thanking God once again there were pictures playing in front of my closed eyes. This was a picture of the Calgary office. There was a knowing that this was Bernice's office yet it was not the same building. This office space was four or five times larger than the current office.

The office was filled with employees in individual cubicles. The walls of this office were covered with pictures. The pictures were of World Vision children. The explanation was that for each consistent increase in business one more child had been sponsored.

The original office space was now shown to me. This office was plastered with pictures of children. There was a knowing that the need to move was due to the business being so successful there was not sufficient space for the employees or the pictures of the sponsored children.

There were no words spoken just an understanding that this was the answer to my previously asked questions, "what does Bernice's company have to do with it?" the previous answer had been to show me Bernice's book. Today this picture was showing me a large successful connection between this company and saving children.

Sharing my visions with anyone but Stefon and at times Valerie was not something I did; mostly because the average person would label me as a nut, perhaps my mother's mental illness had be inherited.

There were occasions when small parts of my visions had been shared with Bernice. She had shared a vision of her own with me, which told me that she would at least be open to the possibility that visions can be real.

The following morning while talking to Bernice on the telephone, I mentioned that Godfrey was my new sponsored child. Bernice also personally sponsored World Vision children. As we spoke, I was relaying my thoughts from the previous day. There had been so much given to me it was time for me to give more.

Bernice's comment was that she would also like to sponsor another child. Her next statement was that she had always wanted to sponsor World Vision children through the office, however her previous partner was not interested in using company funds for such a purpose.

With this statement, every part of me wanted to share the vision from the previous evening. After sharing my vision with the disclaimer that she may think I was nuts. She said, "Wow, this is amazing you don't know how long I have been thinking of exactly that. Adding one sponsored child for every consistent increase in business." As her previous partner was no longer with the company and she had not been replaced. The decision was made that starting today the company would sponsor two children.

Bernice also chose to sponsor one more child and one of the employees sponsored a child. My decision to sponsor Godfrey and share my vision had turned into four more children being sponsored in just one day.

Bernice had been a long time supporter of a local Calgary charity, which helped street kids. On this day, she added that if the Company were to sponsor two children from other countries they would also add the sponsorship of one local street youth through this organization. The formula would be the same, for every consistent increase in business; the Company would sponsor one World Vision child and one youth from the streets of Calgary.

Saving them all was off to a slow start. My interpretation that somehow the ability to finance this Centre would be the starting point of my new mission was now replace with the realization the God may not have intended for me to save them all at the same time. The need to have more resources and to complete my mission on some self determined instant timetable were my interpretations of Gods request.

God made no reference to any timetable in any of our conversations. There were no start dates there were no deadlines. He simply asked me to teach the world to fish and to save the children.

Business levelled out through the following fall and winter months. The Company had made several innovative changes. The expectation was of a busy spring. We found a Company, which serviced my area and were able to install a satellite system for my computer. With the increased speed at which documents could now be transferred, my workload would expand. My office was now able to service clients from the entire Province.

My personal income had increased to a place where there were some months that it was possible for me to save more money than I would have earned in a month in Barriere. The money management and ways of thinking about money T. Harv Eker had taught me my first month in Alberta could now be applied to my daily life.

This money seminar had talked about the realities of today's economy. Lifetime jobs with twenty-year pensions were a thing of the past. In order to protect you from the constantly changing work force five streams of income are required.

Harv Eker's teaching never left me. My initial financial situation required some time to overcome. Harv Eker's formula was implemented the day the seminar ended. My mind had a very different view of money. The logic in my new found knowledge could not be disputed. The words spoken in this seminar were that there were no excuses. If all you have is one dollar, this formula will work for you. Harv was right. Five streams of income are possible even if you have to start with one dollar.

Two and a half years after my arrival in Alberta with a net worth in the negative numbers. I have five streams of income. Three of the five are small trickles. There has been no $2.5 million dollar cheque to deposit. I am hardly independently wealthy. My bills are paid, my savings may be modest but I have savings. The potential to increase each of my five streams of income is endless.

After years of living in the City Bernice bought herself acreage closer to Red Deer. She was now enjoying the country life with horses. One of my five streams of income comes from representing a company, which manufactures health and wellness products. The products used in my home and for my animals are environmentally friendly and safe. As Daniel and one of my grandsons have asthma both Daniel and Laura use only environmentally safe products in their homes.

Bernice has survived cancer not once but twice. She also has several allergies and asthma. While staying with her in Calgary, she introduced me to the products and company, which have made such a difference in her life.

As health, issues have played a large roll in her life Bernice has studied and researched the environment and environmental health in detail. One of her passions Is wellness. She has studied to be a personal health coach. As CEO and founder of three companies including one company which specializes in seminars. Bernice's expertise also includes running a business and multiple streams of income.

In a telephone conversation, one day after Bernice had moved to her acreage; I do not know how the subject came up. For some reason the subject of my Centre, which was part of my visions shared by very few was mentioned. Somewhere in the conversation, I made a comment about Bernice moving to her acreage closer to Red Deer. My comment was that I had a feeling that she was some how connected to the Centre in my vision. I then shared my vision of the Centre in Red Deer where I saw Bernice in a large room teaching an unknown subject. My feeling was that she had chosen to move closer to Red Deer as perhaps the timing to open my Centre was approaching. The exact context of what would occur in this centre was still not clear. Other than to teach something; perhaps hold seminars.

I was beginning to see myself as teaching the world to fish through seminars in this Centre. Once again, Bernice's response was amazing. She said she couldn't believe what I was telling her. Her partner and her had been looking at commercial properties in Red Deer for the purpose of holding seminars on wellness issues and financial freedom. Teaching people about non-toxic environments for their homes as well as sharing her business and wealth building expertise.

Bernice shared a vision she had years earlier. This vision occurred while she was in Mexico reflecting on her life and writing a book. Her vision was also of a Centre. Two visions years apart shown to two sisters who had almost no contact in the past twenty years. Again, I was seeing Jesus take the hand of the little girl in the yellow dress and then turn to say to me, "I will be back for you." Again, this image was telling me that what the future holds included both little girls.

Future conversations would revolve around the images and ideas we each had for the Centre in our visions. The image of a Centre, which offered information and assistance to all, on the subjects of health, wealth and self-awareness, was beginning to unfold. The realities of both of our lives, our experiences, our less than successful beginnings and our incredible journeys to today; perhaps if shared would offer inspiration to someone who may be on a similar journey.

There was no longer the apprehension of sharing my visions with Bernice. As our discussions continued my vision of the wood panelled wall with the words B. Lavis Empowerment Centre in gold lettering and the accompanying phrase, "Teaching the World to Fish (we grow angels) was shared."

Empowerment Centre seemed to be a perfect fit. God had chosen the words to encompass both of our ideas of teaching on the subjects of wellness, financial freedom and self-awareness the title: Empowerment Centre: Self, Health & Wealth was born.

Research would show that Empowerment Centre was being used and was not available to be registered as a Company name. Further brainstorming would result in the birth of the Reach Higher Empowerment Centre. Which encompassed Self, Health and Wealth Empowerment. Partners Bernie Winter (Bernice) & Brenda Lavis (Rose) was officially born November 2006.

The official opening would be in a shared office space in Calgary Alberta and not Red Deer. This would allow the Centre to begin operations and conduct seminars with out the expense of a separate location.

This Empowerment Centre is in its infancy, but it is a reality! The first seminar held at our Centre was called, "Road to Financial Freedom" taught by Bernie Winter beginning March 3, 2007.

The past ten months or so in addition to full time office work I have completed my first children's book. This is the first of many true stories meant to entertain young children while emphasizing the practical Empowerment tools every child possesses.

While watching a television, news special presentation the subject being discussed broke my heart. The name of the news segment was, "Seven." The idea was that the reporter would spend seven days at various locations with various subjects while recording whatever the seven-day event may be. This particular program caught my attention as the reporter stated that he was about to spend seven days at the elementary school, which had been rated as the worst school in BC.

This was a school in a depressed community with much of the student population consisting of aboriginal children. Many of the students in the fifth grade class being visited were fetal alcohol syndrome children. There were a variety of learning disabilities and children with emotional issues in this classroom.

This reporter had no idea what to expect. Clearly after seven days, this man was as heart broken as I was.

I would like to share some of this story. The reporter was having a difficult time retaining the attention of the children. He asked them to each write their names and one thing that was special about themselves on a piece of paper.

Sadly not only were the children not able to think of one thing, which made each of them special; in a fifth grade class room many of the children could not write there own names. When approached individually one young boy was attempting to write his name. He asked the reporter for help to remember the letters. The reporter asked him his name. The answer was Scott. In the fifth grade, this young boy who was clearly concentrating and trying to write his name was not able to pen the letters "S c o t t" without help.

One young girl touched my very soul. She looked to be maybe nine-or-ten-years-old. Such a pretty child; sitting at her desk, her body language was telling me she had no interest in being in this room. Her eyes and her limp movements were telling me this child had lost her spirit. I felt as though I was looking into a mirror at myself in the countless elementary classrooms were I simply existed for the day. The requirement is that children physically attend school. There is no requirement that your mind and spirit be present.

When approached by this reporter who was noticing the blank paper in front of her. He very gently asked if she could tell him one thing that was special about her. She simply answered, "nothing." The reporter was encouraging her to choose something that may be special. She replied, "There is nothing special about me." Every bit of this little girl believed what she was saying. The reporter edited in a comment later in his report. He had learned after this conversation that this little girl was in foster care.

As the seven days progressed there would be other heart breaking stories. There was one young boy who had arrived at school hungry. The reporter managed to find him a banana to eat. This reporter who truly cared for these children was editing his opinion into his report. He believed he was seeing a case of child neglect. After all, what kind of a parent sends their child to school hungry? The intention was to confront this child's parent at the end of the school day.

A slight built, soft-spoken man showed up to pick up his son. The reporter mentioned to the father that his son had been hungry at school and that he had provided him with a banana. The father explained that he knew his son was hungry. He also explained that work was hard to find. He worked three part time jobs. His wife was ill and he had other children at home. He simply said, "some times there is just no food in the house." The reporter's sad narration acknowledged that this child had a loving caring parent who happened to be in an impossible situation.

One of the boys being cared for by his grandfather had fetal alcohol syndrome. A conversation with the grandfather showed a caring loving man. Neither this child nor his grandfather had any idea what it meant to be fetal alcohol syndrome. The grandfather was explaining that he was doing his best to raise his grandson. He ended the conversation with, "I hope one day he grows out of this syndrome he has." Fetal alcohol syndrome is a permanent condition caused by alcohol use by a mother during pregnancy. The brain damaged caused to the unborn child is not something that can be cured or out grown.

One classroom of children in only one school in one province in this Country and yet there were so many lost souls. Part of me could see me as a child in this room and part of me could see a classroom full of Alex's, Nick's and Richard's.

The teachers in this school were truly guardian angels put in an impossible position. Like so many of the teachers in Alex's' world there was no shortage of skilled professionals and others who cared.

In this classroom as in Alex's classrooms the tools required to teach these children who they are and what they are capable of, are what is required. These children need to find their spirits before they find their pencils.

The biggest gift anyone could give to these children would be the ability to answer the question this reporter asked. To be able to tell anyone, one thing that is special about him or her and to speak it from the heart as though they knew it to be true and not as something they repeated from a lesson at school.

The subject of this news program haunted me. That precious little girl flopped over her desk repeating, "there is nothing special about me" with absolute conviction. There was a part of me saying these are the children you are meant to save.

The Richards and Alex's of the world would be a place to start. My life had given me the gift of insight. My experiences with Alex in the classroom may not have saved Alex; they may be usable tools for teachers in classrooms full of Alex's.

This reporter lit a fire under me to create a workable program for classrooms, which may benefit all children including the Alex's in the room. God asked me to teach the world to fish. There was no greater place to start than with the children who needed to be saved the most.

To empower even one child in the fifth grade in the worst school in BC; for even one child to learn to fish in a world full of joy and abundance and not succumb to drowning in circumstances. Perhaps it would be possible to teach one child to turn his or her head to see the ocean without requiring enduring fifty years of fishing in a bucket.

This reporter and this magnificent report haunted me into writing a program for elementary schools. I am in the process of developing a program, which would teach children to utilize the abilities they already possess. This program allows each child to discover that he or she was born with a custom made, one of a kind Empower Tool. The only tool required for a life lived, "Happily Ever After" I hope to develop a unique program to teach each child how to utilize his or her personal Empower Tool brain. This program will enable every child to answer this reporter's question and identify something that is special about him or her. This program is also a guide for teachers, enabling them to enhance the children's spirits, learning potential and desire using non-negotiable and great expectations.

Searching my mind for childhood memories of hardships and accomplishments I was telling myself perhaps some of what I have learned, some of what I have survived may help in teaching others how to fish; especially children surviving abusive or alcoholic homes. Those children like the girl in this classroom suffering from the hole in her soul while in foster care, or as in my case being in the care of who ever may be available.

I began writing each memory as it appeared, hoping to find some useable materials for a school program; children's book maybe even a future seminar. Somehow, my research notes turned into *Rose's World*.

God asked me to "speak and to save the children, all of them from whatever they needed to be saved from." Along the way he has shown me the way to save them all, is to teach the world to fish.

There is no Food Bank or Charity, no matter how large or how efficient; no matter how well intended, which is capable of saving them all permanently. These are necessary and appreciated tools required for those who are still fishing in a bucket.

Truly, the only way to save them all is to teach them to fish in the sea of abundance the universe has provided for all.

It is only with the unwavering realization that one has become a competent fisherman that one can truly see; there is now nothing to be saved from.

What matters most is how you see yourself!
Dare to see yourself as God sees you.
A competent capable fisherman:

Your net worth will improve as your self worth improves.
(Borrowed from an unknown author)

I THANK GOD FOR CHOOSING ME FOR THIS MISSION!
I THANK JESUS FOR DRIVING MY BOAT!

With Jesus driving your boat it is not possible to overlook the gifts in your nets, it is not possible to over fish the oceans.

978-0-595-47559-9
0-595-47559-0